for Charles

God, Where Are You?

*"Wherever & however Charles
happens to be."*

Gerry Hughes

God, Where Are You?

GERARD W. HUGHES

DARTON·LONGMAN + TODD

First published 1997 by
Darton, Longman and Todd Ltd
1 Spencer Court
140–142 Wandsworth High Street
London SW18 4JJ

Reprinted 1997

ISBN 0–232–52226–X

A catalogue record for this book is available
from the British Library.

Designed by Sandie Boccacci
Phototypeset in 8¹/₄/13¹/₂pt Leawood Book by Intype London Ltd
Printed and bound in Great Britain by
Page Bros, Norwich

To Marie

Contents

✎✎✎

Acknowledgements

I THANK Teresa de Bertodano for her careful editing on behalf of Darton, Longman and Todd, and for her constant encouragement, Gerald O'Collins sj, for his detailed comment and expert advice, Brian McClorry, my Jesuit superior, who creates a community which provides the peace for writing and who is always encouraging. I also thank Maggie Hamilton, Margaret Hughes, Michael Ivens, Anne McDowell, Teresa Malone, Patrick Purnell and Margaret Walsh for their useful comments. Finally, I thank all those who have nurtured and taught, supported and opposed, praised and criticised me, and by so doing, have helped me to know the attractiveness of God.

cᏭᎪᏮᎧᎦᏮ

Preface

*A colloquy is made by speaking exactly as one friend speaks to
another – now begging a favour, now accusing oneself of some
misdeed, now telling of one's concerns and asking advice about
them.* (Spiritual Exercises of Saint Ignatius Loyola, s. 54)

'I HAVE NEVER seen You, touched You, heard You, tasted You, smelt
You. You are invisible, yet enveloping all things, elusive yet inescap-
able, remote yet closer to me than I am to myself, unknowable yet
the source of all my knowing, no-thing yet sustaining all things, for
in You all creation lives, and moves, and has its being. In You are all
things: without You there is nothing. Creation is Your sacrament,
Your Eucharist, a sign and an effective sign of Your presence, yet
You are not the sign: You are in it, but not of it, for You are always
beyond, always greater.

'My mind cannot encompass You, but my heart longs for You. It is
in the pain of my emptiness that I glimpse You. I long for You, but
cannot grasp You. That is why You are My Dearest: I long for You
most, but You are also most costly. I know You are not harsh, but
most gentle, that Your generosity is without limit, that there is
nothing You will not forgive, that You exercise the same tender care
for the evil person as You do for the good, that You let Your sun rise
on the just and the unjust alike. It is because You are so attractive
that You are also a source of pain, of terrifying darkness, for to
lose You is to lose everything, to be separated from everyone and
everything I have ever loved and cherished.

'Why write to You, for You know my thoughts before I have formulated them? Before the world was formed You had me in mind. You

already knew my beginning and my end. I write out of my need. I can only come to know You in and through my own experience. You are in every moment of it. You were there when I was being knitted in my mother's womb. You are always there, giving me breath and bread, in every person I encounter, in every step I take, waking or sleeping You are there. But I am short-sighted to the point of blindness. Physically You have blessed me with good eyesight, and mentally You have given me enough intelligence to satisfy examiners, but the blindness that afflicts me is a blindness of soul.

'You taught me a very clear and simple message when I walked to Rome and to Jerusalem: that my destination was the basis of all the subsequent decisions I took, route, maps, equipment, money, direction each day, time for rest, time for walking. It was not that I was continuously thinking of destination Rome, or destination Jerusalem, but subconsciously my destination was the ultimate determinant in every decision. To have ignored my destination would have been to walk blindly.

'By blindness of soul I mean all those attitudes of mind and heart, ways of acting and reacting, which are not anchored in You, my heart's longing, my destination. I may speak Your name, preach and lecture on religion and spirituality, and mean what I say, but my words and thoughts can be proceeding from one level of consciousness, while inner thoughts and aspirations, longings and fears, are proceeding from another deeper but conflicting level, centred on my kingdom, not on Yours, and unconsciously influencing the things I do and do not do. When this deeper level does not acknowledge You as my destination, then I act out of blindness of soul.

'I can see very clearly that our Western spirituality is split, that we have relegated You to what we are pleased to call the sacred; where we show You a reverence which ensures that You do not interfere with everyday life. This split is in me and I want to become more aware of it.

'I can only know You through my own experience, my only access to You. I need the help of other people, of the Church and its tradition, of the wisdom of the ages, in order to learn how to read this experience. But no one can teach me who You are, or what You are like, unless You show me Yourself. My experience is unique to me: it is there and there only that I can catch glimpses of You and know Your attractiveness. In your light, I can see light. So I want to reflect on my own experience in life, hoping that by so doing I shall come to recognise You more quickly, delight more intensely in You, present in all creation, and so let You be God to me, in me and through me.

'You have shown me glimpses of Your goodness and filled me with moments of intense delight and joy, but my memory is short, and although at the time I think I can never forget, I can leave the room of Your presence within me, close the door and return to business as usual, the business of self-regard, self-importance and professional religiosity.

'Although the experience of each of us is unique, yet You seem to have characteristic ways of working in us, with us, and through us, otherwise we could never recognise You. You are the God of truth, of love and of justice: the peace of soul, the tranquillity and strength which we can experience in being true, loving and forgiving, is a sign of Your presence. It is a peace which, provided we remain anchored in it, cannot be shattered by any crisis, however traumatic. Even when we stray from Your truth and love, You are still there nudging us to change, because the bitterness of untruth, of unloving, of seeking our own good at the expense of other people's becomes unbearable.

'There is also a general pattern in the way You lead us both individually and corporately. You led Your chosen people out of the slavery of Egypt through the wilderness and into the Promised Land. Your Chosen people and Your Christian Church have always recognised this pattern. The grumbles of each Israelite as they suffered the wilderness were unique to each, but the pattern of our journey to You remains the same for all of us. In all that we experience, Your loving hand is guiding us, drawing us away from the slavery of our conditioning and the slavery we have imposed on ourselves, into Your own life.

'I want to recognise this pattern more clearly in the events of my own life, so that You become the source, the anchor point of all my decisions, words and actions, not an occasional reference point to which I turn only when things go wrong. You love all that exists. You are at work in every human being, whatever their belief or professed lack of it. I believe that You are in all things, that I meet You in my own experience; but those words can become clichés. Through writing, I want to explore the truth of these statements by looking more closely at my own experience. I shall do so by looking at memories which linger and frequently recur to consciousness, for I believe recurring memories are Your invitation to us to look at them more closely.

'I feel apprehensive about writing in this way. You have taught me the truth of Jeremiah's observation, "O how devious the human heart, perverse, too. Who has ever probed its depths?". You have taught me the dangers of idolatry and the subtle forms which it can take in me, dedication to a cause, religious or secular, which sounds noble and seems plausible but ends in destructiveness because, underlying the fine words and noble ideals, the destructive spirit lurks. Evil masquerades under the appearance of good, nurturing pride which leads us to use the noble cause as a means of self-aggrandisement and the ruthless elimination of anything or anyone who threatens to diminish us. Save me from self-deceit. I need to write in this way for my own understanding, the better to ensure that my heart is more at one with my lips when I say, "You are my light and my salvation, my rock, my refuge and my strength".'

CHAPTER 1

✧✧✧

God Who Does Not Answer

I called: You did not answer me.
Now your answer echoes
Down the arches of the years.

I AM WRITING THIS by a window which looks out across the Firth of Clyde to the hills of Bute and the mountains of Arran. The flat used to belong to my sister, Edith, who died two years ago. A mile away is the house where I was born, so I am living in a place of childhood memories. God is eternal, always in the now, without past or future. In recalling past memories, I now know that memories are not simply records of the past: they are wellsprings of our present. Memories are like energy charges within our being: they can be pleasant or painful, creative or destructive. The life-giving or destructive quality does not lie within the past event, but in the relationship we construct between the past event and the present. We cannot change what is past: the only change we can make is in how we regard it now. That is why I beg for a new spirit within me so that I may see the past in a new way. I love to think of God as the divine alchemist, who can produce something precious out of the base metal of our experience.

Our minds are skilled in blotting out those memories which we would rather forget, but if there are destructive forces within those memories, they continue to work in us, although hidden from our conscious minds. So I pray to God to bring to my consciousness any destructive memories which I have hidden from myself. The opening verse of the Bible describes the Spirit hovering over the chaos at the beginning of creation. God is eternal, always in the present, so I believe that same Spirit still hovers over my chaos, bringing light out of darkness, life out of death.

I met Julia Mckinnon again when I came here. She was now aged eighty-four, mother of nine, grandmother of twenty-three, great grandmother of twenty-four. Julia was nursemaid when I was a child. She reminded me of the day I went missing at the age of three, an event I do not remember. After a long search in house, garden and the road outside, she found me at last hidden behind a cupboard, my face covered in jam. It is as though the mind has a memory filing system, with a large file labelled 'to be forgotten', where we place those events which are less flattering to our ego, or which cause us pain. But there are memories which keep recurring, both painful ones and others apparently trivial, which refuse to go into the forgotten file. I shall look at these recurring memories, whether painful or apparently insignificant, and trust that God will bring up to conscious-ness any forgotten memories which I need to look at.

From my earliest years I was told that God was very important, and I was taught to commend my spirit into God's hands every night before I went to sleep, but I did not know what my spirit was and God seemed very remote.

All my life I have known God to be important, but for much of it God was the distant controller, to be praised, reverenced and served in this life if we were to be happy in the next. God was remote and so had little or nothing to do with those events which have recurred in memory ever since. Now I know that God is not remote and I believe that recurrent memories are God's invitation to us to look more closely. God is in everything, closer to me than I am to myself. God is in every fact, every moment. Everything and everyone is sacred. Every bush is burning, if only we have the eyes to see.

Before the age of five, when we moved from a large house and garden in Skelmorlie, Ayrshire, my memories are all of joy, delight, excitement, of rising early every morning so that I could stand beside my father with my mouth open, waiting for a forkful of his bacon and egg breakfast. When I was two years and ten months old. I informed him that a new baby had arrived and was to be found in bed with Mammy. My brother, Ian, nine years older than I, was away at school at Mount St Mary's, but I remember being carried in his arms around the house when he came home for holidays. Before his death in February 1994, he told me that I had been explaining the house to him as I was carried. I still tend to explain the obvious to those who already know better.

Those early years were ones of delight in the senses, the smell of apples and of scones baking, the taste of food, voracious appetite. I can still hear my mother playing the piano and singing, the crunch of gravel, which meant my father was returning, or a visitor coming. I can hear the creak of the swing hung from a tree at the end of the garden, smell the attic where we played, taste the sweets, called zube zubes, jelly-like with a sugar coating, which my father always carried when he took us for a walk. These are trivial memories in themselves, but through them my father and mother, brothers and sisters are still with me, giving me life. The only time I experienced my father's momentary disapproval was when he took me to the golf course. I chased his ball on the green and brought it back to him. Another memory is of standing in the back seat of the car and shoving against the front in order to help the car up the steep station hill. This last memory is a concise summary of much of my life: an innate impatience and naive belief that I, other people, structures within the Church and within society, can be changed if I shove hard enough.

It was many decades before I began to realise that I cannot change anything. I can campaign, protest, force, coerce: I may alter the pattern of things temporarily, but that will not effect lasting change. All true and lasting change must come from our own minds and hearts. The only thing I can effectively change is my way of perceiving reality. I now understand faith in this way; seeing the world as sacrament, as sign and effective sign of God's presence. As we perceive, so we live. As we are all related and interdependent, not only upon one another but on all creation, so change in our way of perceiving affects everyone and everything for better or worse.

God is the author of all things, of all change. We are channels of God's peace and goodness. When we try to create our own peace, our own goodness, we create discord, bringing out the worst in ourselves and others. Perhaps that is why egocentric people with high ideals can wreak the greatest havoc. That is why the most effective action must begin in stillness, in the ability to listen receptively. In order to do this, we have to learn to let go of our glory-grasping ego.

There are two clear and recurrent memories from those early years which seemed trivial when I first deliberately recalled them. Later, I began to see their significance.

The first is of being put to bed at the age of three, I think by my sister, Marie. She was eight years older and also away at school, so I only saw her in holiday time. In memory I can still see where I was sitting, facing the window with my legs over the side of the bed. I said 'God'. I remember clearly why I said it. I wanted to see what would happen. Nothing happened and I went to sleep.

It is strange that this memory should recur and that I should remember so clearly why I said 'God'. Some part of me must have suspected that God was a God of the unexpected, yet in my conscious memory of childhood, adolescence, and during my long Jesuit training, God was predictable, for God could not change. God was *Rex tremendae majestatis*, Lord of frightening majesty, not interested in childhood play. That call to God when I was a child came from an unspoilt part of me which it has taken a lifetime to begin to recover. A Jewish writer has suggested that at the Final Judgement, God will ask us one question, and one question only, 'Did you enjoy my creation?', and if our answer is 'No', then we are in for trouble! Now when I repent of my past, it includes repentance for my solemnity and over-seriousness, and for the times I have inflicted on others the solemn and constricting image of God which I inherited. I know there is a place for solemnity, for reverence, for penitence and silent adoration. We need those times to become more aware of God and of ourselves, but if our religious practice and teaching is healthy, it must lead us to a deeper sense of wonder and delight in God, the God of infinite possibilities, always new; a beckoning God who leads us on a treasure hunt.

When I said 'God', I received no answer. I have grown accustomed to God's apparent deafness. I sometimes have dreams which are utterly unintelligible, even when I can remember them. They are peaceful but not visual, more like hieroglyphics which have no bearing on anything and no consistency among themselves. I know very little about the Chaos theory in modern physics, but from what I have understood, there is an analogy between that theory and my dreams. It is as though, underlying what we see as the order and pattern of things, there is a fundamental reality which, although it is the source of all that we experience as order and harmony, is utterly different from it, cannot be grasped by our human understanding and will always remain surprising and unpredictable to us. Perhaps this is no new discovery and is only repetition of the traditional teaching that God is both immanent, in all things, but also transcendent, beyond all things, beyond the grasp of our minds.

God is in our minds, in our thinking and imagining, in all our perception. God has given us minds so that we may understand, and hearts that we may constantly seek deeper understanding. It is right that we should use them, that where our heart is, there our brain should be also. It is in our trying to understand that we come to know that there can be no end to our exploration. We can only meet God as the God who is immanent. It is through our encounter with God, immanent in all things, that we catch a glimpse of God who is transcendent. This thought brings me great delight: that we meet God of transcendence, God of mystery, only in the earthiness of things. We have no other way of finding God, and we also have no way of escaping God's presence.

Why did I call on God at the age of three? We were a Catholic family and I was familiar with the name 'God'. On my mother's side my grandparents came from Northern Ireland, and on my father's side from Galway. Every night we said the rosary together as a family before going to bed. We knelt on the floor of the sitting room facing the fireplace, above which was a painting of grandmother, which still hangs in my sister-in-law's house in Glasgow. Grandmother is wearing a large hat, which looks like a miniature rock garden. From it hangs a transparent veil which reaches to her nose. She has beautiful features, but her eyes look sad. Every night we used to pray for grandma, who had recently died. I used to look intently at the picture as we prayed, half hoping, half fearing that she might move in response to our prayers. It is only recently that I have begun to recover the assumption hidden behind this childish fear and expectation. In God the dead are still living and therefore in union with us in a way we cannot imagine. We are part of them and they of us, especially our own relatives, affecting us and being affected by us, not just when we pray, but in everything we do.

My other early memory is not of God, but it reveals an attitude of mind, an early tendency, a momentary unhappiness, which I could not understand at the time. I was standing with Julia by the garden gate when a girl came past riding a pony. Julia chatted with her and then asked me if I would like a ride. I was dying to do so, but said 'No', and afterwards felt very sorry for what I had missed. I still cannot understand why I said 'No', for I have no memory of feeling afraid, and at that age I did not have enough self-consciousness to be shy. It was as though some life-denying and delight-denying instinct, contrary to my real desire, had taken hold of me, leaving me without that for which my heart longed. I believe that we inherit the cell memories of our ancestors, their weaknesses as well as their virtues. Perhaps this delight-denying instinct was something I had inherited, a life-denying tendency, which was later strengthened by the religious teaching I received on the need for self-denial.

At the age of five we moved from Skelmorlie to Glasgow, from a large house and garden to a tenement building in Hill Street, chosen because it was near both the Jesuit Church and College of St Aloysius, and also the Convent School of the Sisters of Mercy. I was delighted at the news because I had stayed with relatives in Glasgow who supplied enormous meals and lived in a house where trams passed by, clanging as they went, and a milkman called every morning driving a horse and cart. O the bliss of unreflecting childhood, which can be totally convinced by its own imaginings!

I had no idea why we were moving. I knew my father was ill: what I did not know till years later was that he was suffering from depression as well as chest complaints. My mother, with six of us still of school age and with no child or health-care benefit, had to return to teaching music to support us. Occasionally, my father would come home, white-haired now, without the sweets, and often ill. Three years later, he died of pneumonia. My mother came to my room one morning, and when I asked how Daddy was, she knelt down and said he had gone to be with God in heaven.

It is difficult enough for an adult to absorb the news of a parent's death, but a child's limited consciousness can absorb very little. I felt sad, a sadness less acute because he had been away so often. That he had gone to be with God in heaven did not help at all, because although God was very important, God was very far away and so was Daddy.

Although my conscious mind could register very little, I was more deeply affected than I knew. It began to feel very strange that I was without a father. When my friends at school talked about their fathers and the good times they had with them, I felt envious. His death left me feeling inadequate, a self-judgement not without foundation, for I disliked my early schooling, had no interest whatever in the things we were taught and came near the bottom of class in the end-of-term exams. From a tender age we were graded, and so most of us learned that we were failures. This did not worry me at the time. What did disturb me was my mother's distress when she read the termly report in which I was frequently described as slow, lazy and a dreamer. Daydreaming was pleasant, but I had no idea then that it might be a gift rather than a defect.

My only interest in life until I was eleven years old was being out in the open air playing games. Doing sums, learning the names of rivers and mountains and Scottish kings seemed a great waste of time, as did learning silly poems and obscure catechism answers by heart. The only interesting school book I can remember in my first three years at St Aloysius Primary School was a geography book with pictures of tropical islands and foreign places. This could start me off on daydreams of sailing towards them, meeting the natives and eating their produce.

My initial enthusiasm for the move to Glasgow quickly died. Playing on the street, or in what was called 'the back' – an empty, grassless space behind the tenement buildings – was like being caged after the spaciousness of Skelmorlie. I became restless at home, an affliction to my sisters, who seemed so well-behaved, and especially to my overworked mother. My brother, Joseph, a name I could not pronounce, so that for years we all called him 'Jofus', until he was old enough to object, was three years younger and seemed incapable of wrong unless I led him into it.

I lived most of the years in Glasgow looking forward to and daydreaming about the summer holidays, when we always went to Ireland and usually had a joint holiday for over a month with the Hackett family, Helen Hackett being my mother's sister. All our holidays together were spent in a remote place in Co. Wexford, called Ballymoney, a few miles north of Courtown. By the shore was an old coastguard station which had now been turned into holiday houses. The furnishings were minimal, the floors bare and the outside toilets were in a shed, a bucket beneath a wooden seat. Drinking water had to be fetched in pails from a well half a mile away and the nearest shop, a tiny Post Office, was a further half mile away. There was a spacious garden which included a bumpy grass tennis court and a croquet lawn. The sea was at the end of the garden and what appeared to be miles of sandy beaches. This place was the answer to my geography book imaginings. My cousin, Joe Hackett, was slightly younger, but we became inseparable friends. When we went off together on meeting after a year's absence, Joe's father once said, 'Goodbye boys. We'll see you at the end of the holidays.'

Each year when we went to Ballymoney there were different families in residence, but always plenty of children about our own age. The coastguard station was owned by a family called Polden. They also owned a cottage opposite, where Niall Rudd and his cousins, Joan and Tony, were always on holiday. Niall Rudd was small, but strong, agile and wiry, with hair which grew brushlike from his head. He had a very loud voice and was given to declaiming, using long words unfamiliar to the rest of us. I can still remember him, at about the age of eight, describing someone as being obstreperous and cantankerous. We swam, played games, spent hours trying to dam a fast-flowing stream which ran from the hills, practised catching eels with our bare hands, caught crabs in the rock pools and played tennis and croquet. I have no memory of ever being bored, and only one memory of brief unhappiness, when having been given a row for some offence, I decided to leave home and started off across the fields. Hunger and thirst drove me back home an hour later and no one had noticed my attempted escape.

Ballymoney was for me a place of bliss, of fun, freedom and delight. The memory of last year and anticipation of the next holiday together were able to dispel any interim gloom. Recently, I was with Joe Hackett in Dublin, now father of nine children and a growing number of grandchildren. The bumpy Ballymoney tennis court had served him well and he later became tennis champion of Ireland, member of its Davis Cup team and played at Wimbledon. Joe showed me a recently published book by Niall Rudd, *Pale Green and Light Orange*. The book is a description of bourgeois life in Dublin, 1930–1950, and includes two chapters on 'Ballymoney'. I had heard that Niall had become a university lecturer and presumed that English was his subject, but Cicero is superior to any English-speaking orator and Niall is now Emeritus Professor of Latin at Bristol University.

Where was God in those holidays in Ireland? If I had been asked that question at the time, I would have said that God was in the rosary every night and at Mass on Sundays. The rosary was less boring when recited with the Hackett family, for they recited the prayers at a rate far surpassing the speed limit which my mother imposed on us. On Sundays we went to a farmhouse near the water well. Mass was celebrated in the stone-floored kitchen, where the open door allowed the hens access.

I did not associate God with my enjoyment of life either on holiday or at home. There were occasional moments when I do remember praying from my heart. These were mostly prayers for my mother, for although I was frequently in trouble and fought with her, the rows were of short duration and I felt anxious for her if she was ever late in coming home from teaching or from shopping. I also remember hearing of the death of Fr Miguel Pro, who had died a martyr in Mexico, shot by the Communists, and I prayed to be brave enough to face a Communist firing squad! I was taught to make the Stations of the Cross and sometimes felt moved when I imagined Jesus' passion. But, in general, nothing that I had heard or learned in church or out of it encouraged me to make the link between God and everyday life: what I did hear and understand discouraged any such connection.

It took me many years before I even began to recognise God in the ordinary things of life, to see everything as God's free gift, to know God as the God of life, who laughs and weeps within us. I was not reflective as a child, was not given to making connections between events; I lived partly in the present, partly in my daydreams, and accepted what I was told uncritically.

At the age of six, when attending the Mercy Convent School, I was prepared for my first confession and first Holy Communion. I felt no fear about going into a little box to confess my sins. To reach the confessional we had to enter the sanctuary and go through a door on the right, being instructed to genuflect to the Blessed Sacrament both on the way in and on the way out. Confession itself was not a problem as we had rehearsed it many times with Sr Mary Agnes. 'Bless me, Father, for I have sinned. This is my first confession', and then we had to tell the priest our wrongdoings. I knew that lying, fighting and quarrelling were to be included, and that helping myself to food outside mealtimes was called stealing, so I was never stuck for things to say. Of grief, sorrow, shame and confusion I knew nothing. Confessing my sins at this stage was no more embarrassing than showing a cut hand or bruised knee.

We got one giggle at first confession. One boy, on leaving the confessional box, genuflected to us and not to the tabernacle. It was not until many decades later that I saw this incident in a new way. The child was confused and we giggled, but the implications are profound. Where is God? God is in each of us. We are temples of God's presence. Whatever sins we have committed, however hope-less our lives appear, God is still there, the Holy One, holding us in being. Our giggling at the other child's mistake indicates that even from an early age we were learning to believe that God was present only in the tabernacle rather than in ourselves. Recently I was working with a group of religious, mostly Chinese, in Singapore. At the peace of Christ during the Eucharist, they turned to one another, joined their hands together, and bowed – a beautiful and very normal form of greeting in the East. If we could all have that respect for one another, we would respect and appreciate our own true worth, and if we could appreciate our true worth, we would have no need to assert ourselves by competing, dominating, oppressing and killing. I love that saying, 'Whenever you approach another person, whatever their belief or lack of it, take off your shoes, for you are entering holy ground, and God has been there before you'.

In preparation for first Holy Communion we were told we were receiving God into our souls. We must receive Holy Communion with great reverence and must not bite on the consecrated wafer, or even allow it to touch our teeth. Cleaning our teeth beforehand was important, but in so doing we must beware of swallowing any of the toothpaste or water, for we could only receive Holy Communion provided that we had fasted from all food and drink from the previous midnight. We were also warned that our minds must be on thanking and praising God, and not on the special breakfast which was to follow.

This is my first memory of a religious scruple. I knew my mind was far more on breakfast than on receiving God in Holy Communion. I tried to banish the breakfast thoughts, but God, in a wafer, was at a hopeless disadvantage. I began to think of God as the anti-breakfast God. Later I would be taught to give up things out of love for God. The teaching was given with the best of intentions, but it made God more remote and forbidding, an anti-pleasure, anti-sensual, anti-sex God, most pleased when we were practising self-denial. This teaching was never counterbalanced with the truth that God enjoys things in us. One of my treasured memories of later life is of giving a retreat to a man from Northern Ireland, who kept warning me that he was no intellectual, had left school at fourteen, and was unlikely to make much progress with St Ignatius' Spiritual Exercises. One day during the retreat he came to my room looking even more cheerful than usual. I remarked on this, and he told me he had just had a cup of coffee, the best he had ever tasted. Knowing the unremarkable coffee the house provided, I asked him what was so special about it.

'I realised,' he said, 'that God was enjoying it in me.' Perhaps those who use the royal 'we' are making a profound theological statement!

In my first thirteen years, I can remember no teaching that ever made God seem attractive in this life, for God reserved all the attractiveness for the next. In this life we were, as the prayer 'Hail Holy Queen' expressed it, 'mourning and weeping in this vale of tears'. As I look back in memory, I recognise God delighting in my growing, in my eating, sleeping, enjoying the present moment, and with me, too, in the love of my family, relatives and friends, working on me in ways of which I was unaware at the time. I have come to know God through everyday events rather than through formal religious teaching. That is why I believe that the most important element in any religious education or training is the genuine love that those in authority have for their charges, and the fact that they show that love in actions rather than in words. It is a sound Christian tradition which made all holy days ones of celebration, feasts and holidays, bearing witness to a God of goodness and generosity, a God of parties and celebrations, for it is only when God is presented to us as attractive, that we can begin to search for that God with all our hearts.

At the age of ten, when I entered the top class of St Aloysius Primary School, classes became interesting for the first time. We had a teacher called Mr Maguire, a story-teller, lover of music, commentator on local news, and a gossip. He also shared with us his current domestic crises. He made us laugh, was never sarcastic, and showed little interest in class marks and places. About this time I began to enjoy reading boys' magazines, *Wizard*, *Hotspur* and *Rover*, before graduating to Richmal Crompton's William books. Fifty years later, I was asked by Aidan, aged eight, to read some William stories before he went to sleep, and was delighted to see him helpless with laughter as he listened.

At eleven I moved to what was called 'the Higher Grade', where we were introduced to Latin and French, Algebra and Geometry, Chemistry and Biology. Study became moderately interesting for the first time. I enjoyed the sound of French, and Latin homework was a challenging puzzle. I could always get help from three older sisters. Marie, now at university, was for me a fount of wisdom. In the

following year, when we encountered Caesar's Gallic Wars, she introduced me to Glasgow's Mitchell Library and taught me how to find
Caesar in English. Every evening after what we called 'tea', which
was, in fact, the main meal, we all sat round the dining-room table
doing our homework till supper and night prayers. When bored with
homework, I would go to the kitchen to chat with Lisa, who came
in a few evenings a week to help my mother. Lisa was from Bridg-
eton, and a born talker, gossip and comedian, but she was also a
good listener and would roar with laughter as I told her of Mr Maguire's stories and domestic crises. She also understood that the way
to a boy's heart was through his stomach. Meanwhile, my mother
was giving private piano and singing lessons in the sitting room next
door after a day's teaching at the Notre Dame Convent.

Although study had become more interesting, I was still restless,
longing for the country and the sea, easily bored and relieving my
boredom by teasing my sisters, especially Margot, who was nearest
to me, and who would get into a temper, which was what I intended.
Then mother would intervene, telling me I was 'driving her to distraction', and comparing my behaviour unfavourably with that of Ian,
my older brother, now studying for the priesthood. I hardly knew
Ian, but even then I doubted if he could be such a paragon of perfection. The rows never lasted long, as far as I remember. My most
lasting memory of those years is of my mother taking me in her arms
and letting me weep and tell her of how caged I felt, how much I
disliked St Aloysius and most of the teachers, how much I loved her
and how sorry I was for being impossible. I can still remember the
lightness, relief and happiness I felt afterwards. This was real confession and reconciliation, so very different from the practice of going
to confession in which I had been trained.

As a child, and until my mid twenties, I never seriously questioned
anything I was taught in religion. Throughout my time at St Aloysius
until the age of thirteen, every schoolday began with catechism questions. Each day a few questions were set for homework, and next
morning there was random testing in class to see whether we had
learned the answers by heart. Failure to remember was punished
with the strap, a wicked-looking instrument shaped like a shoe

insole, but considerably thicker, harder and more pliant. Towards the end of each term, a solemn catechism oral examination was held, conducted by the headmaster himself, in which each boy had to answer any question put to him from those we had learned that term. Called the penny catechism, it was a little fat paperback booklet, the outside cover yellow. It contained several hundred questions and answers, which were, in fact, a concise summary of the decrees of the sixteenth-century Council of Trent, which had been summoned to correct the errors of the Reformation. Although unintelligible at the time to most of us, the words and phrases sank into our minds and affected our perception of God, of the Church, of ourselves and of other people.

The first question was 'Who made you?'. The answer was one of the few easy ones in the book. 'God made me'. But then there was a footnote in smaller print which read. 'GOD: The Supreme Spirit who alone exists of Himself and is infinite in all perfections'. At seven I could rattle this off, pleased to have got it right. It was many years later that I began to understand the effect this statement had on my understanding of God. God was already far distant, but this statement placed him well beyond reach. God was self-existent and perfect, and Jesus told us we were to be perfect as God was perfect.

A few years ago, I gave a retreat to a man of great integrity but fearsome rigidity. When I suggested that he try to use his imagination in prayer, he bristled, saying that his normal prayer was the prayer of stillness, without images or ideas. I assured him that he must pray in whatever way he found helpful, but suggested there was no harm in experimenting with the imaginative method. At our next meeting he told me he had tried this method and knew it was not suitable for him. I had suggested to him that he should try in imagination to accompany Jesus as he went from Nazareth to the Jordan to be baptised by John at the beginning of his public life. He could ask about Jesus' own feelings and thoughts as he began his public life, and talk to him about his own feelings at the prospect of returning to work after the retreat. He told me that the whole exercise had been bizarre. He saw Jesus leave Nazareth, but he suddenly turned into a clown figure, doing cartwheels and handsprings and generally playing the fool, so he stopped imagining and reverted to the stillness prayer.

Imagination, like dreaming, can put us in touch with our subconscious and reveal to us hidden wisdom. As he pondered his reactions to these bizarre pictures, the man realised that for him the divinity of Jesus had almost obliterated the humanity, hence his shock at the Supreme Spirit, infinite in all perfections, playing the clown. And in his following of Christ it was the divinity he was imitating, striving to be perfect and to be alone, existing of himself. I could recognise my earlier self in this reaction.

God was all-important, but remote. He – for there was never any doubt about God's gender – was chiefly interested in our souls. The soul, like God, was invisible, intangible, abstract, but nonetheless all-important, for on its state at death depended our eternal welfare. One catechism question asked. 'Of which must you take more care, of your body or of your soul?', and the answer was 'I must take more care of my soul', and another answer said that the body, 'unless corrected by self denial, will certainly carry us to hell'.

The impression given by our religious teaching was that while the body is sustained by food and sleep, strengthened by exercise, damaged or destroyed by illness, disease or accidents, the soul is sustained by what is called grace, which is supernatural and received principally through the sacraments, but also through prayer, self-denial and good works. The soul can be destroyed through what is called mortal sin and is further damaged through venial sin. It was as though God, in his infinite mercy, had sown this vale of tears with many landmines, some doing us damage, but not killing us and called venial sins: others destroying our souls completely and called mortal sins. God had entrusted the maps locating the landmines to the Pope, bishops and clergy. Transmitting information about these landmines constituted a large proportion of the time spent in Religion classes and it was here that the damage was done. What was or was not a sin could not simply be learned by listening to the ten commandments, for there were also the commandments of the Church, which bound us equally gravely. There was also the detailed application of both sets of commandments to particular circumstances, so that a judgement could be made as to whether a particular infringement was a mortal sin or merely venial. It was these questions which kept the moral theologians busy, and Catholics preoccupied with the question 'How far can you go?'.

It was the teaching on sin which did the damage, for mortal sins included not only mass murder, torture, oppression, but also missing Mass on Sundays, eating meat on a Friday and eating or drinking anything after midnight on the day one went to Holy Communion. To die in mortal sin was to be condemned to hell for all eternity. To take deliberate pleasure in what the catechism described as 'irregular movements of the flesh' was to commit a mortal sin. All sexual actions outside marriage were mortal, and marriage had to be according to the form laid down by the Catholic Church. Catholics who married in a church of another denomination or in a registry office were, therefore, living in a continuous state of sin.

Sin, mortal or venial, could be forgiven through the sacrament of confession, provided one was truly sorry and determined not to sin again, and the priest gave absolution. Sin could also be forgiven through an act of perfect contrition, that is, contrition resulting purely from the love of God. We were told that such an act was very difficult and that contrition motivated by fear of damnation was not enough, so it was safest to keep going to confession.

We were also taught that the Catholic Church was the one true Church. Therefore Catholics were not allowed, in the words of the catechism, 'to attend the services or prayers of a false religion'. 'False religions' included not only all non-Christian religions, but also all Christian denominations, which were not Catholic or Orthodox. While the Catholic Church recognised the validity of Orthodox patriarchs, bishops and priests, Catholics were not allowed to attend their services. The orders of Anglicans and of all Protestant Churches were considered invalid.

Ecumenism was not a word I ever heard in my youth, but we did have prayers for the unity of the Church, called prayers for the conversion of Scotland. When I went to school in England, and later when I went to Wales, there were also prayers for the conversion of England and of Wales. It was only very much later that it struck me as odd that in all our holidays in Ireland I had never heard prayers for the conversion of Ireland! Church unity meant, of course, that all would become Roman Catholic, for this was the one, true, holy, catholic and apostolic Church with a Pope who was infallible, a validly ordained clergy, and sacraments which nurtured the soul with God's grace. So I prayed for the conversion of Scotland, even if the signs were not very favourable. Most of my friends were Catholic and contact with Protestants, as a group, was rare and when it happened, it took the form of stone throwing. In Catholic circles, if any new name was mentioned in conversation, the first question would be 'Is he/she a Catholic?' If he/she happened to be a Protestant, the word was mouthed, or spoken in a whisper, with perhaps 'but a very nice person' added. My mother had a Church of Scotland friend, a former Skelmorlie teacher. When she came to tea, she did not join in our grace, but joined her hands and bowed deeply, a gesture I never tired of imitating.

Although we later heard something of the Church's social teaching, it never ranked as very important, or received the same emphasis as questions of individual morality or dogmatic teaching on the nature of God and of the Church. It is difficult to describe fairly the impression which early religious teaching made on me. Had I been reflective, which I was not, I might have agreed with the Glasgow student whom I met many years later; when I said to her, 'Forget for the moment all the moral teaching you have ever received and ask yourself "What would I most like to do?"', her devastating answer was 'Burn down all churches'!

What I have written so far is true as far as it goes, but it does not include the attractiveness which I sometimes experienced in Church services, learning to serve Mass, singing in the choir, taking part in solemn High Mass with the organ, the choir, the smell of incense, and the flickering candles.

Until I was in my mid twenties, belief in the importance of God remained unquestioned alongside belief in my invisible, intangible soul, which was nurtured by supernatural grace, weakened by original sin, further damaged by venial sin and destroyed by mortal sin. Equally unquestioned was my belief in the fact that I belonged to the one true Church, which could teach infallibly, and the fact that all other religions and Christian denominations were wrong. Heaven and hell were realities, which we would experience only after death when life would continue for ever. The whole point of this life was to avoid hell and get to heaven. Everything else was of minor importance.

As I write, two images come to mind. One is of squeezing a plum with thumb and index finger to see how far the stone would fly. I did not realise it at the time, but it was as though I were caught in a pincer movement between God, source of all that delighted me, who was at work in every moment and in every detail of my life. The other pincer was my ideas of God, the Church, the meaning of life, which were forming in my mind through religious teaching. It was only years later that I began to feel the pain of this.

The other image is of a little wooden statue, which I saw a few years ago on the mantelpiece of a nun, headmistress of a large school. It showed *Christus Pantokrator*, Christ, Lord of all creation, seated on a throne, clothed in royal garments, with sceptre and orb, but holding one hand to his crowned head, and with a look of horror on his face. This statue spoke volumes to me. I could hear Christ saying, 'O my people, what have you done to me?' Sometimes, when praying on Christ's agony in the garden, I have wondered whether part of the agony lay in seeing how his passion and death, in which God enters our sinfulness and pain, would be misused to oppress, control, coerce and dominate.

One day in August 1937, when on holiday at Ballymoney I received news which left me sick with excitement. My mother told me that I would not be returning to St Aloysius College, but going instead to Mount St Mary's, a Jesuit boarding school near Sheffield where my brother Ian had been. My excitement came bubbling up from day-dreams and from an aerial photograph in the school's prospectus. The aerial photograph showed the school set in countryside and the prospectus said that it had its own farm. On two summer holidays, when not at Ballymoney, we had stayed on farms in Ireland and for me heaven was living on a farm for all eternity. In my reading of *Hotspur*, *Wizard* and *Rover* I had formed a picture of boarding schools as places of endless excitement, glorious games and midnight feasts in the dorm.

Although she loved me, my mother did not seem at all disturbed at my eagerness to leave home. She found me impossible to cope with and perhaps hoped that Mount St Mary's would transform me into a paragon of perfection, like Ian. My two sisters, Edith and Margot, were probably glad at the prospect of peace at home without me, and Jofus would find life safer, but I knew that Marie would miss me.

CHAPTER 2

࿇

God, Forbidding Yet
Attractive

While with rifle and fixed bayonet I saluted You,
Disarmingly, You drew me as I prayed.

IF I WERE recalling my conscious relationship with God, I would have little to write about the years 1937–40, for to me God was mostly limited to religion classes and chapel services, statutory periods of boredom to be endured, just another feature in the mystery of the school's curriculum. When I look back now I can thank God not because, as the Eucharistic preface says, 'It is our duty and it leads to our salvation that we should thank You always and everywhere', but because I can begin to recognise God in events which, at the time, seemed to have nothing to do with God. If we let the Spirit hover over our chaos, light does come out of darkness, joy out of tears and sadness, laughter out of events which did not amuse at the time. I used to think of eternal life as meaning only life after death. Now I see eternal life as including God's continuous presence in the now, so that the act of discovering God in our past memories enables us to draw strength from them and is a sharing in eternal life.

In September 1987 I walked across Mount St Mary's College playground, almost fifty years to the day since my first arrival there at the age of thirteen. The large wall in the middle, against which we played a variety of games and where I had carefully inscribed my name, had gone. The rough asphalt surface was now a grass hockey pitch, for the school became co-educational in the 1970s.

As I walked across, memories crowded in. Rudolf Otto, in his book

The Idea of the Holy, speaks of the experience of God as '*Tremendum et fascinans*', both attracting and arousing dread. Otto was writing of mystical experience. My experience of God was not mystical, but I knew dread of God at first and then, later, a strange attractiveness, which did not dispel the dread.

It was all dread as I first entered the vast, forbidding school and climbed the stairs to the dormitory with its rows of iron bedsteads and line of washbasins. I was led to the refectory, where 250 boys were chattering excitedly, ignoring the stranger. On a raised dais sat the six school captains and the senior boys. I felt loneliness for the first time in my life. The food seemed tasteless and there was little of it. After a few miserable days, everything changed, except the food which remained consistently bad, worsening when war began in 1939.

I had not met English boys before, knowing only that they spoke with a strange accent and assuming, from my meagre knowledge of Scottish history that they would be hostile. I was delighted to discover that they seemed quite normal, although they laughed at my Scottish accent. Some Jesuit schools had retained peculiar class names, unchanged since the sixteenth century, so I entered the class of Rudiments, where I was at an unfair advantage at first, having already covered much of the syllabus in the previous year.

After ten days of term we were given a three-day retreat, classes being replaced by talks in the chapel by a visiting Jesuit. In between times we were meant to observe total silence, the only permitted reading being holy books supplied by the Spiritual Father, a large Irishman called John Duffy, known as 'Yan'. My new companions advised on how to survive the retreat. I was to spend all I could afford on sweets, for the tuckshop would be closed for the duration. I should also stock up with books and pamphlets on the martyrs, for the gory details could be more interesting than books on prayer or on the lives of saints who had passed away quietly. They also taught me finger-spelling so that we could continue communicating in silence. Breaking silence was a punishable offence.

I have no memory of the content of any of those annual retreats, was bored by the talks in chapel and did not know what to do in between times other than try to break silence without being caught. After the retreat was over, we still went compulsorily to chapel twice a day – for Mass at 7.30 in the morning, for night prayers at 9 o'clock and frequently for some other service such as Benediction or a talk, or singing practice. I was neither attracted to nor put off religion by these experiences. I was still living very much in the senses. Insofar as I had any intellectual curiosity, it was limited to the intricacies of algebra and geometry and to Latin and French composition. It was as though my mind was being filled with material from study, school life, religious teaching and services, but they were all in separate layers with little or no intermixing.

In religion classes we were taught that the sacraments give grace *ex opere operato*, meaning that by the very fact that a sacrament is celebrated, grace is given, provided that those taking part do not positively reject it at the time. I think it was this belief which encouraged Jesuits and others to submit their pupils to frequent compulsory religious services and to an annual three-day retreat, although it must have been almost as clear to them as it was to us that few of us seemed as grace-filled as the theology books promised.

Every morning at school I used to wake up looking forward to the day ahead, except on Thursdays, when the afternoon was devoted to the Officers Training Corps, the OTC. To be recognised as a public school in England, and to be admitted to the Public Schools Conference, the college had to have an Officers Training Corps. Mount St Mary's, wanting to be so recognised, introduced the OTC in 1937, and was eventually rewarded with official recognition in 1941, acquiring a coat of arms. This brought the Jesuit rector great delight but left most of us unmoved, for we took pride in being a small school, undistinguished academically or, at that time, in sport.

On Thursdays, before lunch, we had to don the khaki uniform of the 1914–18 war, with breeches which came just below the knees; our legs bound in puttees, a kind of khaki bandage which covered the heel of the boot and had to be carefully secured at the base of the breeches, otherwise it would unroll as we marched, bringing shame, confusion and disgrace. Morning recreation was spent in polishing brass buttons and boots. Immediately after lunch we paraded in the playground, marched up and down to the uncertain notes of a bugle band, practised arms drill, sometimes with fixed bayonets, and had occasional mock battles in the playing fields with blank ammunition.

I loathed the OTC from the start, not from any pacifist leanings, but because of the discomfort of the uniform and the mindlessness of most of our military activity. Above all, I disliked the effect donning a uniform seemed to have on some normally amiable boys. As they climbed the promotion ladder to lance corporal, corporal or sergeant, they became more monstrous, barking commands and rebukes at their subordinates, revelling in their brief moment of superiority. In general, it did not ruin friendships, because most of us recognised this military behaviour as play-acting, but it has left me with an abiding dislike of the potential for inhumanity inherent in every form of hierarchical organisation, the dislike becoming the more intense as I found myself caught up in it.

In spite of the OTC, the poor food and compulsory cricket in the summer term, when I practised daydreaming in the outfield, I enjoyed my time at Mount St Mary's. Compulsory chapel attendance, although it bored, did not trouble me. I never doubted God's existence, nor the teaching authority of the Church and I would occasionally pray on my own for my father and for the family, but any religious leanings had to be in moderation, for the more obviously pious were mocked, and the more studious were disliked.

It was in my first year at Mount St Mary's that I learned that masturbation was a mortal sin and that even sexual thoughts could be mortal sins if consented to fully. This set up the beginnings of an internal tension, but it never became the nightmare for me which it became for many boys, some contemplating suicide because of the desperation they experienced at not being able to overcome the masturbation habit, which, they believed, doomed them to hell-fire. Because my religious experience was somehow sealed off from everyday life, I could happily talk, laugh and think about sex on the way to and from the chapel, but knew I must not continue thinking this way in chapel, because God did not approve of sex except in marriage. Outside of marriage it was dirty and sinful.

Sin means separation, separation from God, from ourselves and from others. The way in which sexual morality was taught to us was, in itself, sinful, for it encouraged this triple separation deep in our psyche. The split is not just a split between ourselves and our sexuality, for our sexuality is integral to our being human, but it engenders an inner violence which expresses itself in violent attitudes towards others, leading to inhuman behaviour, to militarism, sexism, racism, to treating others as objects rather than as persons. The moral teaching we received did not itself cause the split, but was the effect of a split which affects religious and irreligious people alike. Sexuality is thought of as somehow separate from our essential being, a separation reflected in our language, so that we speak of the sex life of an individual as though it is separate from the rest of life. Sex becomes an object, a thing, something to be exploited or, with the spread of AIDS, to be feared. Whether exploited or feared, and whether experienced through abstinence or through promiscuity, the separation violates our very being and robs us of integrity.

In 1939, the major who ran the OTC announced on parade, with tears in his eyes, which he dried with a brightly coloured handkerchief, that he was off to the war. His place was taken by Fr Dignam, who changed on Thursdays from Roman collar and Jesuit gown into military uniform, insisting on being called 'Sir' and not 'Father' when in his military role. I found this switch of roles difficult to cope with. On one occasion, I worked this normally very gentle Jesuit into a rage. I was summoned to the Orderly room and greeted him with 'Good morning, Father'. He corrected me first on this form of address, then reprimanded me for being disgracefully inefficient on a recent field exercise. I had given my section a fire order using, as the prominent object from which shooting directions could be given, a moving herd of cattle. At the end of it all I said, 'Sorry, Father' and it was then that he exploded. Fr Dignam was also our class master and enlightened us on the course of the war, forecasting the invasion of Denmark and Norway long before it happened. At first, the news of war was a cause of excitement and some boys ran away to join the forces, lying about their age. The excitement abated when we began to hear news of the death of some who were a year or two ahead of us, and when we had to spend the night in air-raid shelters, as happened occasionally, listening to the bombs falling on Sheffield, a few miles away. In 1987, when I revisited the college, I stood in the entrance to the chapel, read the lists of names of those who had died during 1939–45, inscribed on wooden panels, and remembered the many who had been boys at the school in 1937. It was a strange experience, for I could see them as though they were present, felt great sadness, and prayed that we may all know the stupidity, barbarity, and wastefulness of war as a means of settling differences.

In 1940, the school offered a scholarship to those in their School Certificate year, a reward which would cover our school fees for the next two years. I decided to try for the scholarship, and spent more time in study. I thought prayer might improve my chances, so I visited chapel in my free time, reciting many Our Fathers and Hail Marys. Occasionally I would stop babbling and just kneel there. I had no visions or ecstasies like the saints I had read of during retreats, but I did experience a strange attraction, and an inner longing that it should continue. My friend, Robert O'Neill, won the scholarship, but praying had become attractive and I continued, using fewer set prayers. The saints about whom I had read, besides ecstasies and visions, also practised great austerities, so I gave up sweets for a time. Then I noticed a change in my attitudes. I was no longer engrossing myself in daydreams of my own pleasures once free of school and was becoming a little less self-centred, quarrelsome and greedy. I felt lighter and happier.

There was a strange custom in the school which decreed that elder brothers should pay little or no attention to any younger brothers they might have there. Joe had also come to MSM in 1939 and I had followed the custom for two terms, but after the prayer experience I met with him every day, not as a duty, but because I wanted to. In vacations at home I never remember a row after this year, but much laughter and long conversations in the evening sitting by the fireside with my mother, often after all the rest of the family had gone to bed. She was a good listener and let me prattle on about school, telling me about her own schooldays at Notre Dame, Blackburn, at the turn of the century, a regime which made Mount Saint Mary's seem wildly liberal.

Marie and I used to go for walks. She had now graduated and was teaching music in Glasgow. She took me one day to a tearoom in Drymen, near Loch Lomond, where we could eat as many cakes as we wanted for half a crown, and afterwards we walked by the Loch. She also took me one day to the Glasgow University Catholic chaplaincy, a small house, which was adequate for the small numbers of Catholic students then at the university. One year, during the Easter holidays, we had a week together in a flat we had rented in Skelmorlie. I began writing short plays in which all the characters were our relatives and friends. I would then recite them to Marie, imitating the voice and mannerisms of each until she was helpless with laughter.

Marie asked me what I wanted to do with my life and I told her I wanted to study medicine, if I could. In those days there were no university grants, but Marie assured me that she would see me through as she was now teaching. One day I told her that I would first join the air force. She did not approve, saying that I might be killed. I can remember saying to her, 'But that doesn't matter, for I shall go to heaven.' She was lost for an answer, but remained disapproving.

In the summer term at Mount St Mary's we celebrated the Feast of Corpus Christi with a solemn procession of the Blessed Sacrament through the school grounds. The procession began from the chapel and was headed by the smallest boys bearing baskets of rose petals which they strewed as they went. Appointment to this role was hard to live down subsequently. Behind the flower boys came two more boys bearing the front poles of a canopy. Beneath this canopy was the celebrant holding the gold monstrance containing the Blessed Sacrament, with the two rear pole bearers behind him. The Jesuit community, fully vested, followed, then the choir, with the rest of the school following behind. There was a Benediction service on the lawn a few hundred yards from the chapel and the procession then returned to the chapel for a final Benediction.

When the Officers Training Corps was introduced, there was an addition to the procession, a Guard of Honour. Six boys dressed in military uniform, bearing rifles and fixed bayonets, flanked the pall bearers, three on either side. At the moment of Blessing, when the celebrant held up the monstrance to the congregation for adoration, the Guard of Honour gave the royal salute with a clatter of their bayoneted rifles, and a bugler played. In 1940, being of suitable height, I was chosen for the Guard of Honour. We practised the slow march and general salute for hours beforehand. During the procession I tried to pray. Despite my loathing of the OTC, I was glad to be chosen and it never struck me as incongruous that we should accompany the Blessed Sacrament with rifle and fixed bayonet.

This is not a memory which gives me life, for it raises uncomfortable reflections on the mind's openness to conditioning, so effective that we think we are right in acting according to it. It took me twenty years to break through this particular conditioning. Another twenty years on I met George Zabelka, an American Catholic priest, who was an air force chaplain during the war. He had blessed the *Enola Gay* before it flew to Hiroshima to drop the first atomic bomb in August 1945. He told me that it had taken him twenty-five years before he realised, with horror, the enormity of what he had done. He had spent the remainder of his life preaching peace, and when I met him he was with an ecumenical group of pilgrims for peace, who were walking from the west coast of America to Jerusalem.

Occasionally, thoughts of priesthood crossed my mind, but I dismissed them. At the end of the School Certificate year we had to opt for either science or arts during the next two years in preparation for the Higher Certificate. I chose science, not because I liked it, but because it would be required for medical school.

When we returned to school in 1940, there was a new Prefect of Studies, a forbidding-looking man, who interviewed each of us going into the sixth form. He asked me what I intended doing on leaving school. I told him medicine, or the air force, adding that I had been thinking of priesthood. 'What kind of priest?' he asked. 'I don't know, except that I don't want to be a Jesuit.' 'Why not a Jesuit?' 'Because I don't like most of them.' He laughed and told me that if ever I wanted to talk more on the subject, he would be happy to listen.

I did go to him and told him what I had been thinking and feeling. He seemed interested and I began seeing him regularly. He encouraged me to pray on my own, and gave me a book called *Christ in Us* by Raoul Plus sj. With my literal mind, I could not grasp this notion of Christ within, but felt it must be important.

The Prefect of Studies also encouraged me to practise mortification by taking the discipline, a whip of knotted chords held in the right hand and landing on the bare back, a practice which was common in religious orders at that time, performed to control the body and express love of God! I dreaded taking it, but like foul-tasting medicine, I thought it would be good for me. Certainly it concentrated the mind wonderfully, but I became spiritually overheated. My friends noticed the change in me and did not like it. I was becoming too intense, too serious, could no longer laugh at their jokes and became very self-conscious, verging on the scrupulous. By this time I was thinking of becoming a Jesuit despite my previous reservations. A friend of mine, Patrick Purnell, had decided to go to the Jesuit noviceship in September 1941, and I knew that another friend from Glasgow, John Hughes, was also going.

In the summer term of 1941 I let up a little on the mortification regime, felt happier and more normal and began having doubts about becoming a Jesuit. Reporting this to my spiritual mentor, he said the change of mind was because I was growing slack. His comment worried me. I had felt a strange attractiveness in prayer and knew that following this attraction was the only thing that really mattered. I wanted to give my life to God and reasoned with myself, 'There is no greater sacrifice than that a man should lay down his life for his friends'. Shooting down German bombers would be putting my life at risk for my friends. The RAF was much more attractive than the Jesuit noviceship, and I still thrilled at the thought of the Battle of Britain in 1940 when, in Churchill's words, 'Never had so much been owed by so many to so few'. In spite of my spiritual mentor, I still did not know what I should do.

When I told my mother that I was thinking of becoming a priest, she advised me to keep my thoughts to myself for I could easily change my mind. She knew me well. We had our summer holidays in Skelmorlie. One evening I was listening to music and gazing at a most beautiful sunset over the Firth of Clyde. I knew then that I had to become a Jesuit. While part of me was repelled by the thought, at another level I knew this was what I must do. I never wavered after this and felt more at ease in spite of the physics and chemistry studies, which I now knew were not my real interest, but it was too late to change.

The last year at MSM was by far the most enjoyable. We were a small group at the top of the school with our own study dormitory which no one supervised, and our own private room downstairs where we had tea every afternoon. In memory, it was a year of laughter and long conversations about the war and our own futures. The thought of Higher Certificate examinations did not weigh heavily on us and we were not distressed at the school's lamentable rugby results.

Had I been asked before I departed for the Jesuit noviceship, 'Are you acting freely?' I should have answered without any hesitation, 'Yes'. If asked further, 'Is this what you really want to do?', I should have answered, 'I dread going, yet feel I have to go.' 'Does it attract you in any way?' 'From what I already know of Jesuits, and from what I have heard about the noviceship, it does not attract me, but God does, and I believe this is what God is asking me to do.'

What I had experienced at the age of sixteen in prayer, undertaken to help me pass an examination, and what I had experienced subsequently, especially when listening to music as I gazed across the Firth of Clyde, was so attractive to me that I knew nothing else could satisfy. I believed that by entering the Jesuits I could best give my life to God. In my mortification phase I had thought of the Carthusians, because they were more austere, but the austerity attraction did not last long.

At the time, I was unaware of any conflict between my ideas about God and my experience in prayer. I had felt God's attractiveness, but I had a mental understanding of God and of the Church which was abstract, unattractive, fear-inducing, unrelated to everyday experience and potentially dangerous and divisive.

In my thinking, God was the Supreme Spirit, all-powerful, almighty, in heaven, and therefore distant and separate. God would be all-important for us after death: in this life God's main interest was in our deviations from divine perfection. Jesus proved he was God by rising from the dead: that, we were taught, was the meaning and import of his resurrection. He had founded a Church to teach and instruct us on our way to heaven and to nourish and strengthen our souls with its sacraments. By becoming a Jesuit I would be joining a body of men, disciplined papal shock troops, leaders of the counter-reformation, dedicated to working for God's greater glory and for the defence and spread of the Catholic Church, which was, I then believed, identical with God's kingdom on earth.

Although I had occasional moments when prayer was attractive, most of the time I was bored, distracted, and soon away on my daydreams, growing anxious if they meandered into sexual thoughts and feelings. I had been taught that feelings do not count: it was faithful perseverance in prayer that mattered, and avoiding sin outside it. My notion of sin was very narrow and very individualistic. Sexual sin was the main danger, but honesty, obedience, acting against selfishness, doing kindnesses, trying to be generous and to love one's neighbour were also important. I had no doubts about the moral rectitude of what we were doing in the war against Germany. I had seen poverty in Glasgow and had found Marie one day in tears. She had just visited a family in Glasgow's slums and was appalled by what she had seen, but it never occurred to me that there could be anything wrong with the structures of our society, still less with the structures of the Church. I knew that there were Communists, who besides being atheist, denied our right to private property, a natural right according to Catholic teaching. Every day at the end of Mass there were special prayers, said in English, for the conversion of Russia, which meant, of course, conversion from Communism. The conversion of England and Scotland was less urgent and those prayers were said only at Sunday evening Benediction.

Had I been asked at the age of eighteen, 'What matters to you most in life?', I would probably have said, 'Finding God and doing his will'. What I did not realise at the time was that it was my relationships within my own family, with my relatives and my friends which mattered most to me. It was when I was on good terms with them that I was happy and enjoyed life, but I was not at all aware of God in those relationships, nor in moments of delight in games, or at seeing something beautiful. My understanding was that God was somehow outside of all this, and that my attachment to family and friends, to delight and enjoyment in cycling, cross-country running, swimming, rugby, golf, to reading, listening to music, going to films, to good meals, was somehow a weakness. I must be dedicated to God alone. Fortunately, I was neither very reflective nor very consistent, so when I went to the noviceship I was still healthily attached to my family and friends and still capable of enjoying life without suffering scruples, but I was heading fast towards becoming the oddity against which my mother had warned me when I told her I wanted to become a Jesuit.

I was also lacking in self-confidence, for although I was reasonably good at some games and won school prizes, including the debating prize, I had been told by one teacher that I was slow, unintelligent and ignorant, a judgement with which a deep part of me concurred. I was also shy and desperately anxious for approval and acceptance, especially by those in authority. Together with this diffidence I had a strong streak of competitiveness. If I could be top in studies, or in games, perhaps I could make it in holiness. I would never have admitted this to myself explicitly, but the seeds of pharisaic self-righteousness were in me and were about to fall into rich soil.

Today, I shudder at the rise of fundamentalism in all its forms, but especially when I see it in the Catholic Church. I know the state from personal experience and realise the damage that it does to fundamentalists, robbing them of their humanity in the name of God, and leading them in the name of Christ to adopt attitudes and religious, social and political values that are the very opposite of those which Christ proclaimed and for which he was crucified. The most effective policy for all true enemies of religion is the encouragement of fundamentalism in every way possible.

On the other hand, I believe that God is at work in everyone, even in the fundamentalist. We need to encourage one another rather than condemn. In spite of all my narrowness, rigidity, ignorance, hidden self-righteousness and deep egoism, I knew that God was leading me in ways I did not understand.

Years later, after I had been ordained a Jesuit and had a little more self-knowledge, I wondered about my reasons for becoming a Jesuit. Was my going to the Jesuit noviceship simply the result of the same conditioning which had allowed me to march beside the Blessed Sacrament with fixed bayonet? Was it based on a false theology of the Church and of religious life, which led me to think that I could serve God generously only by becoming a priest and joining a religious order? Were I eighteen again, would I now make the same decision? This question worried me for a long time, for I thought that if I could not give a clear and definite answer, then I could not, with integrity, remain a Jesuit. Now I see the question differently. I have no way of proving that my original decision was really free and could give many convincing arguments against its freedom, but I can still remember what I felt when I made it, best expressed in Luther's words: 'Here I stand: I can do no other.' When I consider the question now, I am not worried by the possibility that my original decision may have been conditioned, but see it as a question for now, 'Do I want to remain a Jesuit?'. There are layers of my consciousness which would like to be free of being a Jesuit, a priest in the institutional Church, but when I think through them, I reach that same point as fifty years ago, 'I can do no other'.

The night before I left home for the Jesuit noviceship I had a dream. I was in a very bright room with beautifully covered armchairs and sofas and outside the French window was an enormous garden ablaze with flowers. This, I thought, must be St Beuno's, the Jesuit noviceship. Even my subconscious is naive. Saying goodbye was very painful. My mother's last bit of advice was 'know you are always welcome back again, and don't become odd like so many of them'. My brother Ian, who was home at the time, suggested I should buy a return ticket, just in case. Marie was in tears.

CHAPTER 3

❦

You Have Seduced Me,
Yahweh

*God is not to be blamed for our religious stupidities: we are to
blame if we do not acknowledge and learn from them.*

WHILE WALKING TO Rome in 1975, I spent one night in a chalet in
the French Alps, overlooking the snow-covered slopes of La Meije.
In the evening light its colours changed from delicate pink to lilac,
then to deep purple as night fell. At first I delighted in the view,
seeing it as a manifestation of God 'in whom all creation has its
being, heavenly and earthly, for all things were created through him
and for him'. Then my thoughts took another turn and I began to
see the same scene very differently. I have described this change in
In Search of a Way:

> Then another voice began in me. 'You are escaping into vague
> and woolly thoughts, the result of pleasant physical tiredness, a
> good supper and a bottle of wine, but those thoughts are unreal.
> Even your vision of the mountains is unreal. They are seductive,
> cruel and savage. They cast a spell on people, draw them on and,
> when they are near the summit, let loose their avalanches
> and hurl them down their icy flanks to death. A sign of God's
> presence! A splendid sign of his presence, because God, too,
> seduces men and women and draws them to throw their lives
> away, to renounce father, mother, brother, sister, possessions,
> independence, in order to serve God. Off they go, full of hope and
> expectation to climb the mountain of God, entering the gates of
> the seminary or noviciate. There they meet 'safe' guides who

show them how to scale the heights by observing 'the rule', putting in the statutory time in 'spiritual duties', attending three meals a day punctually and with due religious decorum and obeying their religious superiors as if they were obeying Christ himself. And in your name, and out of love for you, they keep their rule, not because it is easy or pleasant, but because they have faith in you. So they live in arid isolation awaiting your coming, more dead than alive. If they complain that their life seems to them, in their more honest moments, to be a waste of time, then they are told that they must pray more and beg for faith.

I set off for the mountain of God in September 1942 along with two other Glaswegians whom I already knew, Lachlan Hughes and John Campbell. We were wearing the regulation dress prescribed for novices, a dark suit, black tie and a hat, an article I had never before possessed and have never since worn, until very recently as a protection against the Australian summer sun.

The place of the noviceship in North Wales, called St Beuno's, was built in 1846 as a Jesuit house of theology. Beuno was a sixth-century Celtic monk who wandered through North Wales and made such an impression that his tomb at Cynog Fawr is still a place of local pilgrimage. There is a stained-glass window in the St Beuno's chapel which depicts him replacing a severed head on Winifred, his niece. Winifred had refused the advances of the wicked Prince Caradoc, who cut off her head. A spring welled up on the spot where the head had fallen, which became known as Holywell and is still a popular healing place. As the first biography of Beuno did not appear until eight centuries after his death, there was plenty of time for oral tradition to develop!

Since 1927, when the theology centre moved to Heythrop, Oxfordshire, St Beuno's had become a house for the final year of Jesuit training, called the tertianship, and also a retirement house for old Jesuits. In 1940, when the bombs started falling on London, the tertianship was suspended until the end of the war and the noviceship moved from Roehampton in London, to North Wales. The house, built by Hansom, better known as the designer of Hansom cabs, is situated on the side of a hill overlooking the Clwyd valley and across to the mountains of Snowdonia and the sea. Its gardens matched the beautiful garden of my dream, but the interior of the house did not. There were spacious corridors with tiled floors. The bedrooms had bare wooden floors, a minimum of furniture, not an armchair in sight, and there was practically no heating. The food, however, was excellent, as the college had its own farm.

The noviceship lasted for two years. It was designed to be an introduction to religious life, primarily a spiritual formation with only a minimum of study in elementary Latin and Greek. It was, in fact, a monastic kind of existence, bearing little resemblance to what St Ignatius Loyola intended, but I only discovered this decades later.

Ignatius of Loyola was a sixteenth-century Basque nobleman, brought up in the Spanish court. In his late twenties he was defending the city of Pamplona against overwhelmingly superior French troops when a canon ball wounded one leg severely and injured the other. The city surrendered and Inigo, as he was then known, was carried off home to Loyola, in northern Spain, where he spent many months waiting for his legs to heal. He whiled away his time, Don Quixote-like, in dreams of valour and of the great lady he would win once his legs had healed. Bored with his daydreams, he asked for novels. There were few in existence in those days and none at Loyola, so he was given a life of Christ and a book of lives of the saints instead.

Inigo began daydreaming again, but this time he was outdoing the saints in holiness and feats of austerity. For weeks he alternated between the two sets of daydreams, until he spotted something which was to change his life; it has affected millions since, and is the reason why you are now reading this. He noticed a qualitative difference in the after-effects of the daydreams. Both sets were enjoyable at the time, but dreams of valour and of winning the great lady left him bored, empty and sad, while dreams of outdoing the saints left him happy, hopeful and strengthened. This experience he was later to call his first lesson in discerning the spirits; we might call it reading our moods.

Having decided to outdo the saints, he went limping off on a

pilgrimage to Jerusalem. In those days pilgrimage was a risky undertaking and pilgrims were advised to make a general confession
before setting out. Inigo stopped at the shrine of Montserrat to make
his confession and, having a lot to confess, spent three days over it.
He then stopped at a place called Manresa, where he remained for
nine months, undergoing spiritual experiences of inner darkness and
light. It was out of this experience that he began writing his Spiritual
Exercises, a series of scripture-based, Christ-centred meditations and
contemplations. He believed that those who made these Exercises
would themselves become more conscious of the creative and the
destructive movements within them and, by choosing to follow
the creative and avoiding the destructive, would discover the will
of God.

Inigo reached Jerusalem, but the Franciscan authorities would not
allow him to stay there. Returning to Spain, he began giving the
Spiritual Exercises until the Inquisition caught up with him. The
Inquisition could find nothing unorthodox in his Exercises, but
forbade him to give them until he had learned some theology, for he
was at this stage academically and theologically untrained. At Paris
University, where he studied, he met a group of friends, some of
whom were to become the first Jesuits. The Jesuit Order was the first
religious Order in the Catholic Church which was not monastic, and
therefore not obliged to daily recitation of the Divine Office in choir.
Jesuits were to be a mobile force within the Church, ready to go to
any part of the world where the need was greatest. To preserve this
mobility and availability, Jesuits were not to undertake jobs which
would tie them down to one place. They were to live in the world,
responding always to the greater need.

At St Beuno's, we lived in seclusion in an all-male house, visiting
the outside world only on Sundays when we were allowed to go for
a walk in the immediate neighbourhood, wearing our dark suits,
black ties and hats. We walked in threes, our walking companions
being chosen for us. Apart from Sundays we could wear ordinary
clothes, but over the top we had to don a Jesuit gown, a shapeless
black garment with two black 'wings' hanging from the shoulders.
St Ignatius had worn such a gown when he was an undergraduate

at Paris University. But we had an addition to Ignatius' uniform: a little blue schoolboy cap which we always had to wear in the grounds. Failure to do so upset the master of novices, who saw any infringement of the many regulations as an incipient sign of disobedience. Only obedient men could become Jesuits.

Our timetable varied little from day to day. We rose at six, had an hour's meditation in private, Mass at 7.30, breakfast, then a half-hour period of kitchen work, usually peeling vegetables, during which time someone read from *The Practice of Perfection and Christian Virtues* by Alphonsus Rodriguez SJ, an arid treatise of the seventeenth century by an author who anticipated Jansen, a theologian who reckoned most of the human race was destined to damnation. Rodriguez left us with the impression that God would have been wiser to create us without bodies. At potato peeling time, the lighter chapters of this heavy treatise were read to us, in which the teaching 'is confirmed by sundry examples'. These were always stories from the Fathers of the Desert in which monks who had disobeyed their abbot met with grave misfortune. This was followed by a lecture from the novice master on some aspect of the spiritual life of Jesuits, lectures which we had to write up afterwards.

The rest of the morning was spent in housework, cleaning, scrubbing, or possibly gardening. After lunch and after supper we had three quarters of an hour for what was called recreation, either walking up and down in the grounds, or sitting in the common room. We had to recreate with whoever happened to be nearest to us as we reached the door leading to the garden. It was remarkable how many shoelaces needed attention just as we were moving towards the door! Official recreation was the only time when we were allowed to speak with each other in English. At all other times we had to speak in Latin, this being the universal language of the Catholic Church. With our elementary knowledge of Latin, most of us managed by putting Latin endings on English words. The afternoons were spent in gardening, in which most had neither interest nor ability. In the evening we had to read and summarise Alphonsus Rodriguez privately.

Shortly after arriving in the noviceship we were told to study and make notes on Rodriguez' treatise on Charity. It began with the text 'Unless you hate father, mother, brothers and sisters, you cannot be my disciple'. It was years later that I learned that Hebrew does not have the equivalent of our word 'prefer', so in order to say, for example, 'I prefer apples to oranges', one has to say 'I hate oranges, but like apples'. Alphonsus Rodriguez, unaware of this distinction, exhorted his readers to break free of all family ties, suggesting that the reason the family clung to us and did not want to let us go was because they were after our wealth! In spite of my naivety and gullibility, I knew that this was nonsense and found nothing helpful in all my reading of Alphonsus Rodriguez. Sometimes we had an evening lecture, and before supper we had another half-hour of silent prayer, but this time we were all together in the chapel. Before going to bed we had night prayers, followed by a quarter of an hour's reading over the next morning's meditation topic, then another quarter of an hour's examination of conscience. The only break in this regime was a two-week period in the summer when the rule of silence was relaxed and we had tea every afternoon in the garden.

There were about twenty of us in the two-year noviceship, most aged about eighteen, but there were a few in their twenties. Some of the more intelligent and tougher-minded saw the defects in the training at the time, but they endured it as a necessary obstacle to be overcome if they were to be Jesuits, just as those in the armed forces endured the inanity of much of their training. Most of us were from Jesuit schools, knew that religious life would demand sacrifice and trusted that this training, which had been established for centuries, would form us as it had formed the Jesuit saints and martyrs. We trusted the training would teach us humility, the source of all virtues, and we knew that in order to be humble we had to renounce our own will. As most of the timetable was certainly not according to our own will, we presumed its observance would one day make us humble!

The novice master had lectured in philosophy before taking on our spiritual formation. He was a very disciplined man, with a clear head but a not very warm heart. In lectures he was always lucid and precise, teaching which appealed to the head rather than the heart.

He put great emphasis on indifference. In his Spiritual Exercises, St Ignatius states, 'We must make ourselves indifferent to all created things, as far as we are allowed free choice and are not under any prohibition. Consequently, as far as we are concerned, we should not prefer health to sickness, riches to poverty, honour to dishonour, a long life to a short life' (s. 23). In another part of the Exercises Ignatius writes of what he calls 'The Third Kind of Humility'; 'Whenever the praise and glory of the Divine Majesty would be equally served, in order to imitate and be in reality more like Christ our Lord, I desire and choose poverty with Christ poor, rather than riches; insults with Christ loaded with them, rather than honours; I desire to be accounted worthless and a fool for Christ, rather than be esteemed as wise and prudent in this world. So Christ was treated before me.'

The ideal put before us was that of indifference, also called detachment, presented to us as meaning the overcoming of all our natural inclinations, choosing instead that which we found difficult or even repulsive. The ideal Jesuit would always choose the worst things in the house for himself, would deny himself what gave pleasure, would shed all personal possessions, rejoice in obscurity, in being criticised, misjudged and insulted. The Jesuit was also to excel in obedience to the Pope, to religious superiors, and to those in charge of any work in which he was engaged, so that in obeying the orders of the cook in the kitchen, or the novice who was in charge of gardening, we were, in fact, obeying God's will. Obedience, we were taught, was not simply carrying out the orders of a superior: we must also practise obedience of the mind and heart, convincing ourselves that the superior was right, even if we thought him wrong, and performing the ordered task as though we really wanted to do it. Frequently we heard readings of St Ignatius' letter on Obedience, which he sent to the scholastics of Coimbra, who were proving difficult.

The absurd regime of the noviceship was based on a misunderstanding of the meaning of detachment. If detachment simply means overcoming all our natural inclinations, choosing instead what we find most difficult or repulsive, then the more inhuman, monotonous and unpleasant the regime, the greater the opportunities offered to practise detachment. But detachment practised in this way is destructive of our humanity. If the practitioner succeeds, such 'success', far from leading to true detachment, can lead to a sterile pride in one's high degree of detachment, oblivious of the fact that we are now firmly trapped in our own egoism. True detachment is the attainment of freedom, so that we are no longer crippled by our own fears, imprisoned in our own false securities. It can only be practised safely if our attachment to God is stronger than our attachment to wealth, status, health, honour, power, and so on. That is why desire is so important: and everyone is led by desire. We were taught to ignore, or if that was not possible, to overcome our feelings, yet it is upon noticing feelings that the whole of Ignatian discernment is based. I was completely unaware of the fact that I was becoming attached to my own practice of detachment, an idol, as damaging to the soul as attachment to wealth, status and honour, but far less enjoyable.

After two months in the noviceship we made the full Spiritual Exercises of St Ignatius, lasting for thirty days and ending on Christmas Day. The retreat was given by the novice master who talked to the group four times each day for about forty-five minutes. After each session we had then to pray privately on the matter presented in the lectures. We were told beforehand that this was the most important month not only in the whole noviceship, but in the whole of our lives, and that our future as Jesuits would depend upon the way we made this retreat. We had to observe silence throughout the month, apart from three rest days when we had less prayer and two limited periods of recreation.

I made this retreat as though my life depended on it, praying for a spirit of total detachment, for the grace of 'shame and confusion because I see how many have been lost on account of a single mortal sin, and how many times I have deserved eternal damnation, because of the many grievous sins I have committed' (s. 48). I prayed too 'for a growing and intense sorrow and tears for my sins' (s. 55), contemplated the torments of the damned in hell and prayed 'for a deep sense of the pain which the lost suffer, that if because of my faults I forget the love of the eternal Lord, at least fear of these punishments will keep me from falling into sin' (s. 56).

I remember thinking of the Jesuit, George Tyrrell, as I contemplated hell. He had studied theology at St Beuno's, became a modernist, was excommunicated, and when he died was not allowed Catholic burial. He was mentioned as a grim warning of what can happen when a Jesuit becomes disobedient. In the noviceship there was a man in his late sixties training to be a Jesuit brother, which meant that he had chosen not to be ordained priest and was, during the 1940s, likely to be engaged in domestic tasks. This brother novice told me that he used to serve Mass for Tyrrell at Farm Street, the Jesuit church in London, and was always struck by the beautiful way in which he celebrated. It was decades later that I came to appreciate George Tyrrell through his writings.

The meditations on sin were followed by contemplations on the life of Christ, the petition always being 'for an intimate knowledge of our Lord, who has become man for me, that I may love him more and follow him more closely', praying, too, to imitate him 'in bearing all wrongs and all abuse and all poverty'. During the contemplations on Christ's passion, we prayed 'for sorrow with Christ in sorrow, anguish with Christ in anguish, tears and deep grief because of the great affliction Christ endures for me'. As the retreat came to an end we were contemplating the resurrection and praying 'for the grace to be glad and rejoice intensely because of the great joy and glory of Christ our Lord'.

The retreat ended on Christmas Day, my first experience of an unhappy Christmas. My homesickness was acute, made worse by letters and presents from home. All the presents had to be handed in, as we were allowed to keep nothing for ourselves. I was worried at my inability 'to be glad and to rejoice intensely because of the great joy and glory of Christ our Lord', and felt that I must have failed in this retreat. I could enjoy watching the sunset over the Clwyd valley, could long to be at home with the family, but the resurrection of Christ left me feeling utterly indifferent.

During the month's retreat we saw the novice master individually on two or three brief occasions when he would ask very general questions as to how we were, and whether we were being faithful to the prayer times. I prayed as instructed, but instead of 'shame and confusion, tears and intense sorrow for my sins', I felt fear 'seeing how many have been lost on account of a single mortal sin', for there were so many possibilities of it. In contemplating the life of Christ, however, I again felt the overwhelming attractiveness of God, and if 'insult, injury and abuse', self-denial and choosing the worst things for myself was the way to find God, then I was ready to try.

At the age of eighteen I accepted this strange way of life, trusting that it was the way of finding God, because approved and sanctioned by the Church. It was as though God had shown me a wonderful spring of living water when I began praying for exam success at the age of sixteen, and again on that evening overlooking the Firth of Clyde when I knew I must become a Jesuit, but the stream then went underground and I was following through barren wastes, because convinced that those in authority knew that this was the right direction. Saints and martyrs of the past had been trained in this way, and what was good enough for them was good enough for me.

One of the Jesuit saints recommended to us for imitation was the Polish Stanislaus Kostka, who had died as a Jesuit novice, manifesting his holiness by doing ordinary things extraordinarily well, so we dug the garden, washed the dishes, peeled the potatoes, swept and scrubbed floors extraordinarily well. Another recommended saint was a Dutchman, John Berchmans, whose outstanding virtue was his fidelity to the Jesuit rule, and who declared that his greatest mortification was community life! As described by his biographer, I could find nothing to commend him. We were also told that if we kept the rule, the rule would keep us. A third model was St Aloysius Gonzaga, an Italian, presented as a model of chastity. I was not attracted by any of these saints, but I did believe that the sincerity of my love for God was to be proved in observing the rule with exactitude, being faithful to prayer and practising constant self-denial. In spite of the excellent food, I lost weight in the noviceship and suffered chronic constipation, which I did not then recognise as the body's healthy objection to the regime I was imposing on it.

The noviceship regime made sense if one misunderstood detachment as being a virtue in itself, because almost nothing in the day, apart from meals, was according to any human being's natural inclinations. Holiness, the following of Christ and dedicating oneself to the greater glory of God, was translated into fidelity to the rule, doing what we were told extraordinarily well, overcoming our natural inclinations, avoiding every form of criticism, obeying not only in performance, but with our minds and hearts. To encourage us in this and to help us in self-awareness, there were occasional sessions with the novice master when a novice had to kneel in front of the assembled novices, who were then asked to comment on that novice's faults. The more kind-hearted would say they had noticed no faults, or would mention something trivial, but the more serious and devout would pass severe judgements and the novice master would add a few comments of his own. These sessions, called 'Rings', could do immense harm to more sensitive individuals, undermining their confidence and sowing the seeds of resentment against those who had made the accusations. One novice, with whom I was sharing a room, woke up screaming on the morning of his Ring, having been badly mauled by the more conscientious novices in his previous session. Six years after the noviceship, I was on holiday and sharing a room with a friend. 'Do you remember,' he asked, 'your accusing me of brooding in a noviceship Ring? I've been thinking about that, and it is not true!'

I think most of us regressed in many ways during the noviceship. As we had no personal responsibility, no decisions to make on our own, we remained immature. The enforced silence and lack of normal companionship intensified my self-consciousness and I began to dread recreation times, for I felt I had nothing to say. The undermining of self-confidence was the most damaging result of the noviceship for me and, I think, for many others. Brainwashing is only successful if self-confidence is first destroyed: then individuals will readily grasp whatever means of salvation their mentors prescribe, and they will cling to it for dear life. It is totally contrary to the scriptures, in which the most recurrent phrase is 'Don't be afraid'. To diminish self-confidence is to incapacitate for life and to rob of the ability to make a real act of faith. The need to be faithful to Mass daily and to one hour's private prayer was greatly emphasised, alongside examination of conscience twice a day, spiritual reading, preparation of the next day's prayer and the constant practice of self-denial. The result was that it took many of us years before we could begin to feel at ease outside the noviceship framework. The exigencies of the study years which followed would leave us too exhausted to give all this time to prayer, and then we would feel guilty and remember all the warnings we had been given that once prayer was neglected, then loss of vocation would surely follow. 'Woe to those who turn back once they have put their hands to the plough' was a text we heard frequently.

What saved us from insanity was the natural resilience of youth, our ability to laugh and the support, often wordless, which we felt from one another. We were warned of the dangers of what were called 'particular friendships', which, although most of us did not realise it at the time, was a warning against homosexual relationships. I understood it to mean having no friends in particular and being ready to accept anyone who came along as companion for a walk, or for recreation. To choose someone you did not like was, of course, success in detachment and gave greater glory to God!

I was not miserable in the noviceship. At this stage I was not reflective, not given to asking questions unless the matter touched me as an individual. I trusted the process, which I did not try to understand, but I was inwardly censorious of those who did criticise. I was also desperately anxious for approval and the way to gain it was to be the perfect, unquestioning novice doing ordinary things extraordinarily well. I was happy not to be studying and enjoyed working in the garden, scrubbing floors and washing dishes. At the time I did not realise the effect the noviceship way of life and teaching was having on me and the problems it would cause in the future. Twenty years after the noviceship I heard a prison governor lecture on aftercare for prisoners. He described an illness which the Germans had detected and named 'Stacheldraht Krankheit', 'Barbed-wire fever'. Symptoms included a tendency to withdraw from other people, especially strangers, an inability to sit still and enjoy a film, play or reading a book, a constant restlessness. I recognised the symptoms!

In spite of its many and serious defects, the noviceship did provide a structure in which we were forced to draw on inner strengths if we were to survive, and it gave us the time and opportunity to pray on our own. We were taught to meditate and to pray with our imagination. Unfortunately, we were also left with the impression that feelings do not count and that it is the will which is all-important. Consequently, if our prayer was arid, sterile and full of distractions, we were never, as far as I remember, invited to reflect on the reasons for this, but rather exhorted to persevere until the time for prayer was over, or even to extend the time of such prayer, for it was the will, the intention to praise and glorify God which was important, not what we thought we were getting out of it! There was a measure of truth in this advice, because in all prayer it is the intention of our heart which is all-important rather than the feelings and thoughts which may flicker in our consciousness, yet the advice encouraged us to ignore rather than to take notice of the feelings and thoughts arising in our prayer. Consequently, our prayer could become a form of inner violence, for in ignoring feelings and thoughts we were learning to ignore the needs of body and mind, so rendering ourselves insensitive to the promptings of the Spirit.

Although we lived in St Beuno's as three different communities – novices, lay brothers and elderly retired priests – and although the strange living conditions fostered eccentricity, there was a sense of peaceful purpose, of unity and of humour in the house, however mistaken the lifestyle may appear fifty years later.

Reflecting on this noviceship now, I understand more clearly some of my present reactions when I hear or read lectures or books on prayer and spirituality. If the speaker or writer appears to be presenting images of God or ideals which are not grounded in our ordinary human experience, then I feel an inner revulsion, which springs from unacknowledged pain in my own past, when I was striving to batter my way to God with acts of the will. Yet in some mysterious way, God remained not only all-important, but also attractive. To follow this attraction I dedicated myself to a system which nurtured my narcissism, nourished my attachment to other people's approval, and fostered a deep-seated egoism, an uncritical acceptance of human authority, a fear of myself and of God. Although

I could not distinguish between my service of God and my observance of human conventions, I still had glimpses of God's attractiveness. To know, love and serve God was the longing implanted in me, and I believed that living as a Jesuit was the only way for me to do this.

Consequently, on September 8th 1944, dressed for the first time in a Roman collar and black suit, our uniform for life, we took our first vows of poverty, chastity and obedience, vowing also to remain within the Society of Jesus. We had been told many times that these vows were binding for life and that to break them would be a betrayal. As far as we were concerned, these vows *were* for life; the Society of Jesus, however, would not accept us for life until we had taken our final vows at the end of our training. In my case, this would not be until 1960, sixteen years later. I had no hesitation about making these first vows, and I particularly looked forward to the day because my mother and brother Joe were coming to visit me.

CHAPTER 4

⊷ⓒ☙

The Dark Side
of God

*Why should I be out of mind because I am out of sight? I am
waiting for you, for an interval, somewhere very near, just round
the corner. All is well.* (Henry Scott Holland)

AFTER TAKING VOWS, those who were older, or better educated,
departed to Heythrop College in Oxfordshire to begin their three years
of philosophy, and the rest of us remained at St Beuno's for another
two years for what was called 'the juniorate'. Its purpose was study,
to prepare us for philosophy, and possibly for a university degree.

Instead of scrubbing floors, weeding and digging the garden and
having lectures on Jesuit spirituality, we now studied Latin, Greek,
French, English, History, and a few studied Mathematics. In charge
of us was Fr Tom Corbishley, a man I later came to like and admire.
At the time I was in awe of his knowledge and intelligence and
wrongly interpreted his shyness as stand-offishness, but I enjoyed
his teaching and preaching, which revealed a world interesting and
worthwhile in itself and not something God had made so that we
could practise detachment. He also seemed to trust us and was not
fussy about rules and regulations.

We still had to meditate every morning for an hour, attend Mass,
examine our consciences twice a day for a quarter of an hour, spend
half an hour in spiritual reading, a quarter of an hour preparing the
following day's prayer, recite the rosary privately and pray before
the Blessed Sacrament for a quarter of an hour. We also had to
attend night prayers except on feast days, when there was evening
Benediction. In the noviceship we had frequently been warned of the

dangers of becoming lukewarm, an inevitable consequence of neglect of what were called our 'spiritual duties', a temptation which, we were told, would assail us when we went to study philosophy at Heythrop, a place we pictured as little better than Sodom and Gomorrha.

Today's young Jesuits would find our juniorate regime intolerable, but to us it brought relative freedom. We no longer had to spend our afternoons in gardening but were free to play games, walk or go running. Cross-country running had been forbidden in the novice-ship. I delighted in it now and in the occasional full day's walking, not only for the sense of well-being I experienced in the activity, but also for its after-effects. We enjoyed one another's company and I have no memory of rows or serious tensions between us in the two years.

We had a few classes each day, leaving us plenty of time for private study. Having studied Physics and Chemistry in my last two years at school, my knowledge of Latin was elementary, of History and English Literature rudimentary, and of Greek non-existent, apart from the alphabet. Most of my contemporaries were much more advanced and I felt myself to be a slow learner. I plodded away, getting some delight from discovering that I could understand the occasional Greek sentence. The first piece of Greek literature that I painfully learned to read, with the help of a dictionary and an English translation, was Plato's *Apologia* – the account of Socrates' last hours before being put to death for corrupting the youth of Athens and not believing in the gods in whom the city believed. At the time I did not know why this book so attracted me.

It was only years later, when I was giving retreats, that I began to learn the importance of noticing what lingers in memory and affects our feelings. It is as though our subconscious is more intelligent and less timebound than the conscious mind. Perhaps we are closer to God in our subconscious than in our conscious, reasoning minds. Perhaps that is why the psalmist writes 'be still and know that I am God', why alert passivity is so important in prayer, and why use of the imagination can be so helpful and revealing. I soon noticed in giving retreats that a word, a phrase or an image which appeals to someone early in the retreat, is like a seed planted in them, which will grow and develop, provided they keep returning to it. The portrait of Socrates in the *Apologia* appealed to me and kept recurring in memory. Later in life, I was to run into conflict with myself, and with Church authorities, because I could no longer accept those images of God and of the Church which had been presented to me. I also loved Socrates' notion of wisdom as the ability to recognise our own ignorance, and when I have remembered to remain in touch with this wisdom, it has always been consoling, strengthening and freeing. Socrates was much more attractive to me than most of the saints I had read about in the noviceship, whose sanctity appeared to consist in the severity of their austerity.

With slightly less difficulty I struggled with Latin authors and had my first introduction to Tacitus, whose terse style I admired and longed to be able to imitate. We were introduced to English poetry and encouraged to learn passages by heart. I liked the sound of Gerard Manley Hopkins when read aloud, as I once heard him read by the actor Robert Speaight who was visiting Fr Tom Corbishley. But I could make no sense of most of Hopkins' writing and failed to understand other people's enthusiasm. I was pleased to discover later that most of Hopkins' contemporaries shared my difficulty.

Because life was now less strained and artificial, my prayer became less arid, but I did not recognise the connection at the time. I used to find myself praying spontaneously outside prayer time, usually when walking in the garden, but I never counted this as 'real prayer', nor did I realise that I could pray much better if I stopped making such an effort and gave God a chance.

Over Easter 1945, my three sisters, Marie, Edith and Margot, came to visit me for a few days and I had been looking forward to their coming. Marie looked older, had some grey streaks in her black hair, and she seemed tired. I enjoyed showing them around, but once they had given me the news from home, of relatives and friends, I felt I had nothing to say. I also felt strange, dressed in my black suit and Roman collar, as we strolled through Chester one day. It was very painful, for I felt separated from, awkward and self-conscious with those to whom I was closest, something I had never experienced before. At the time, I did not understand that this pain was an indication of my own separation from myself and from God, because I was trying to force myself into becoming the perfect Jesuit. We had been told in the noviceship. 'If you keep the rule, the rule will keep you'. We had also been taught that pain was something to be offered up to God, then ignored. To dwell on the pain was giving in to self-pity: one must bash on regardless.

After Easter I was summoned one day by Fr Tom Corbishley, who told me I was to go to Hodder, the Stonyhurst Preparatory School for boys aged 7–11. Hodder needed someone for a term to teach the most junior class. Untrained and unqualified, I duly tried to teach. One benefit of the experience was an abiding interest in the question 'How do we learn?' During the following year I read a book on education in which the author made some very obvious comments, which were new to me. He claimed that all knowledge begins in the senses, a truth which St Thomas Aquinas had noted seven centuries earlier with his '*Nil in intellectu nisi prius fuerit in sensu*', 'There is nothing in our minds which was not first in our senses'. The author also stated that we make the most important educational leap before we go to school, when we learn to say 'I want' or 'I won't', or to ask 'What's that?'. The child crawls along the floor, touching, tasting, smelling its surroundings, is fascinated by colour and movement, reacts to sounds and imitates them. To form concepts from sense experience is the first great educational leap. Therefore, in all education, the senses must be stimulated, imagination nurtured, and the child must be encouraged to explore and experiment, for it is out of this process that ideas are born.

It is all so obvious, yet it had been largely ignored in my own education so far, and would continue to be ignored in the long years of study ahead, when we were constantly given answers to questions we had neither asked nor had any interest in asking. Our own experience was never considered to be a subject worthy of study. At school, the only subject in which we had been encouraged to experiment was in Science, but the experiments consisted in following prescribed procedures and noting the predictable result. Imagination was rarely encouraged, daydreaming deemed a fault and the senses judged unreliable.

I was interested in these educational ideas, but it took me many years before I understood their implications, especially for religious education and spiritual development. Nor, in all the retreats I had made and lectures I had heard on Jesuit spirituality, did it dawn on me that these ideas on education were also at the heart of St Ignatius' Spiritual Exercises.

While on a bus returning to Hodder from Preston, I heard the news that the war had ended. During the noviceship, we had had no access to newspapers and heard only those snippets which the novice master saw fit to pass on, so my knowledge of the war was slight. I did not discover until later the extent of the devastation in Europe, knew nothing of the holocaust, nor of the twenty million Russian casualties. We were still praying for Russia's conversion from Communism to Catholicism.

I enjoyed the three months at Hodder, relished the freedom to swim every day in the Hodder river, explored the beautiful Ribble valley by bicycle, made occasional visits to Stonyhurst itself, an awe-inspiring building half a mile from Hodder, described as a large museum with school attached. Life at Hodder was much less regimented than at St Beuno's. We had conversation at meals instead of sitting in silence or being read to. It was also good to have some responsibility for others and I enjoyed trying to teach. I returned to St Beuno's physically stronger and fitter, but vaguely uneasy about my spiritual state. I read an article once entitled 'Feeling bad about feeling good', an affliction of conscientious Christians whose basic image of God is such that if they are enjoying life, they suspect that something must be amiss. I had often heard that God had told St Teresa of Avila, 'I send suffering to those I love', and that she had replied, 'Then it is not surprising that you have so few friends'.

Although I never formulated it in this way at the time, God was to me a jealous God, demanding everything in this life, but promising in return eternal life in heaven. Any delight in life, absorption in any activity other than prayer, church-going, scripture or spiritual reading, was somehow a reneging on wholehearted service of God.

It was as though my life with God and my everyday life ran on parallel lines, which crossed only when I sinned or was tempted to sin. God was primarily a God of individual morality, who was generally in the very distant background at all times other than those of formal prayer or religious services. Occasionally, when I felt God's attractiveness, usually when I was gazing at the Clwyd valley without a thought of prayer in my head, my conscious mind would discount the delight as coming from a contaminated source, the material world. My delight, as with that of the saints, should come from 'heavenly things'.

There are two images from these years which keep coming back to me. One is of riding a bicycle which has no chain: the other is the picture of a sturdy novice pumping the chapel organ. Recurrent images are fascinating: they contain in microcosm the basic pattern of our thinking.

Every year throughout our Jesuit training we made an eight-day retreat. The retreat-giver talked four times each day for about three quarters of an hour, and for a further three quarters of an hour we had to reflect and pray over what we had heard. The talks were based on the key themes of the Spiritual Exercises, which became increasingly boring as they became more familiar. It was during one of these retreats that I first became aware of the image of riding a chainless bicycle. I tried to pray, wanted to pray, struggled to keep awake and dispel what were called distractions. In those days I thought that anything which was not explicitly religious and consciously centred on God, was a distraction. When the retreat was over, I felt very much as I did before it began, and all my efforts to pray seemed to have little or no connection with everyday life. The chainless bicycle image reflected this experience, which was not limited to retreats, but reflected my normal daily experience of prayer most of the time. The image was a true reflection of what was going on inside. I was trying to find a God, who was separate from everyday experience, the transcendent God of mystery, of pure love and of goodness. To find such a God I must raise my mind and heart above 'the things of earth' and find God, in spite of my material self, in 'the things of heaven'. I had no notion then, nor for many years, of the sacramentality of all creation, nor did I realise that I was trying to force myself to find an abstract God, while ignoring God at the heart of everything, closer to me than I am to myself and whom I could only find, because of my creaturehood, in what my eyes saw and my ears heard in the world around me.

The second image was based on a reality. It was a warm summer's evening in the St Beuno's chapel choir loft, during Benediction, and the novice who had to pump the organ was tiring. By the pump there was a chord, weighted with lead and bearing a cardboard arrow, which registered the air pressure. In order to generate adequate air pressure, this moveable arrow had to be below, or at least aligned with, a fixed arrow on the side of the organ. Reckoning that as long as the moveable arrow remained below the fixed one all would be well, the novice stopped pumping and pulled hard on the chord. The chord snapped: the organ sighed into silence. This image was giving the same message as the chainless bicycle. My effort to find God through religious activity, ignoring ordinary everyday experience, was like the novice pulling on the chord. My notion of God and of religion was too abstract, too theoretical, not sufficiently rooted in experience. This image recurs frequently, especially at religious services and meetings when we pray, or are exhorted to pray, for global issues, as though prayer is an alternative to the hard thought and hard work that is necessary if we are to achieve that for which we long. Again, we are pulling the chord without pumping the organ. Whenever I hear politicians assure us that if we can keep inflation down, all will be well with the country, or promising more prisons and longer sentences to reduce crime, I remember the novice pulling on the chord instead of pumping.

After my first year in the juniorate, Fr Tom Corbishley was appointed Master of Campion Hall, Oxford, and Fr Conyers D'Arcy took his place. He was an older man, even more shy, retiring and lacking in small talk. On my producing a piece of Latin translation, he told me that Latin was probably not my subject, which shattered my dwindling self-confidence.

On March 26th 1946, Fr Conyers D'Arcy summoned me and told me I was to go to Glasgow next day as my sister, Marie, was seriously ill. He had no details he could give me. I can still taste the brown bread sandwiches in my dry mouth as I travelled by train to Glasgow, my mind in torment about Marie's illness and dreading that I might not see her again. At Central Station I was met, not by my mother, but by Fr Willy d'Andria, the Jesuit Rector of St Aloysius. On the way to my home he broke the news. Marie was dead, her body found in Loch Lomond. She had gone shopping, after recovering from 'flu, and had never returned. When I met my mother, she said nothing but held me as we both wept. I could not absorb the shock, nor cope with the pain. I locked it away in a corner of my consciousness, where it has been working its way out ever since.

I could not understand Marie's death. Someone told me that depression was not uncommon after 'flu, a kindly thought which did not help at all. How could God have allowed this to happen? In those days God was for me the almighty, eternal, all-powerful God, creator of all, but remote from all. I had no notion of God sharing Marie's and the family's pain. Marie had served God faithfully, went to Mass regularly during the week as well as on Sundays, and she had made the nine Fridays. To a seventeenth-century French visionary, Margaret Mary Alacoque, God had promised that those who attended Mass and received Holy Communion on the first Friday of every month for nine successive months, would be assured of a holy death. I knew that Marie had made the nine Fridays many times, and I had never had a moment's doubt about the truth of the promise. She was also the kindest, truest, gentlest, most generous person I had ever known and had always come to the rescue when I was in trouble.

Suicide was considered such a grave sin that those who died in this way were not allowed Christian burial. Fortunately, this sanction was not observed and Marie was buried after a Requiem Mass at St Aloysius. We were not encouraged to talk about our feelings in those days, but were expected to carry on courageously. Such was the shame, confusion and shock that we hardly spoke about Marie's death even within the family. I did not initiate a conversation on Marie, nor inquire too closely about the circumstances of her death, for I did not want to cause any of the family more pain. It was only much later I realised that my fear of causing them pain was really a fear of my own pain.

When I returned to St Beuno's I told others that Marie had died after a severe bout of 'flu. Many must have known of her suicide, but no one mentioned it to me or asked me about it, until Fr Paul Kennedy, the tertian instructor, did so fourteen years later. Thirty years after her death I spoke about it to a group of people with whom I was working, and wept.

My reasoning mind caused me agony. Catholic teaching was clear. Suicide was a mortal sin. Those who die in mortal sin go to hell for all eternity. I never believed that Marie was in hell, but I could not bear to think of the possibility. Consequently, although I prayed for Marie, I could not bear to remember her. A great darkness enveloped a deep part of my soul. It is difficult to describe this inner state. I did not doubt God's existence. Perhaps God was so remote and abstract for me that God's existence or non-existence was not a real question. To one part of my mind, God was still God the almighty, all-powerful, source of all goodness, my eternal destiny. But in another part of my mind, which I did not dare acknowledge, there was a dark and terrifying side to God. I believed that my prayers could help Marie, so endlessly I prayed the Our Father, Hail Mary and Glory be to the Father, especially every November, because there was a Catholic belief that each time we prayed each prayer six times, we would gain what was called 'A Plenary Indulgence' whereby a soul would be released from purgatory. I must have released hundreds!

Apart from saying prayers for her, I could not remember Marie for many years without feeling pain and sadness. In recent years I have felt closer to her than to any living person, and I now see that she has always been close to me. In imagination I speak to her and to the rest of my family, who are all now dead. The conversations are not formal: it is as though they are all there with me, wherever I am, sharing in whatever I experience, delighting when I am glad, supporting me when sad. This has helped me understand a suggestion which Ignatius makes in the Spiritual Exercises, when he writes, 'I behold myself standing in the presence of God our Lord and of his angels and saints, who intercede for me' (s. 233 and 151). At first, I was put off by this suggestion. I could only visualise holy pictures with harp-playing angels and haloed saints, and felt no great enthusiasm for their company. Now I see it differently, thinking of all those who have died as still living in God. Like God, they must be all around us, with and for us, longing for our good.

Although it has taken many years for me to realise it, I believe that Marie has been with me, guiding me through the inner darkness which enveloped me after her death, guiding me towards a God who is no longer remote, no longer the almighty, all-powerful God of judgement, primarily interested in our moral faults and failings. This God is so near to us that even our ideas and images of God can become a barrier. God is closer to us than our own consciousness, sharing everything with us, our delight and our sorrow, a God of compassion who loves all creation and whose living Spirit is in all. Whenever I say 'I', it is God, rather than my conscious self, who is the ultimate reference point to which 'I' is pointing, beyond the 'I' and greater than it, yet within it.

I returned to St Beuno's and tried to carry on with the life and studies, but it was as though my soul was numb. After Easter I was again summoned by Fr D'Arcy and told that I would be spending the following term teaching at St Peter's, Southbourne, a small Jesuit secondary school in the south of England, which had a few student boarders. It was a wise move for me at this time, for my attention would have to be fully engaged in preparing and teaching classes of fourteen-year-olds, as well as helping with games and with the boarders during weekends. There was a pleasantly sleepy atmosphere in the Southbourne school, its pupils affable but not demanding, and I enjoyed teaching.

At the end of the school term, I returned to St Beuno's and remember hearing the news of the atomic bomb on Hiroshima and of the end of the war with Japan. My immediate reaction was relief that the war with Japan was over. I never thought of questioning the morality of dropping the atomic bomb, or of the carpet bombing of German cities, nor do I remember the question being raised by any of the Jesuit community, the only world with which I had contact at the time.

Before moving from St Beuno's to Heythrop to begin a three-year philosophy course, I had a few days at home with the family. We had moved to a new house in Glasgow with a large garden. My mother, Edith and Margot seemed well and to be coping with life: my brother Joe was still in the navy.

Heythrop was a massive mansion in the Cotswolds, to which two wings had been added, one to accommodate philosophers, the other for theologians. The main chapel, which was large and dark, was a converted indoor tennis court. Next door was the refectory, a vast T-shaped room, full of light and with a magnificent view over rolling woodlands. Philosophers and theologians, though living under the same roof, were not allowed to communicate with one another, except on feast days, when philosophers could play on the nine-hole golf course, reserved normally for theologians and lecturers, the latter always referred to as 'professors'. We also met for very occasional football matches. Our limbs could not have endured too many, for they were always the roughest and dirtiest games. To live in the same house with others but without verbal communication is very bad social training. My friend, Lachie Hughes, having lived in the Jesuit community in Farm Street, London, went off to work in South Africa. On returning to Farm Street six years later, he met an older member of the community in the lift, who greeted him with 'Oh, haven't seen you for a while. Been away for a bit?'

The community at Heythrop numbered about a hundred and fifty, including Maltese, Spaniards, French, Germans, and eventually a number from Eastern Europe, many of whom had been in concentration camps. Life was much less regimented than at St Beuno's, but we all had to rise at six, appear in chapel just twenty-five minutes later, then proceed to our rooms to pray for an hour before Mass. The mornings were taken up with lectures and there were occasional evening lectures. Talking was officially allowed inside the house only at the two recreation times, after lunch and after supper. At other times we were supposed to communicate in Latin. We usually ignored these regulations, but I found the noviceship training in fidelity to all rules took time to wear off.

The grounds of Heythrop were extensive. Past generations had built huts in the woods, where we could have tea in the afternoons, and spend our weekly day off, which was Thursday. The huts were an escape into relative normality, where we sang, talked, reflected and shook ourselves free of some of the scrupulosity which the noviceship had induced in many of us.

Life in a country mansion with private parkland was a strange training for men who prayed to be 'poor with Christ poor', and who planned to work in the world preaching the Gospel to the poor and outcast. Some who found the studies irksome and who were much more at home in the woods than in lecture rooms have, in fact, spent the rest of their lives in a hutlike existence in remote parts of Guyana or Zimbabwe.

Those who did not spend Thursdays at the huts used to put as much distance between themselves and Heythrop as possible by going hitch-hiking. One man started keeping a log of journeys made and people met on these expeditions, inviting others to contribute. I came across this log recently in the house library in Birmingham and it makes fascinating reading. Most of the unfortunate drivers who offered us lifts were then engaged in a religious discussion, in which the philosopher argued against the driver's Communist, atheist, humanist, Protestant or Anglican views, presenting instead the truth of the one, true, catholic and apostolic Church!

Philosophy began with a six-week course on minor logic, given by a man whom one wit described as having a mind 'as sharp as a razor and about as broad'. Using illustrations from *Alice's Adventures in Wonderland*, he taught us how to put statements into syllogistic form and how to spot logistic fallacies. A syllogism is a method of argument in which a conclusion is derived from two propositions, called a major and a minor premiss. A simple example is 'All human beings are mortal' (major premiss), 'Socrates is a human being' (minor premiss), 'therefore Socrates is mortal', (conclusion), which is not a very exciting piece of information, but the method can enable us to spot logical fallacies in ordinary discussions. This course in minor logic, given in English, was fundamental to the methodology then practised at Heythrop, a method which had been used in medieval universities. Almost all the other lectures were given in Latin and based on St Thomas Aquinas' thirteenth-century *Summa Theolo-gica*, a many-volumed work, which we carried to lectures in a small portable bookcase. During philosophy I had an operation to remove a knee cartilage and was told to exercise the leg by sitting on a table, attaching a weight to my foot and then raising it. I spent more time with St Thomas' *Summa* resting on my foot than open on my desk.

The lectures were given in thesis form. A statement would be made. One, which I never believed, was 'Animals are without intelli-gence'. Those who opposed this doctrine, known as 'the adversaries', were then listed, their views summarised in a brief sentence or two. The arguments for the thesis were then presented and any possible objections refuted. At the end of each year there was an oral examin-ation in Latin on the theses covered. Four examiners would propose a question and the philosopher would then prove the thesis and answer objections. The final examination was also oral and in Latin. It lasted for one hour and examiners could ask any question covered during the last three years.

The method was archaic, but it did help us to think clearly, if not profoundly, and to develop an ability to think on our feet. Most of us found it difficult to understand what philosophy was about and why we should be submitted to three years of it. We were constantly told that we would understand its relevance later, when we came to do theology, for philosophy was the *'ancilla theologiae'*, 'the handmaid of theology', and theology was 'the queen of the sciences'. When theology was completed, many of us were still asking the same question.

I studied this philosophy in much the same way as I had dug the garden at St Beuno's and scrubbed the floors, with little real interest in the subject itself, but seeing it as a duty to be performed. Having a reasonable short-term memory and an ease with basic Latin, I could satisfy the examiners. The only subjects which really interested me were not on the examination syllabus, lectures on the History of Philosophy by Frederick Coplestone, and a few lectures on experi-mental psychology.

The subject I found most obscure was ontology, the study of being. It was all so abstract, and the various theses on the analogy of being contained most complex terminology. It was only years later that I began to understand the importance and relevance of this subject. As I write, the press and media are full of reports and commentary on an Anglican vicar, who has been expelled from his parish by his bishop because he says he no longer believes in God. In the ensuing controversy I have heard nothing on St Thomas' teaching on the analogy of being. I am a being, you are a being, and God is a being, but God's beingness is not the same as yours and mine. The word 'being' can only be used analogously of God, because God is always beyond, always greater than anything our minds can conceive or imagine. In our human sense of being, it would be true to say that God is not a being, as we experience being, and it is therefore true to say that in our sense of exist, God does not exist.

When people say, 'I no longer believe in God', their assertion must be respected, but they must be encouraged to examine what it is they no longer believe. To question the notion of God which we have been taught is a necessary stage in the faith journey. If someone says, 'I no longer believe in God', meaning that they can no longer accept the notion of God as a separate, all-powerful super-being external to us, who controls all things, but whose beingness is the same as ours, only greater, then that person may, in fact, be moving to a deeper understanding of God, 'no longer believing in the gods the city believes in'. God is not an intellectual problem. When treated as such, there are no fully convincing arguments for God's existence. God is. We and all creation are in God. God is mystery, and so are we. Life is a journey into mystery. God can never adequately be known by our reasoning, as though we could prove God's existence, and then, having filed God, get on with life. I now no longer feel disturbed if someone says, 'I no longer believe in God'. I feel much more disturbed when I meet someone who has never entertained a doubt and claims to have an unshakeable faith in God.

As far as I can remember, my prayer life did not change during these three years. I was still trying to reach a still form of prayer without ideas or images, and the result was long periods of dryness. When I told this to the spiritual father, an affable old man in retirement whom we had to visit once a month, he would counsel perseverance, adding that we all find prayer difficult, but that it is our faithfulness to it and the purity of our intention that matters. I did not find these sessions of formal spiritual direction helpful. We were questioned, always gently, as to whether we were being faithful to our prayer and spiritual duties, were exhorted to be even more faithful, and then we would chat about the latest news, or on whatever interested the spiritual father. At Heythrop, the spiritual father was very interested in his own health and would discourse at length on his many operations.

In spite of the ontology lectures on the analogy of being, I never doubted God's existence, nor did I doubt that the Catholic Church was the one, true, holy, catholic and apostolic Church. My doubts were more self-centred. My admiration for Socrates in his pursuit of truth left me worrying about my own integrity. How far was I really God-centred? I was troubled by temptations against chastity. The usual answer given was that as long as one does not give consent to the thoughts, then there is no sin. This did not help me, for I felt that the very fact that I was tempted must mean that I was consenting in some way. I was on the road to scruples. My whole spirituality, although I did not realise it at the time, was dangerously self-centred. I was striving to 'be perfect as your heavenly Father is perfect', but interpreted perfection, not as St Luke does in terms of compassionate love, but understood it as meaning correct behaviour. I knew nothing in those days of Jung's shadow self, nor had I grasped, although I had heard them many times, Ignatius' rules for the discernment of spirits. My philosophy studies had also added to the doubts, for there was a whole treatise on epistemology, which considers the question of how we can know that we know. I applied this question to my own relationship to God. How did I know that I was really living in the grace of God? It took me many years before I could delight in giving myself the answer, 'I don't know: I trust.'

These questions about my own integrity, my own belief, my own relationship to God were useful in themselves, but because they were so me-centred they were unhealthy, making me far too self-absorbed. Deep selfishness can take many forms. The conscientious religious person is always at risk of deep self-centredness.

The spiritual journey is perilous. I hate that saying of Jesus about the way being narrow and few taking it, but I know it is true. It is as though the harder one strives to come close to God, the nearer one also comes to the demonic. The person who lives a self-indulgent life, enjoying as much pleasure as possible, probably does less harm to self and to others than the devout religious who is intent on spiritual perfection, but whose striving is totally centred on their own ability to reach what they conceive to be the perfect state.

At the end of philosophy I went to France for six weeks to polish up my French, staying most of the time at Vals, in the Haut Midi, and spending a short time in Paris. The young French Jesuits seemed much more alive to and interested in the world about them than the rural Jesuits of Heythrop. They were politically and socially alive, still divided among themselves over the question of the wartime Vichy government, a division manifested in their dress, the pro-Vichy wearing a cloth soutane belt while the resistance men wore leather, and the resistance men's soutanes were usually shabbier. The French were less preoccupied with sport, using up their energies in endless conversations on the 'Question Sociale'. Many intended becoming worker priests, who would take on ordinary jobs, living a simple life among the people with whom they worked. I joined the French scholastics in their eight-day retreat, felt very drawn to the 'Question Sociale' and wanted to do further study and work in that area.

Three years of philosophy were normally followed by a period of three to six years called 'regency', when scholastics, as Jesuits in training are called, either went to university to obtain a secular degree or to teach in a Jesuit school, or did both. After regency, we would begin four years' study of theology.

Every year on the feast of St Ignatius, July 31st, the provincial sent to each house a list of the appointments for the following year. In those days there was not much consultation beforehand. God's will was delivered by the postman. I was hoping to go to university to take a degree in Latin and Greek, but when I read the list I saw my name down for Stonyhurst.

CHAPTER 5

⌒⌒⌒

God Who Fails the Verification Principle

There are more things in heaven and earth, Horatio, than are dreamt of in your philosophy. (Hamlet)

During the noviceship I had prayed the prayer Ignatius gives at the end of the Spiritual Exercises. 'Take, Lord, and receive all my liberty, my memory, my understanding and my will, all that I have and possess. You have given it all to me: to You I return it. Take me, Lord, and do what You like with me, only give me Your grace and Your love and that is enough for me.' Later, I found the prayer too wordy and summarised it into 'Take and receive the whole of me and give me You instead'. But now I pray again 'Take and receive my memory'.

Our past must be in God's present, for in God there can be no before or after. For us too, past memories are, in a sense, present, for they are affecting us now for better or worse, depending on how we look at them. Truth is so clear when once I see it, but it has taken me years to see that what is true of memories is true of everything that we experience, that the effect depends ultimately not on the event itself, but in the way I see it now, and therefore react to it. That is why I find praying to God to take my memory is so important, so that past memories, however unpleasant the event remembered, do not blight the present, and also so that I do not try to escape painful memories, either by repressing them, or distorting the truth to save myself discomfort, for the truth always catches up with us in the end.

I can look back on my two years teaching at Stonyhurst followed by four years at Oxford, so focusing on my failings that I make more of them than of God's goodness. It has taken me years to realise that focusing on my failings to the exclusion of God's goodness is not only destructive and depressing, but is a sin of pride, not letting God be God to me. It is true that I went to Stonyhurst, as I had gone to the noviceship, with a desperate need to be approved, thought well of, to be considered 'a good Jesuit'. It is true that both at Stonyhurst, and later at Oxford, success was very important to me, and success meant being well thought of by those whose opinion I valued. I was not aware of this at the time. Had I been asked, I would have said 'God is all-important and I only want to do His will'. This was true, too, but God was still a distant God, God of the supernatural, God of the commandments, God whose orders were passed down to me by the authority of the Church. Because God, whom I must love with all my heart and soul, mind and strength, was not of this world, any enjoyment I experienced in an activity not specifically religious had a hint of disloyalty. Now I can be grateful for all the enjoyment of those years and see them as God's gift.

Stonyhurst College in Lancashire was given to the Jesuits in 1793 by Thomas Weld, a former student at St Omer, in France, where the Jesuits ran a school for the sons of English gentlemen, when the practice of Catholicism was a treasonable offence in England. The main entrance is by an avenue which bends at right angles at the top of a hill and reveals, half a mile away, the Elizabethan manor house with its twin towers surmounted by eagles, the avenue flanked first by playing fields, then by two long ponds. I was overawed at first by the beauty and grandeur of the place, full of reminders of England's Catholic past and of its continuation through penal times into the present.

The Jesuit teaching staff numbered about twenty, living separately from and having little communication with the small lay staff, who had a separate refectory and common room. The lay workers who were not on the teaching staff were mostly local people, but a few lived in, also having their own quarters and refectory. It was a very self-sufficient, hierarchical society. Once slotted into the organisation, it was possible to become totally absorbed in an inner Stonyhurst world, a pleasant, regulated and very predictable world, with which most members seemed to be content, dedicated to defending its ways and customs against the inroads of modernity.

Although I felt very inadequate, I fitted in well, teaching all subjects, apart from French and Science, to a class called 'rudiments', consisting of thirteen-year-old boys. Most public schools are divided into houses, each house containing older and younger boys together. Stonyhurst, on the other hand, was organised on an age division, the divisions called 'playrooms', each playroom having a playroom master, responsible for all out-of-class activities. I was appointed assistant playroom master to an impressive-looking man of delightful simplicity called John Firth, who was in charge of Fourth Playroom, the youngest age group. He had reduced education to a few clear principles. Boys were to keep the rules and were to be punished if they did not. They must never be allowed to be idle, must play games with enthusiasm, take plenty of exercise, say their prayers and have regular haircuts. The insistence on haircuts was because long hair would interfere with their performance at games!

I spent the two years trying to keep a little ahead of the class, which contained some of those annoyingly bright boys who can quickly spot a teacher's mistakes and who delight in pointing them out. When not engaged in teaching, preparation and correction of their work, we had to supervise all their other activities, refereeing rugby and cricket matches and taking them on cross-country runs whenever rain stopped play, which, at Stonyhurst, it often did.

In my second year, John Firth moved on and I was put in charge of Fourth Playroom. I asked him for some guiding principles for the coming year. The first, he told me, was to ensure that they all ate porridge at breakfast, as this would give them a foundation for the day. The second was to warn them against sitting on radiators, as this led to 'horrible diseases'. Looking after about fifty Fourth Playroom boys was an exhausting job when I was also having to teach, but I enjoyed being with boys of thirteen before sophistication has set in, and I could happily envisage a future spent teaching at Stonyhurst. In vacations I explored the countryside by bicycle and by cross-country running, and kept up study of Latin and Greek, hoping eventually to be allowed to go on to Oxford. I knew that if I were to teach competently, I needed further study.

I came to know some of the non-teaching staff. I was appointed stage manager, about which I knew nothing, and relied totally on the college carpenter, a shrewd Lancastrian called John Embly, who would speak naturally in Shakespearean English. John kept a notebook of every carpentry job he had ever done in the college. I asked him why he kept such a detailed record. He told me that every new rector made changes, and he had learned that doors he had removed or walls he had broken down would have to be replaced a few years later on the appointment of a new rector, so it saved him time to keep a careful record. I also got to know some of the cleaners, who worked long hours for very little pay, yet were devoted to the college and enjoyed their work. My interest in the 'Question Sociale' was so general that it did not lead me to question the structure of Stonyhurst society, or the place and status of those who were called 'the servants'. I had my niche and was content. Neither did I question the religious services of the school – Mass at 7.30 every morning, which all boys had to attend, and two Masses on Sundays, one before breakfast at which they could receive Holy Communion because they had been fasting from midnight, or the High Mass later in the morning, with full choir, at which no one apart from the celebrant, could receive.

The two years teaching and the demands of playroom mastering saved me from the neurosis of total self-absorption which earlier training had encouraged. I prayed regularly and I prayed for those I taught, but God was still remote, God of the catechism and of RE classes, God full of disapproval of the world, the flesh, and of Jesuits who did not keep the Rule. I never questioned my belief in God, the Church, or in my life as a Jesuit, and felt uneasy when I heard some of the lay staff criticising the Jesuits and the college organisation. I could see no reason for change either in the Church or the college, defended both, and reckoned that the critics were lacking in detachment! I did occasionally feel envious of some of the married lay staff, who could go home to a wife and family, but dismissed these thoughts as temptations against my vocation.

We are creatures of our environment. The more sheltered and circumscribed it is, the more cocooned will be our world view. Few of us will be changed by any amount of reading, or listening to lectures, however broad and enlightened. It is only when circumstances break the cocoon of our environment, or we deliberately move out of it, that change can happen. Those Catholics who have never encountered at a deep level people of other denominations, or of a different faith, are unlikely to understand or have any interest in ecumenical or inter-faith work. Those who have never tried to get inside the mind of the atheist or the humanist are unlikely to have an appreciation of their own religion, however aggressively they may profess it. Had I remained at Stonyhurst for life, I would probably have ended my days with much the same vision of reality as I had when I began. Life would have been more peaceful and I might have been more content, but contentment has never rated highly in my value scale except when I am caught in a crisis.

After two years at Stonyhurst, I was told I would be going to Oxford to read Classics. One older member of the community at Stonyhurst, on hearing this news, commented, 'In my day, only the best were sent to Oxford.'!

The Jesuits have a house in Oxford, called Campion Hall. We were a community of about thirty undergraduates, graduates and tutors, including Jesuits from the USA, Australia and India. The Master of Campion Hall was Fr Tom Corbishley, whom I already knew from St Beuno's, and for a time the Spiritual Father was Archbishop Roberts, a Jesuit who had just retired as Archbishop of Bombay. He was a man who appeared to be in constant good humour, lived very simply and for whom titles meant nothing. The first five terms at Oxford were spent in reading Latin and Greek classical authors in the original and learning to write Latin and Greek prose compositions. The more gifted also wrote Greek and Latin verse. Although I could speak and understand ecclesiastical Latin, my knowledge of classical Latin was elementary and of Greek prose composition almost non-existent, so most of my time was spent in study, with very little social life outside Campion Hall, apart from games.

For the first time in my life since leaving Skelmorlie School at the age of five. I was being taught by people who were not Roman Catholic and not Jesuit, studying with men and women, most of whom appeared to have little or no interest in religion and who were puzzled by the whole idea of religious life. At first, I felt like a stranger from outer space, a feeling accentuated by the black suit and Roman collar which was then compulsory uniform. I felt more at ease in the afternoons when we could go off, collarless, to play rugby or squash, playing for St Catherine's College which was then struggling at the bottom of most sports leagues, but making up for in enthusiasm what it lacked in skill.

Lectures at Oxford were not compulsory, but two individual tutorials, one in Latin prose writing, the other in Greek, were compulsory, each lasting for one hour. I was struck by the intelligence, courtesy and patience of both tutors with my attempts to write Latin and Greek prose after the style of the classical authors whom I could understand only with difficulty. One tutor, having corrected my many mistakes in Greek or Latin prose composition, would then hand me a model version: another tutor used to correct my mistakes and then produce a model version based on my own effort. I would now be incapable of writing a Greek or Latin prose composition, but that tutor gave me an insight which I have never forgotten, for his method of teaching helped me to see God as God who creates out of our mistakes and our sins, always creating something new and original in every single human being.

Because of my tutors, and through some of the friends I made through games, I first consciously asked myself the question, how is it that these men, so gifted, intelligent and good, cannot see the obvious truth of Roman Catholicism? I prayed for their conversion along with the conversion of the rest of Britain, and of course, Russia.

At first, I was so busy trying to translate the prescribed Latin and Greek texts that I did not appreciate their content, but as I became more adept, I began to enjoy what I was reading. As special topics, I studied Lucretius' *De Rerum Natura*, 'On the Nature of Things', and Plato's *Phaedo*, in which Socrates discourses on the immortality of the soul. Lucretius, in particular, fascinated me, although I did not know why at the time. He predated Christ and devoted his life to teaching atheism. He delivered his teaching in six books of beautiful, if somewhat complicated, poetry. In contrast to the *Phaedo*, Lucretius did not believe in human immortality. According to him, we are like everything else in the universe, a bundle of atoms. Everything could be explained in terms of bombarding particles. In life, we consist of a particular conglomeration: in death, the pattern breaks up, and we are no more. The important thing in life is to live as pleasurably as possible while our atoms are in place, without worrying about our future destiny, for we have none. He believed that the source of disorder in human life sprang from fear, especially fear of the gods and of the punishment they will mete out after death to those who displease them in life. He illustrates this strikingly with the story of Iphigenia's death. On the way to Troy to rescue Helen, who had been abducted, Agamemnon's fleet is becalmed near the island of Aulis. Agamemnon calls on his seer to ask what he must do that the gods might grant favourable winds. The seer tells him he must sacrifice his daughter Iphigenia to the winds. Lucretius describes the death of this beautiful, innocent girl, ending with the thundering lines, *'Tantum religio potuit suadere malorum'*, 'To so much evil can religion lead'.

These lines of Lucretius were touching off something in my sub-conscious, at which my conscious mind was not ready to look. Lucretius' explanation of the universe in terms of bombarding par-ticles, which he had learned from the Greeks, was to have a long run up to our own times. God, the soul, personal immortality, religion, have no more substance than a whistle of steam: remove the steam and there is no more whistle.

While Lucretius' theory of bombarding particles as the explanation of all life was false, his analysis of the danger inherent in all religion was profound. We all tend to make God in our own image and likeness, then use God as a means of ensuring our own security, oppressing and dominating others in the name of God. Because we are afraid and uncertain of ourselves, we readily submit to this form of domination, whether by the Church or the State. While I was reading Lucretius, I was dominated within myself by an authoritarian system. I was not aware of this at the time, but a hidden part of me knew and was attracted by the freedom which Lucretius' theory promised.

After five terms we had the first part of our degree examination, consisting of eleven three-hour papers. I can still remember the anxiety I felt while waiting to enter the examination room for the first time. When the examination began, someone fainted and had to be carried out. I survived, better than I had expected.

At the time, I never made any link between what I had learned in the noviceship about detachment and what I was now experiencing at Oxford. It is natural to feel apprehensive about examinations, but my anxiety to do well was deeper in my soul than I realised. I prayed daily, 'Thy Kingdom come'. There was a group of undergraduates, mostly from Jesuit schools, with whom I used to meet regularly for discussion and prayer. Someone asked one day, 'What does "Thy Kingdom come" mean?' None of us had a clear answer. The only answer I could think of was that the whole world should eventually become Roman Catholic. I did not then realise that the Kingdom of God is a state of being, not a structure or organisation, that it means letting God be God to us, within us, and through us at all times and in all our activities. The kingdom which really engaged my energies and attention was my kingdom, that I should do well and be well thought of. Dedication to the Kingdom of God as it really is would have enabled me to find more enjoyment in studying Homer and Virgil, Plato, Aristophanes, Euripides and Aeschylus, recognising God in their truth, wisdom, wit and insight. I would have been far less anxious about my success or failure in the examinations, because God would have been in reality, rather than just notionally, my rock, refuge and strength and the prospect of failure would not have worried me unduly. The basis of my confidence would have been more secure than any success I might achieve, or any regard I might win, whether from my peers or from those in authority. I can be grateful now for all I learned from those ancient authors, and I am also grateful to those tutors who taught me so much more than Latin and Greek by their courtesy, intelligence, patience and honesty. They were teaching me more than I realised about the nature of the Church and the meaning of God's Kingdom.

The competitive spirit was nurtured not only by the examination system; we also competed with one another in conversation, but subtly, because any obvious boasting was bad form. Cleverness and wit were more appreciated than sensitivity to its victims. Success, whether in examinations, or in any other area of life, is not wrong in itself and the pursuit of excellence is to be encouraged, but it carries with it an infection which works very quietly and secretly in the soul. It was only very gradually that I became aware of inner attitudes of superiority over those who did not possess my knowledge or skill, slight as it was. I would not admit this feeling to myself, but it would reveal itself in a failure to listen and consequent boredom in conversation.

As Oxford's terms lasted only eight weeks, most of the year was spent in vacation, when we were not allowed to remain at Campion Hall, but were sent off to other Jesuit houses, where we were free to get on with our work and expected to put in at least thirty hours of study each week. I used to return to Stonyhurst every summer, and spent the Christmas and Easter vacations at another Jesuit school, Beaumont College, Old Windsor.

After the first examination, the remaining seven terms were given to ancient Greek and Roman history and to philosophy. I found ancient Greek history fascinating; the development of the city state, the growth of Athenian democracy and Thucydides' history of the Peloponnesian wars, which is an analysis of the nature of war itself. Philosophy, on the other hand, baffled me at first, for the style and content of the teaching was so different from what we had experienced at Heythrop, where we had to learn, and reproduce for the annual oral examination, innumerable theses, answering in syllogistic form objections to the thesis we had propounded. At Heythrop we had had no private tutorials and scarcely any written examinations. At Oxford, we had two tutorials each week, one in history, the other in philosophy. For each tutorial we had to produce a 2,000-word essay for which our tutor provided a large reading list of books and articles. We read the essay to the tutor, who would then comment on it and give us a topic and reading list for the following week. The method was demanding, stretching and rewarding. It trained us in the ability to spot quickly and summarise concisely the main points of a book or an article. Most of us soon learned short cuts, leaving the recommended books unread and finding short reviews instead. The method taught us to weigh up historical evidence or the strength of philosophic arguments, to form an opinion of our own and to express it clearly. We were being encouraged to discover for ourselves, to think for ourselves. I was lucky in my tutors. They did not appear to be concerned with any tenets of orthodoxy, but with the truth of the argument. They were also encouraging. If they found my essay inadequate, confused or badly presented, they pointed this out very gently, but they also commented on anything they found good, and they encouraged me to trust my own judgement. This is the greatest service any teacher can give, while to undermine self-confidence is the worst damage a teacher can do. I am glad that corporal punishment is banned in state schools, but I wish that sarcasm and any other method of undermining confidence could be similarly banned.

It took me another twenty years before I realised that this Oxford method of teaching was, in fact, closer to Ignatius' principles in the Spiritual Exercises than was Heythrop's. If we are not encouraged to think for ourselves, to discover for ourselves, then we are likely to find a ready-made God, a God of convention, not the God of life, who is constantly calling us out of the prison of our own inherited thought system to a sense of wonder and to freedom.

Oxford philosophy at that time was concerned mainly with linguistic analysis, the meaning of meaning. Instead of theses being propounded, questions were asked. At first, I found the questions niggling and could not become interested. 'It looks like a banana, tastes, feels and smells like a banana. Is it a banana?' or, 'If I ask a wax policeman the time, what kind of mistake have I made?' How are we to know whether statements have any substance, any meaning? In his book *Language, Truth and Logic*, A. J. Ayer asserted that a statement has meaning only if it can be in some way verified. As another writer put it, 'If I come across a garden in the middle of the jungle, is it meaningful to say there is a gardener? If I fence the garden round so that no one can enter or leave, keep watch over a long period and find no evidence of a gardener, then what meaning can there be in the statement that there must be a gardener?' So what is the meaning of the statement 'There is a God', or 'Our souls are immortal'? Once this question, 'What does it mean?', gets into the mind, the effect can be very unsettling. What do you mean by God, the soul, heaven, resurrection, essence or substance of a thing as distinct from its accidental qualities? Philosophy at Heythrop had been peppered with metaphysical terminology: theology later was to be even more peppered. What does it mean? Is there any way of discovering what it means?

If we keep asking questions about meaning, we are threatened by the fear of meaninglessness: if we do not continue asking, we become imprisoned in our thought system, and if we are religious people, we can end up worshipping a God in our own image and likeness. Constant questioning is uncomfortable and threatening, but if we fail to question, our faith cannot leaven everyday life and we do not meet God in ordinary events. It is as though we have to travel this questioning route until we are exhausted and terrified that it will end in an abyss of meaninglessness. It is then that we can discover God's presence with a knowledge which is deeper than our sensibility and rational thought, and which enables us to live with uncertainty and ambiguity at one level of our being, while knowing we are enveloped in God at another and deeper level.

One evening in vacation I was walking up and down a path in the grounds of Beaumont College. Suddenly the thought came. 'What if the Christian creed is really based on a fiction, has no real meaning, and the Church is just a human organisation which generations have created to give themselves reassurance, to help them feel secure?' This was not just a speculative question. St Thomas Aquinas' *Summa Theologica* is full of questions and objections to Christian beliefs. The question which came to me that evening was very different. It was as though the ground on which I stood was opening up, revealing a threatening void. I felt a momentary panic, interpreted the experience as a temptation, prayed to be rid of it and tried to forget it. The intensity of the feeling did not last long and did not precipitate any crisis. Later, I told a spiritual director that I had been having temptations against faith. He put his hands to his head and said, 'Oh, my God', which was not very encouraging. I did not realise at the time that this was a potentially creative moment, for it was inviting me to look at my idea of God in the light of my experience, especially that of the last few years in Oxford, and to integrate into my relationship with God all the other thoughts and feelings I was experiencing through life in Oxford. It was an invitation to move from belief in a remote and threatening God to a different kind of belief, in a God 'closer to me than I am to myself', a God both familiar and mysterious, whom I could both know and not know, yet with whom I could be at peace in the not knowing. Interpreting the experience as a temptation, I did not accept the invitation.

Since Marie's death I had visited home several times and my mother, Edith, Margot and Joe occasionally visited me at Heythrop and at Stonyhurst. My mother had always longed for what she called 'a little house in the country'. In 1951, the family had moved to Ayrshire. The house was not as remote as my mother would have liked it to be, but remote enough to be difficult for the rest of the family who were all working in Glasgow. My mother knew she would have to move nearer to the city, and her weekly letters showed her anxiety about this. About five weeks before my final exams at Oxford, Edith phoned to tell me that my mother was seriously ill and that I should come as soon as possible. Every week until her death, my mother had written to me, and one of my regrets about my attachment to detachment is that I never preserved her letters. I went to Ayrshire and stayed four weeks, taking my notes and a few books with me.

My mother was in bed, fully conscious, but her breathing was distressingly laboured. I could never remember her having taken to her bed before. She would not hear of going to hospital and insisted on having the doctor who had attended her since youth, an elderly general practitioner, who would arrive by car on his daily visits from Glasgow anytime between midnight and 2 am. On one occasion he cheerfully announced that he had fallen asleep on the way down, adding that it was just as well he knew the road so well. He always gave my mother an injection, which would ease her breathing and enable her to have a few hours' sleep.

My sisters, Edith and Margot, and my brother Joe were all at home. Edith had stopped working to look after my mother, while Margot continued teaching. Joe, who had served four years in the navy, was now studying accountancy and was the proud owner of a two-seater car, which I had to push every morning to get him started on his way to work. Edith and I worked in shifts to be with my mother when she was awake. In between times I would try to do some study, but my heart was not in it.

There are memories which have a sheen on them. When recalled they are encouraging and strengthening, as though there is an aura around them. Those four weeks still retain their sheen. Although it was distressing to see my mother fighting for breath and to hear her struggle, it was as though her body was labouring while her spirit remained free. She was naturally a worrier, often about trivialities. In her illness, she would occasionally express some trivial worry, but most of the time she was very peaceful. When the breathing eased she would talk, much of the conversation being about family and relatives, about her own childhood, her parents and younger sister, Helen, and about her schooldays at the Notre Dame Convent in Blackburn, where she had been a boarder. Most accounts I have heard, or read, of convent boarding schools at the turn of the century have been horror stories. For my mother, her days at Notre Dame were bliss, for there was great emphasis on music, singing and acting, all of which she loved. When she tired, she would ask me to read some scripture to her. Her favourite passage was John c. 6, 'Yes, it is my Father's will that whoever sees the Son and believes in him shall have eternal life and I shall raise them up at the last day' (v. 40) and 'Whoever eats my flesh and drinks my blood lives in me and I live in them' (v. 56). Then she would start worrying that I was not getting enough time for study.

As her breathing grew worse and the doctor's daily arrival time became more erratic, we decided that my mother needed hospital care and a change of doctor. By this time, she realised the need herself and agreed. She was moved to the Bon Secours nursing home in Glasgow, where she improved immediately under new treatment, and I thought it safe to return to Oxford. When I saw her in Bon Secours she was sitting up, looking very peaceful, and she said she was glad to have made the move.

A few days later, back at Campion Hall, I had a phone call from Edith. When I reached Bon Secours my mother was already unconscious. She died later that night. Finals began two days after the funeral and there was a rail strike at the time. My cousin, John Murray, who was also at Oxford, drove me back overnight, a horrific journey through mist and fog. We arrived in Oxford in the early morning, giving me twenty-four hours to prepare for finals.

My mother's death had banished all the pre-exam anxiety which had afflicted me before her illness. The exam no longer seemed all-important. I survived, Zombie-like, and realised at the end of some of the papers that I had neither remembered accurately nor thought clearly, but I passed with a second-class degree. Her last gift to me was to teach me that examination success is not important.

Years later, after a bout of depression, I talked about my childhood and my relationship with my parents to a psychologist. I don't think he believed me when I said that I loved them and felt no anger or bitterness towards them. He suggested that I had buried my resentment and anger. The only anger and resentment of which I was conscious was momentarily directed against the psychologist himself and was misdirected in this case, for he was generally helpful. Later, I realised the anger was directed at a cluster of experiences in which some people in authority, whether teachers, spiritual directors or religious superiors, had succeeded in undermining my own self-confidence, leaving me with an abiding hatred of manipulators who sap our confidence in our own experience and claim that they know best. While it is true that I can bury in my subconscious truths I may fear to acknowledge, and that another may be able to spot what is hidden, that knowledge can only be helpful to me in so far as I can be helped to see it for myself. Those who undermine another individual's self-confidence also undermine faith, for faith in God necessarily involves faith in our own judgement.

I had felt anger and resentment against my mother when I was a child. As I grew older and came to know her, the resentment and anger vanished. She apologised later for being over-strict when I was a child, saying that it had been difficult for her to know what was best after my father's illness and death. Her own religious education had been narrowly Catholic and as a child I grumbled at having the rosary every night, at being sent to Benediction as well as to Mass on Sundays, and at being sent back to Mass again if I arrived even a second late. Places for summer holidays could be chosen only if they were within reach of a Catholic church on Sundays. My mother was not over-affectionate, but was not afraid of showing affection, and an abiding memory is of her letting me weep in her arms when I was twelve. She survived my father's illness and death, and above all the death of Marie, to whom she was very close, without breaking down or sinking into a depression. She lived for us, but without becoming over-possessive. The memory of those last weeks with her retains its sheen.

After my mother's death, the family decided to move back to Glasgow. I stayed with them for a few weeks, helping with the removal. The following September I returned to Heythrop to begin theology.

CHAPTER 6

God Who Is Always
Greater

If we want to bring together what is divided, we cannot do so by imposing one division upon the other. If we do this, the union is not Christian. It is political, and doomed to further conflict. We must contain all divided worlds within ourselves and transcend them in Christ. (Thomas Merton)

EXCEPT FOR THAT one brief moment of doubt, the questions which Oxford raised for me had not affected my religious belief. It was as though my psyche contained a number of well-insulated compartments, the religious compartment of childhood upbringing and later Jesuit training being especially impervious. I did not doubt the existence of God, in spite of the verification principle – that only what can be empirically verified can have any real meaning – nor did I doubt that the Roman Catholic Church was the one true Church. After the experience of being with my mother in her illness and death, I felt confirmed in my Jesuit life. The noviceship teaching on the need for detachment, and on suffering and self-denial as a means to attain to it, was still strong. I prayed to suffer more, believing that this was the way to purification.

Religious language is full of ambiguities. It is true that to find God we must learn to be detached, to be poised over against everyone and everything, so that we never invest our whole being in any created person or thing, otherwise we abandon our freedom and sentence ourselves to slavery. It is also true that we need to practise self-denial, but we need to understand the self we are denying. Like the Gerasene demoniac in the Gospel, 'there are many of us', innumerable urges, desires, ambitions, fears. If we follow whatever we happen to be feeling at the moment, we tear ourselves and other people apart. We have to learn to distinguish the true self from the false self, the deep-down self from the superficial. Simply to deny ourselves indiscriminately and to go against every inclination is to destroy ourselves.

It is also true that suffering can purify, but it more often destroys. In Christianity, writers, commentators and preachers on the meaning of Christ's passion and death, have often divinised suffering, glorified pain, as though pain and suffering were in themselves good. In many biographies of the saints, the reader is left with the impression that holiness and the ability to endure suffering are in direct proportion, whether the suffering is inflicted by others or self-inflicted. In themselves, pain and suffering, are an evil and to be avoided, but I did not understand this when I went to theology, so I prayed for suffering. It came, but I do not believe it was in answer to my prayers. I do not believe that God punishes us as we punish one another. I believe God is continuously leading us out of darkness into light, from slavery to freedom. The pain comes because we have grown so accustomed to the darkness that we prefer our prison to the risk of freedom. God is both with us and ahead of us on the journey, as with the chosen people in the wilderness, sharing our pain with us. For Christians, the clearest manifestation of this truth is in the life, passion, death and resurrection of Jesus.

I returned to Heythrop to begin theology in September 1955, glad to be back with friends, some of whom I had not seen for six years, glad to be free of the pressures of Oxford and to have the time to find answers to some of the questions which Oxford had raised for me.

The method of teaching in theology was as it had been in philosophy, with three or four compulsory lectures each day, topics being taught in thesis form. A statement is made; for example, that Christ is really present, body and soul, in the sacrament of the Eucharist. The statement is briefly elaborated on and those theologians who have held unorthodox opinions are mentioned. The thesis is then proved with reference to scripture, to the tradition of the Church and to human reason. Finally, objections are answered, and a brief summary of the whole thesis usually presented to us by the lecturer on two sides of A4 paper.

Given that the lecturers had to present a basic theology course to students of very mixed ability to enable them to teach, preach, administer the sacraments, counsel and guide, it was not an unreasonable method. In the skeletal theses presented, references were given to the scriptures, to early Fathers of the Church, Church Councils and to the work of modern theologians. Those who had the interest and aptitude could pursue questions in greater depth in the excellent Heythrop library, and in my experience, professors were always delighted if anyone showed any interest in their subject and they were very ready to help.

At first, I studied the subjects presented without any great interest. It was for me like surveying a desert landscape – dry scrub and only the occasional oasis. The interest came later when the study years were over.

Theology is the study of God, which at once raises a problem. For God, being beyond definition, cannot be an object of study. All that we can safely state about God is what God is not, for God cannot be encompassed in any human formulation, a truth which led Pascal to say, 'I am amazed at the audacity with which some people speak about God!' Jung wrote, 'I cannot define for you what God is. I can only say that my work has proved empirically that the pattern of God exists in everyone, and that this pattern has at its disposal the greatest of all energies for transformation.'

Men and women struggle to express their religious experience in words, and from their writings and sayings comes that body of knowledge called theology. Among the Jewish people, the prophets uttered the inspiration they experienced. Their words resonated in the minds and hearts of others and so the scriptures came to be written over many generations. The early Christians, inheritors of this Jewish tradition, wrote of 'what their eyes had seen and their ears heard'. They struggled to put into words their experience of Jesus Christ who lived, died and rose again, expressing it in concepts which were familiar in the Graeco-Roman world. At first, there was no distinction made between spirituality and theology, nor between moral and doctrinal theology. In later centuries the work became systematised and theology came to have a life of its own, which did not necessarily have any connection with the spiritual experience of the writer. All theology has its origin in human experience, and theology adrift from religious experience can become a very arid subject.

In the first year we studied four main subjects – the nature of the Church, moral theology, Church legislation (known as Canon Law), and a subject called fundamental theology. I was soon in difficulties. Fundamental theology included questions about the nature of faith, whether God could be known by natural reason, and on the origins and nature of scriptural writing. The catechism had stated that, 'Faith is a supernatural gift of God, which enables us to believe without doubting whatever God has revealed'. Supernatural gifts of God did not therefore seem to be open to verification. How are we to know whether we really have faith or not? If faith is a supernatural gift, then there is obviously no natural way of knowing whether or not we have it, yet faith is necessary for salvation. That was one part of the problem of which I was aware, and it touched off deep anxieties. How was I to know whether I was, in fact, living in the grace of God? This question worried me for a long time. I grew even more worried when I came across a statement in some Church Council decree which stated that no human being can have the certainty of living in the grace of God. Then it slowly dawned on me that this must be true: if it were not true, there would be no need for faith in God, and this dawning truth brought peace and an end to that particular worry.

But there was another problem about the nature of faith which was more fundamental. At that time, I thought that the primary meaning of faith was believing all that the Catholic Church teaches. This was later to become the source of many difficulties, as I found myself questioning one belief after another. Were these doubts signs that I was not really living in the grace of God? It took me many years before I began to realise that faith is not primarily about belief in doctrine, but primarily an attitude of trust, trust in God, present in all things, in every circumstance, every fact, every detail of life. Faith, in this sense, is not separated from the rest of life; it is faith in the sacrament of the present moment. Faith in this sense is quite compatible with confusion, bewilderment, doubt, and ignorance of many things, including the teachings of the Church. It is an attitude of deep confidence in life which remains unshaken by uncertainty about its details. 'Unless you become as little children, you cannot enter the Kingdom of God.' In order to have trust in parents, the child does not have to walk around with bulky documentation proving its paternity, maternity, and the trustworthiness of both parents. Faith is an attitude of the heart, not primarily of the intellect, an attitude which, as St Anselm expressed it, 'seeks understanding'. Von Hügel later expressed it as, 'Where your heart is, let your brain be also'. The primary object of faith is God: all the doctrines and teachings of the Church are means to help us in that journey of faith. If they become the object of our faith instead of a means leading us to faith, then they become an obstacle to our finding God. Nothing so masks the face of God as religion.

Moral theology, which is concerned with Christian behaviour, raised even more questions. Is there a natural law, and if so, how can we know it? If it is natural, why is there so much disagreement among those who all share the same nature? The reason we spent so much time on moral theology – the course lasted for two years – was to enable us to hear confessions after we were ordained. A penitent told the story of going to confession to an aged Jesuit whom she heard snoring as she confessed her sins. She finished what she had to say: the snoring continued. She coughed loudly: the old man woke up and said, 'Would you kindly speak up, that I may assess your guilt?' There was, in my day, an emphasis on assessing guilt, on being able to apply general principles to particular cases and so assess whether a particular action was a grave offence against the natural law, the law of the Church, or the code of Canon law, and therefore qualifying as a mortal sin. Later, I once saw an examination paper in religion, set by a Jesuit for fourteen-year-old boys, in which the examiner gave a list of misdemeanours and asked candidates to separate them out into two columns, one headed mortal sin, the other venial!

The examination for hearing confessions was popularly known as the B.E.F. exam – meaning, back every fortnight – for if failed, the candidate had to try again a fortnight later and could not be ordained until he had passed. The more intelligent and thoughtful candidates usually failed frequently.

We need moral guidance and I am not arguing against moral theology itself, but against the manner in which it was taught to priests in training and the effect this had on so many conscientious Catholics, for it confirmed their image of God as judge, primarily interested in our faults. This led the more conscientious to scrupulosity, and others to abandon the practice of church-going altogether. Later I was to experience the devastation in people's lives which insensitive and ill-applied confessional practice so often caused, especially in the area of sexual morality.

Although unhappy with many of the theses presented in fundamental theology, and still more unhappy with the way in which natural law was presented in moral theology and applied to particular cases, I never doubted, at this stage, that anything the Catholic Church declared to be gravely sinful was, in fact, gravely sinful.

The course, *De Ecclesia*, on the nature of the Church did interest me. As a child in Skelmorlie, where everyone greeted everyone else, I was puzzled by the changed relations on a Sunday. As we were climbing the station hill on our way home after Mass, the Protestants were descending on their way to the Church of Scotland. Instead of the usual greetings, brief bows were exchanged across four centuries. At Oxford, where for the first time in my life I had come to know and admire Christians of other denominations, I became interested in the question of Church unity and discovered that it was now called ecumenism, spelt in those days 'oecumenism'. I read with interest about the new Church of South India, in which Anglicans and Free Church congregations were uniting, the Free Churches agreeing to have bishops. Fr Maurice Bevenot, a patristic scholar with a particular interest in St Cyprian, the third-century bishop of Carthage who wrote a treatise entitled *De Unitate*, encouraged and helped me pursue this interest. He kept pointing out interesting books and articles on ecumenism written in German, so I started to learn the language and hoped to spend the following summer in Germany.

On the evening of New Year's Day 1956, I had a phone call from my brother Ian in Glasgow. Margot was dead. Her body had been found in a canal in Glasgow. Edith, Joe and Ian were at home and my mother's sister, Helen Hackett, had come over to be with them. People react differently to devastating news, some breaking down completely, others able to absorb the shock at the time and to operate outwardly in what is considered a normal manner. Edith, who was always the quietest member of the family, was rocklike, as she had been after the deaths of Marie and our mother. None of us broke down. It might have been better for us if we had, but this was the kind of blow from which it takes years to recover and affects the way we look on life and therefore the way we react to it.

I was benumbed by the news. When feeling did begin to return, it was a feeling of bitter regret that I had been away from home and unaware of what Margot must have been going through. As a child I had constantly teased and baited her, and she never failed to rise to it. Like Marie, she was musical, and later taught music. She was more interested in practical matters than in ideas, and as we grew older I could never share ideas with her, as I could with Marie.

After my mother's death, when we were preparing to move house, Margot grew snappy with the rest of us one evening and I, self-righteously, snapped back at her. We made it up next day and my last memory was of hugging and kissing her goodbye at Central Station and thinking how well she looked. I have never been afraid of rows and have often had friendships which began with a row, or been greatly strengthened by rows, but what I find most difficult to bear are rows which cannot be mended. Margot's and Marie's deaths have left me with an abiding awareness that in any friendship we do not have each other for long, and so I find it very difficult to cope with lingering rows.

At Margot's funeral, a priest who had known her told me that she was over-scrupulous. Her death and Marie's have left me with a special sympathy for all who suffer from depression, and a horror of any form of preaching, teaching or writing that could in any way nurture scrupulosity. Later, I was horrified in pastoral work to meet so many sensitive and imaginative people whose lives had been blighted by the fears and scruples which Church teaching, especially on sexual morality, had induced.

The pain of Margot's and of Marie's deaths lasted for many years and will never completely disappear. The worst, most lasting and most devastating effect of Margot's death was the fear that I, too, having the same genes, could end by committing suicide. The most destructive mixture in the human psyche, and therefore in life, is fear plus imagination. My fear was not simply of committing suicide, but of the fact that I was flawed in some way and could never be certain, no matter how sure I might feel, that I was acting reasonably. This undermined my confidence at the deepest level and linked in with previous questions as to whether I really was living in a state of grace. I felt confirmed in my flawedness whenever I heard talks, or read books on prayer or on Christian or religious life, which spoke of the wonderful peace and happiness which God brings. It is hard to write accurately of states of mind without giving wrong impressions. After Margot's death, I did not live constantly in a state of dread about my present condition and future fate, but the fear was always lurking there in the depths, and any crisis could bring it to the surface. Particularly painful were remarks passed on to me later that two people, both authority figures, had stated that I should not be listened to because of my family background. My sister Edith suffered the same fate. She wanted to join a religious order, but was turned down because of the death of her two sisters. Edith took this without bitterness, and lived happily as a laywoman, but the rejection hurt her.

Especially in recent years, I have known that Margot, like Marie, is close to me, a strengthening, reassuring presence. In death, life is changed, not ended. I believe the dead, especially the dead of our own family, live on in us. No analogy is adequate to describe the effect of this belief, but it is as though the dead pass on their baton to us, the baton containing their hopes, longings and aspirations, and they are cheering us on as we run our race. Somehow, their good and my good are identical. I have no way of proving this, but I sense this identity and that my actions and aspirations now affect them, as theirs affect me.

When I returned to Heythrop after Margot's funeral, I told a few close friends of what had happened, then I tried to carry on as usual, but it was like crossing bleak moorland in heavy mist. Edith and Joe came down to Heythrop for Easter, a visit which helped us all, and in June, Joe married Margaret O'Brien. Their home became Edith's home for many years, and they always made me feel that it was my home, too.

After Margot's death, I wondered sometimes at my own ability to continue studying theology, for I could make no sense of Margot's death, nor of a God who could have allowed this to happen. I still do not understand, nor can I explain rationally why I can now feel at peace within myself with Marie and Margot, and with God. Sometimes I wonder whether, for my own security and sanity, I have unconsciously constructed an image of God to shield me from pain I cannot bear. But I can face that thought and know that with regard to Marie's and Margot's deaths it is not true. In one retreat, years after their deaths, I deliberately spent time standing at the end of my bed imagining I was having a conversation with Marie and Margot in turn, then with my father and mother. It was an extraordinary experience, for I felt peace and delight welling up within me as I spoke to each. There was nothing forced: the effect took me by surprise and has never left me. God is the God of mystery, beyond my thinking and imagining. Even if Julian of Norwich had never said it, I would know from that experience that 'All will be well, all manner of things will be well'. I know that with my deepest self.

When I asked if I might spend the summer of 1956 in Germany, the dean of studies suggested that as my interest was in ecumenism I should go to Germany for the remaining three years of theology.

The Nazi threat had brought the Christian Churches in Germany closer together, a bond strengthened after the war by the threat of the Communist East. The Allied bombing had destroyed most of the churches, so that in 1956 there were 2,000 Catholic churches which were also used by other denominations. There was also a vigorous ecumenical movement in Germany called 'Una Sancta', founded by

Franz Josef Metzger, a diocesan priest, executed by the Nazis in 1944. Metzger was in the army in the 1914–18 war, from which he emerged as a pacifist and he was prominent in international peace efforts until the late Twenties. He also founded houses of 'Christ the King', hospitality houses for the hungry and homeless. When I was walking to Jerusalem in 1987, I called in at one of these houses by mistake, thinking it was a bed-and-breakfast place. I was made most welcome, given a towel and a bar of soap and told to take a shower before meeting the other hungry and homeless people for supper.

Metzger came to believe that peace between nations could come about only if the Churches were reconciled and united. The aim of the Una Sancta movement was not that all the other Churches should become Roman Catholic, but that each denomination should be true to the scriptures and to their own tradition. The underlying belief was that it is the Holy Spirit alone who can bring about unity. What form that unity may take, we cannot predict in detail. Insofar as each denomination strives to be open to the Spirit, the Spirit will draw us into unity. In pursuit of this aim, besides sharing churches, there were frequent public meetings of Catholic, Lutheran and Evangelical churches, in which doctrines which unite and those which divide were explained and discussed. In consequence, a flood of books and articles on ecumenism appeared. Besides, it was in Germany that the Reformation had begun, with Luther, and Oxford had taught me always to go back to the sources, so I left Heythrop for Germany in autumn 1956, to spend the next three years at Sankt Georgen, the Jesuit house of theology, in Frankfurt/Main.

Like almost every other city in Germany, Frankfurt had been heavily bombed during the war and was still showing its scars. Sankt Georgen was in the suburbs, set in a flat plain in the midst of garden allotments, a large functional white building, still being constructed and smelling of concrete and paint. When I arrived, the library was a small room with few books. Before the war, the German house of theology had been in Falkenburg, in Holland, and the books had not yet been recovered, nor the library built in Frankfurt to receive them.

There were about a hundred scholastics, mostly German, but with a sprinkling of other nationalities, including four Americans and two

Irish. Everyone was dressed in black, wearing a long soutane and black girdle. I arrived with my mind well stored with wartime anti-German propaganda and first impressions did nothing to dispel my prejudices. There was an inpersonal feel about the house, a heavy seriousness. Shortly after I arrived, we had an eight-day retreat, the four talks each day given by a visiting Jesuit, the personification of gravitas. During his talks, the Germans were busy note-taking. My German was still elemental, so I simply made a note of any unfamiliar words I could catch, looking them up in the dictionary later. After one talk I looked over my translation, which read, 'sin, destruction, eternal loss, devastation, corruption, poison, despair, anxiety, torment'. The retreat improved my German and forced me to pray for perseverance.

When lectures began, there were many each day. The method of teaching was the same as at Heythrop, but the thesis summaries supplied were longer. The German students studied these assiduously, marking out passages with coloured pencils and retyping them in summary form, which sometimes turned out to be longer than the original. I was intrigued by one scholastic whose coloured pencils included a white one. When I mentioned this to a friend, he suggested that the white pencil was for underlining the unimportant bits!

The lecturers were all Jesuits, and some were very scholarly men with international reputations in their field, but too many years of listening to lectures had left me incapable of attending for much more than ten minutes unless the subject was exceptionally interesting – a rare occurrence. As soon as concepts were introduced which seemed to fail the verification principle, I lost interest and fell asleep, or doodled. There was one lecturer on Church history who never sent me to sleep. Lecturing on the Reformation, he spoke of Luther with enthusiasm, describing him as a deeply religious man, praise which I had never heard before from a Catholic lecturer. Another lecturer spoke disparagingly of Pope Pius XII. I had never heard such criticism from a Catholic priest before and felt inwardly censorious for my notion of loyalty to God and loyalty to the Catholic Church, the Pope in particular, were not yet differentiated. Another excellent lecturer on scripture began his lecture on the day after Pius XII's death with 'We must make as much progress as possible with our scripture studies while the keys of Peter are at rest'. It was from his lectures that I was introduced to the demythologising of the scriptures, including the New Testament. This raised all kinds of questions for me. If the infancy narratives are not historical accounts but the language of myth, what about the other events in the Gospels, the passion accounts and the resurrection appearances? To my rigid religious thought patterns, these were very disturbing questions.

It was mostly through private reading and discussion with others that I became more interested in theology. The Jesuit Fr Karl Rahner, probably the most outstanding theologian of the twentieth century, was then lecturing in Innsbruck, and was beginning to produce his volumes of *Theological Investigations*. From scholastics studying at Innsbruck we were also getting some of Rahner's typed notes on the doctrine of grace, the relationship between the natural and the supernatural, the Doctrine of Original Sin, and also a large manuscript of thirty lectures which he had given on St Ignatius' Spiritual Exercises. Karl Rahner's German style was tortuous and obscure, with sentences sometimes more than a page long. His brother, Hugo, is reported to have said that he would spend the rest of his life translating Karl into German! At first, I found that attempting to read Rahner was like trying to chew granite, but I had learned to persevere with difficult texts at Oxford and soon began to see the importance, and at least some of the practical implications, of his writing.

Ideas, like groceries, can be looked at, picked up, quickly assessed, then either returned to the shelf or put in the trolley. Grocery shopping is a waste of time unless the purchases are eventually eaten by someone. The same is true of ideas, but it takes much longer to assimilate ideas than it does to digest food. I picked up ideas in Germany, but it has taken me decades to assimilate them, to understand their implications and try to live them in practice.

Rahner explored the relationship between grace and nature, the natural and the supernatural. In my thinking, the natural and the supernatural existed in two separate tiers. There was this material world with ourselves in it, each of us wrapped around in a material body. This material world had a reality, but a transient one. True and lasting reality was God and the world of the spirit, a distinction reflected in our language and behaviour. We speak of natural and supernatural, grace and nature, sacred and secular, holy and profane, as though they were separate realities. In life, I believed that the supernatural mattered above all; keeping in the right relationship with God, giving him our worship and praise in prayer and receiving God's grace through validly celebrated sacraments. Rahner's point was that there is nothing in existence which is not supernatural. God freely chose to create a world, to identify God's very self with it, in Christ. All creation is called into unity with God, and God is constantly drawing all things into that unity. Everything is sacramental: every bush is burning, if only we have the eyes to see. In every conscious act we make, we are either saying 'yes' or 'no' to God.

Karl Rahner's writings also made clearer to me the essential nature of the Church, that it is to be a listening, discerning Church, listening both individually and corporately, to the Spirit which is its life. The structures of the Church are essentially provisional and are to be seen as a means to make us more perceptive and more responsive to the Spirit. God, not doctrine, is the primary object of faith: 'God alone shalt thou worship, God alone shalt thou adore'. Faith is not primarily an assent of the mind, but an entrusting of our whole being to God. Because the natural and the supernatural are not two separate layers of reality, faith in God is also trust in God's presence in whatever we experience, and in whomsoever we encounter. Obedience is not primarily about obeying those in authority over us, but about listening carefully to God in every circumstance of our lives. Church unity is not about a takeover bid by one Church of all the other Churches, but about listening to one another across the denominations, working together in obedience to the Spirit, the Spirit of unity and of peace poured out on all peoples. Church doctrines are given to us not as definitive answers to problems, but as ways of keeping us open to the mystery of God and life, and in order to encourage us to explore further. One of Rahner's seminal articles was 'God in the New Testament', showing the variety of ways in which the writers present God, the phrases they use and the images they employ all indicating the unknowableness of God and the inadequacy of all human ideas and images to express who God is. Consequently, there must be a measure of agnosticism in every true believer. He wrote, too, of the anonymous Christian. Men and women who are true to their own consciences, who may profess no religion, attend no services, receive no sacraments, may be closer to God than an observant Christian. I was to meet many such people later. God is at work in everyone, of whatever faith, or no faith.

As my German improved and I came to know individual Germans, I became more aware of my own prejudice and racism. To my prejudiced mind, Germans had all been lumped together without distinction as being heavy, industrious, wooden, humourless, unquestioningly obedient and prone to appalling inhumanity. I came to realise that among themselves they differ as much as the British, and I was able to see the danger of generalising about any nation or group. Most Germans had been through traumatic experiences during the war, and shared the national shame and guilt. One evening we were shown a film of the concentration camps, taken just after the war. At the end of the film, the Germans were in tears. If there was a certain heaviness at Sankt Georgen, it was understandable.

How was it that a nation so intelligent, cultured and religious, could have been taken over by the Nazi party? Some individual Christians did speak up against the regime and the persecution of the Jewish people, and many were imprisoned and executed for doing so; but the Churches as a whole did not stage any mass protest. The question intrigued me at the time and has intrigued me since. Many Germans summed up the answer in the phrase. 'We lacked discernment'. The phenomenon of Nazism is not just a problem which Germans have to ponder: it is a problem for every nation, every church, every religion. We are all just as likely to succumb to nationalism, race hatred, religious fanaticism, sectarianism, when we identify ourselves with any 'ism'. That is why I now see the role of the Church as being the critic, the questioner, in the spirit of the prophet Elisha. 'Throughout his life no ruler could shake him, and no one could subdue him. No task was too hard for him'. (Ecclesiasticus 48:13).

As I shed my prejudices and became more fluent in German, life in Sankt Georgen became less baneful, the heaviness much alleviated by my American and Irish colleagues. A German priest, who was chaplain to one of the American army camps and also to the American military prison, used to invite me to do the preaching for him, so I had plenty of practice in preaching before ordination. Vast numbers used to attend Mass at the American camps. I did not meet any who had any problem in combining enthusiastic Catholicism with membership of the armed forces, nor at this time did I. In the prison, numbers were smaller, but all the Catholics attended Mass. I later discovered that the largest prisoner of all, who was doing time for violent assault, ordered the other Catholics to come.

At the end of my second year at Frankfurt I was ordained priest. There was a rule at that time that Jesuits studying abroad had to be ordained in their place of study. Ian, Edith, Joe and Margaret, and my Aunt Helen Hackett came over to Frankfurt by car for the ordination. I approached the rector and asked if I might return home for a few weeks after ordination. He looked puzzled and asked why I wanted to go home. 'Because it is home,' I said. He replied that I must have an academic reason, so I told him that I was very interested in Scottish theology, whereupon he agreed to my going!

At ordination to the priesthood and for several weeks afterwards, I lived in a state of bliss inside my religious cocoon, so out of touch with reality that I mislaid my passport, which Joe helped me to recover from my suitcase while we stood searching for it in a thunderstorm. In those pre-Vatican II days, the celebration of Mass was regulated by innumerable rubrics, giving an exact description of every gesture, every movement made during the celebration, and directions as to which prayers were to be said aloud, and which *sotto voce*. We had many rehearsals, so that when the time came to say Mass for the first time I was not too bothered by the detailed instructions. Celebrating Mass for the first time, I felt a great happiness which had the same overpowering quality I had first experienced at the age of sixteen. It was as though I had found a stream of life-giving water at the age of sixteen, so attractive that I had to follow it for the rest of my days, but when I began my Jesuit training, the stream had gone underground. I plodded on, believing that I was still on its tracks, and it had reappeared at this Mass.

After ordination I had to return to Germany for a final year of theology. The last term was lecture-free to give us time to study for the final examination, a two-hour oral exam with four examiners, conducted in Latin and covering the whole of theology and philosophy. I survived the examination, then set off with a Dutch priest to take part in a 'Kapellenwagen Mission' to the Protestant parts of Germany, which had no Catholic churches, but now had large numbers of Catholic refugees from the former German Sudetenland, now part of Poland. We travelled in a caravan which carried a large marquee. We would set up in a field, hold two services each day in the tent and visit as many people as we could. The hospitality of these peasant people was overwhelming and we were invited to different families for all meals. Sudetenland fare was usually stew and dumplings, even when the temperature was 90 degrees. I heard vast numbers of confessions for which my training in moral theology was of little help, for often I could not understand their dialect, nor did I know how to assess guilt when the confession took the form, as it often did, 'It is twenty years since my last confession and I have sinned in thought, word and deed'.

I also spent a few weeks at an Ecumenical Institute in Paderborn, where the director suggested that I should return later, offering to supervise me while I studied for a doctorate at Münster. I was flattered by the offer, but although I wanted to work on ecumenism, I knew I was not suited to academic work. The director also offered to take me to meet a group of Catholic and Protestant theologians who were having a five-day meeting on the theology of the Eucharist. When I wrote back to England to ask if I might spend the rest of the summer in Germany, I received a curt reply, telling me that I did not appear to appreciate the apostolic needs in Britain, and that I should return as soon as possible to help out in a parish in Preston.

CHAPTER 7

৵৩৫৩৵

God Who Shakes the Foundations

It is through the tragedy of freedom that Christian renaissance on a world scale will take place. The Christianity of the future will be a Christianity of freedom of the Spirit which has successfully passed through the trials of freedom by overcoming the temptation to oppose them. (Berdyaev)

IT WAS RAINING as I walked from the station to the parish where I was to answer Preston's urgent spiritual needs. The parish priest greeted me, 'You must be Hughes. Don't quite know what we are going to do with you for the next few weeks, but you can help out with Masses on Sundays.' This was my first introduction to the active apostolate for which I had been in training for seventeen years.

Almost the last words spoken by an elderly Jesuit philosopher as he lay on his death bed were, 'I think God created because He was bored'. After some events, such as my arrival in Preston, I have sometimes wondered whether God might not have created for a laugh, a thought which soon vanishes, for it would mean God is cruel. But our gift of laughter must derive from something in God. All our humour, from the crudest to the most sophisticated, springs from false expectations, from the gap between reality in itself and our perception of it. To be able to laugh, we have to distance ourselves from the situation we laugh about. We can laugh at two people having a screaming match with one another, and the more pretentious the contestants the funnier we find them, provided we are totally detached from both. This is why the ability to laugh at ourselves is a gift from God, for it demands that we step outside our own ego, that we let go our own self-importance, that we begin to see others and ourselves from a new standpoint. If we could really do this, we would not have to wait for TV sitcoms; every hour of every day would provide rich comedy. That is how I now understand and relish prayers which ask God to keep our minds on heavenly things, not on the things of earth, but I wish they were expressed as 'O God, infect us with Your laughter and help us to see the absurdity of our own self-importance'.

While God was still for me 'the Supreme Spirit infinite in all perfections', I never made any connection between God and laughter. Now I can look back on my Preston sojourn and on many other past incidents and laugh, but at the time I was not amused. I felt frustrated at being imprisoned in this parish with very little to do, when I could have been having a most interesting and useful time in Germany.

I remember the outline of a sermon I preached while in Preston. There had been much in the press about the first space rocket, so I compared the Church to a space rocket, guaranteed by the highest authority, scripture and tradition, as the one and only reliable vehicle. I quoted the catechism's description of the Church as 'the one ark of salvation for all', using the patristic phrase, *'Extra Ecclesiam nulla salus'*, 'Outside the Church there is no salvation'. The Church takes us from earth to a new and everlasting life in heaven. I elaborated by comparing the sacraments to the food to be taken on the journey, enabling us to keep alive and well on the spacecraft, and preparing our bodies for the new kind of existence to which we would be introduced in heaven, quoting Ignatius of Antioch's description of the Eucharist as 'the medicine of immortality'. I was rather pleased with this analogy and it pleased a few of the congregation, which is said to be a rare event in Preston. However, the sermon showed how little I had really assimilated in my theology studies. I was still thinking in terms of a two-tiered reality, consisting of natural and supernatural. Parish life, as I first experienced it in Preston, was uninspiring, undemanding and boring, but perhaps this was the price one had to pay for administering supernatural life to God's chosen!

It was now seventeen years since I had entered the noviceship at the age of eighteen. A few years later, as a playroom master at

Stonyhurst, I was giving a sixteen-year-old boy his half-term report, summing up briefly and, as I thought, gently, the adverse comments which his teachers had made and adding a few of my own. He was apparently unperturbed, then commented, 'The trouble with you, Father, is that you haven't had enough experience'. I knew he was right. I was full of ideas and ideals, untested by practical experience, and emotionally I was half frozen. The final year of Jesuit training, called the tertianship, was described by St Ignatius as a *'schola affectus'*, a school of the affections, for he recognised the dangers of emotional dessication after long years of study. Nowadays, Jesuits do their tertianship only after they have had a few years of practical experience, but my generation was summoned to the tertianship immediately after theological studies.

In September 1959, I returned to St Beuno's for tertianship along with thirty other Jesuits, mostly British, but with a few from other countries. We shared the house with some elderly retired Jesuits, one of whom, entering the refectory on our first morning, complained in a loud voice, 'Can't move for bloody foreigners'. The tertian instructor, Fr Paul Kennedy, was still learning his trade. He was Dublin born and Stonyhurst educated. He had entered the noviceship straight from school, but his Jesuit training and very Celtic temperament never quite blended. In 1959, his Jesuit training still dominated, so he tried his best to run the tertianship on traditional lines, as a return to the monastic life of the noviceship. Every now and again, even in the middle of his lectures, he would break into laughter, as if to say, 'It's all very absurd'. This laughter was his saving grace. He never took anything too seriously, least of all himself, so he was constantly seeing the funny side of things. Later, as he studied Jesuit sources, Paul Kennedy became an inspiring instructor for many Jesuits, introducing them to the Spiritual Exercises as they were originally given, namely individually, and not, as we had always known them, through lectures delivered to large groups. American, Canadian and Australian Jesuits who came under his influence then returned home and set up centres of Ignatian spirituality where the Exercises were given individually. Fifteen years after my own tertianship, I visited Jesuit centres in the USA and Canada to learn from

Paul Kennedy's former pupils the art of the individually given retreat, which was still unknown to most British Jesuits.

After a few months' tertianship, I was walking with a melancholic Belgian who shared his reflections on Jesuit training so far. 'In the noviceship,' he began, 'they take away our humanity. In philosophy they take away our reason. In theology they take away our faith. And in the tertianship they say "Now get going".' Apart from the six weeks of Lent, when we left St Beuno's to do apostolic work, and a three-week period working in a hospice for the dying, I did not find the nine months of tertianship a profitable experience, certainly not a '*schola affectus*'. After so many years of study and seclusion, I was longing to engage in apostolic work of some kind. In prayer, the image of riding the chainless bicycle kept recurring and also the image of the novice who stopped pumping the organ and tried instead to pull the indicator chord to the right position. In the tertian-ship seclusion I was in danger of becoming too introspective, mentally spun around by the doubts and questions in my own mind, whether I was essentially flawed, whether this Jesuit training was preparing us to engage in real life or simply providing an uncomfort-able form of escape from reality.

My doubts were confirmed by the visits of two outside speakers. One spoke with enthusiasm on liturgy. When asked how liturgy relates to everyday life, he looked puzzled, as though the question was an impertinence. The second speaker spoke on the role of the parish priest. He had two main points: the first was the care to be taken in keeping a baptism register, and the second was that we should exercise similar care in keeping the parish accounts.

With hindsight, I now recognise the value of these doubts, but at the time I felt enveloped in a dark cloud. The doubts were forcing me to question the relationship between faith and life, between the supernatural and the natural, sacred and secular. I could not see the connection between liturgy and life, between the cultic side of Church life and life itself. I did not recognise the root of all this unease at the time. It was only much later that I realised that the source of unease lay in my own split spirituality. God was still in a separate compartment of my psyche, but I projected this question outwards and so felt annoyed both with the liturgy lecturer and the parish expert, but had no awareness that I was the real cause of my own annoyance. I now see the importance of reflecting on our inner moods and feelings, tracing their origin, as far as we can, then presenting our findings to God in prayer and asking for enlightenment. I cannot now remember in detail how I coped with the questions swirling around in my mind during the tertianship, or with the emotions, but I know I would have prayed to be strong in faith against the many doubts, and to be delivered from anger, irritation and moodiness with individuals and with the whole tertianship. I still did not realise that the doubts and negative feelings could be God's invitation to look more closely at their roots. I still thought that if I was close to God, then I should be free of doubts and of any negative moods or feelings.

Consequently, in order to be close to God I must first rid myself of all doubts and negativity, asking God's help, certainly, but never for a moment suspecting that God might be in the doubts and in the negativity.

This time of monastic seclusion in the tertianship was, of course, broken by our two periods away from the house. In the first period, lasting three weeks, we were sent to work as untrained orderlies in a hospice for the dying in Manchester, which was run by a religious order of brothers. As it was open to all denominations, we were cautioned beforehand not to pray with the patients or talk religion unless invited to do so. The brothers lived an austere life, rising at five-thirty and working long hours on menial tasks, only a few of them being qualified nurses. At six we had to wash patients' faces and hands, then give them a cup of tea. One patient always greeted the first touch of my ministrations with 'Bugger off'. We then had rapidly recited morning prayers, followed by Mass and breakfast, before returning to the wards. After breakfast, patients were wheeled into a large dull room, where they sat against the wall, mostly in depressing silence, broken only when tea arrived at eleven and by further complaints when dinner and tea appeared, after which we wheeled them back to their wards and put them to bed for the night.

For ten days I did night duty, sitting with the dying and helping to lay them out after death.

The hospice was a sad place. It looked after the physical needs of the dying patients, but most of the staff had neither the time, energy or skill to listen to the pain of individuals in their helplessness and anxieties. Some never received visitors. One, a wealthy man, had relatives who used to come occasionally. They did not enter the building, but looked through a window to see how near he was to the end. I had read books and articles on the theology of death, on the importance of this moment when our eternal destiny is determined. Those facing death in the hospice had obviously not read these books and articles, for they seemed blissfully unaware of the drama. Most seemed peaceful before dying and simply wanted to go to sleep.

The best and most profitable part of the tertianship was the six weeks of Lent when I was sent to help Fr Benjie Winterborn, the Jesuit chaplain to Catholics at Manchester University. He lived in a damp, cold and crumbling building, a former hotel, and ate inadequate meals, which somehow fuelled him with abundant energy. He was raising funds and had architectural plans for a large new chaplaincy for the increasing number of Catholic students and staff, most of whom he seemed to know by name. His proposed chaplaincy, like so many Catholic buildings of the 1950s, sprang from a theology of the Church which saw it as the one ark of salvation for all, so the bigger, grander and more solid it was the better. Its upkeep was to prove a heavy burden for his post-Vatican II successors and most of the building has now been let out for business purposes. Although he was engaged in long-term planning, Benjie's method of running his chaplaincy was to answer immediate needs as they arose, so he would ask me to take a group of medical students for medical ethics at one hour's notice or less, or talk with another group on the nature of faith. When I would reluctantly agree, he would give a broad smile, say 'jolly good', and fly off to his next engagement. He was an inspiration to work with, and loved by the students and staff for the constant encouragement he gave them to think for themselves. Years later I visited him in hospital where he was suffering from an incurable illness. He was still peppering every statement with 'jolly good' and had a typewriter in front of him. He was writing his memoirs.

These weeks at Manchester restored my hope in Jesuit life. Towards the end of the tertianship we were given time to prepare eight-day retreats, which every Jesuit was supposed to be ready to give on request. At that time, these retreats were given exclusively to Catholic religious men and women, and occasionally to secular priests, and consisted of four talks each day, so we had thirty-two lectures to prepare which were to cover all the main themes of the full Spiritual Exercises. I had a typed copy of thirty-two talks which Karl Rahner had delivered in the course of an eight-day retreat given in Rome, so I translated this into English for the benefit of the non-German speakers among the tertians and had my thirty-two talks in hand. They served me well for many years, until I eventually realised that giving talks is not the way to give the Spiritual Exercises, and that to try to squeeze the full Spiritual Exercises into eight days is to fail to understand their purpose.

Towards the end of the tertianship the provincial came to let the British tertians know where they would be working the following year. I was still hoping to do further studies in ecumenism, not in order to lecture in theology, but to enable me to return to Scotland to work ecumenically. The provincial heard my request, then produced an enormous folder containing the staff at every Jesuit institution in Britain. He told me I was needed at Stonyhurst to teach Latin, Greek and Religion. I accepted this decision as the mysterious will of God, but without any enthusiasm.

On Sunday afternoon during vacation time, Stonyhurst was open to visitors. One Jesuit suggested that a suitable opening sentence for visitors might be, 'The Jesuits first came to Stonyhurst in 1793: little has changed since'. There were many more lay staff and some changes in the Jesuit staff, but the general running of the school was much the same as when I left it in 1951. However, the Sixties were beginning and not even Stonyhurst could remain unaffected by the decade of the Second Vatican Council and by the counter-culture. I had a timetable of Latin, Greek and Religion classes and was also playroom master to those at the top of the school. Religion classes took me hours of preparation. I was trying to teach what I had learned in theology, presenting it in simpler form. Within minutes of beginning class I could see a glazed look come over the eyes of my audience. Some looked out the window, others examined the ceiling's cobwebs or their finger nails. They were all suffering from a surfeit of religious instruction and practice, with compulsory Mass at seven-thirty in the morning daily and night prayers at nine o'clock. Very few professed disbelief: most accepted what they were told and did not have enough interest to ask questions. At that time I agreed with the compulsory daily Mass, night prayers and Sunday evening services, for I still believed that they were a means of grace, even if participants were paying little or no attention, and that their souls would benefit just by being there. As Mass was compulsory, I decided to give one particular class a course on the Mass, how it had developed historically and why it was the central act of Christian worship. I studied a two-volume work by Jungmann, then the leading authority on liturgy, and felt confident as I took my first class, a group just beginning A-level work. Five minutes later I knew I had failed again. At the end of class, one youth, John Bickerton, approached me and said, 'I suppose you realise you are wasting your time?' Suspecting he was right, I asked, 'Why do you say that?' 'Because half of us are atheists.' 'Which half?' He said he could not reveal this without consulting the others first. 'How long have you been atheist?' 'Ten days; he replied. Later, he came to see me with the atheist list. When I explained the difference between an atheist and an agnostic, he decided that he and his friends, being open-minded chaps, would be more accurately described as agnostic. We then founded the agnostics' club, which used to meet regularly in their free time in my room, where we discussed whether or not God exists. That group taught me a very obvious lesson about religious or any other type of education, that one has to start from where people are, and it is useless trying to give answers to questions they have never asked. I also began to see that the questioners were more open to truth, and therefore to God, than those who accepted what they were taught but were not sufficiently interested to question.

At the top of the school, the only boy who did seem to pay any attention in my RE classes was Eric Kemmet, known to his class as 'the atheist'. Easter fell early in 1961, so term did not end until Easter Monday. The boys attended all the Holy Week services, culminating in High Mass on Easter Sunday, which they attended in military uniform, ready to parade in the playground afterwards and perform a march past, while the rector took the salute, standing on a raised dais and wearing Jesuit gown and biretta. Early on Easter morning I met an enraged colonel in charge of the Combined Cadet Force. He took me to the playground. The rector's dais had disappeared overnight and was now floating on the pond. On a large wall in the middle of the playground someone had painted the nuclear disarmament sign, and below it, 'March begins here. (No children please)'.

I was in charge of the criminal investigations. I suspected that Eric Kemmet was the leader, but my heart was not in the task of tracking down and punishing the criminal; for the crime raised for me a question which I had never faced before. Was it not more criminal to encourage children to celebrate the feast of the resurrection with the weapons of death than to float the saluting base on the pond and paint the playground wall with a peace sign?

The question came as a whisper at first and I could easily ignore it. It is a noble thing to risk one's life in the service of Queen and country. Stonyhurst was proud of its war record and the refectory contained seven portraits of old boys who had won the Victoria Cross. I had friends in the armed forces whom I admired and respected, and other friends had given their lives for their country. Besides, the Church had taught the doctrine of a just war for over fifteen hundred years. What would have happened to our world if the Allies had not resisted and overcome the Nazis? But the whispering voice persisted in spite of all my loud arguments against it. The initial question then bred a host of others with which I am still struggling thirty years later.

What is the relationship between faith and life? How do our specifically religious beliefs and activities relate to our everyday conduct as individuals, as a group, as a Church, as a nation? Is saving our souls a purely private matter between God and ourselves?

The writings of the Jesuit anthropologist Teilhard de Chardin, including *The Phenomenon of Man* and *Le Milieu Divin*, appeared in English in the early 1960s. I read both books and was particularly struck by *Le Milieu Divin*, which demolished my belief in the super-natural and the natural as two separate layers of reality, a demolition which Rahner had begun. God is in everything. In all our activities and our passivities, in all our decisions, actions, reactions to events, whatever they are, we are encountering God.

I began to understand more clearly why my RE classes bored my pupils. Their subject matter was not related to the boys' own interests and experience, which is the only place in which they can find God. I also began to acknowledge that much of what I was teaching bored me, too. Within my own psyche, I had not allowed God freedom of movement, although I did not realise this at the time, nor did I realise that to give God freedom of movement is to invite trouble.

If God is in all things, then God must be at work in other religions and in people of no religion. I began reading a little on comparative religions and was amazed and delighted to see the convergence there was in the beliefs of major world religions. I read, too, some of the classical humanists, Comte, Feuerbach, Bertrand Russell, in order to understand why they rejected the notion of God. At first I was alarmed, because I found myself in agreement with much of what they wrote. Because God was so divinised, human beings were dehumanised and held in subjection to those who claimed to know the will of God. These classical humanists were echoing the ancient line from Lucretius: *'Tantum religio potuit suadere malorum'*, 'To such evil can religion lead'. The most striking and disturbing article I read was an address which Albert Camus, an existential atheist, had deliv-ered to a group of Dominican priests in France at the end of the war. Camus told them that he was not able to share their belief in the divinity of Jesus Christ, but pleaded with the Dominicans to be true to Jesus' teaching in the Sermon on the Mount, and to join with the atheists in hungering and thirsting after justice.

Camus sent me back to a reading of the Old Testament prophets. I began with Amos, the first of the recorded prophets, a poor shepherd from Judaea, called by God to preach to the affluent and sophisticated people of the north. God gave Amos an abundance of zeal and eloquence, but left him short on tact. He addressed the fashionable ladies of Samaria:

> Listen to this word, you cows of Bashan
> living in the mountain of Samaria,
> oppressing the needy, crushing the poor,
> saying to your husbands, 'Bring us something to drink!'
> The Lord Yahweh swears this by his holiness:
> The days are coming to you now
> when you will be dragged out with hooks,
> the very last of you with prongs.
> Out you will go, each by the nearest breach in the wall,
> to be driven all the way to Hermon.
> It is Yahweh who speaks. (Amos 4: 1–3)

In another passage, Amos addresses the exploiters:

> Listen to this, you who trample on the needy
> and try to suppress the poor people of the country,

The exploiters of Samaria continued to have religious services. God, through Amos, comments:

> I hate and despise your feasts,
> I take no pleasure in your solemn festivals.

To one of my RE classes I gave a course on Communism. In preparing classes, I was struck by the similarities between Karl Marx and Amos. In class I pointed out the similarities. Some time later the rector received a letter from an angry parent, complaining that I was teaching Communism to her child.

In the Spiritual Exercises Ignatius has a meditation called 'The Two Standards'. In it he takes the theme, to be found in every religion, of the struggle between good and evil, but sets it in his own conceptual world. He sees the struggle as a warfare between Christ and the evil one, whom he calls Lucifer, the light-bearer, because the evil one operates under the appearance of good. The prayer of the meditation is for the grace to be able to recognise Lucifer's deceits and to guard against them, and to know the attractiveness of Christ's teaching and embrace it. He pictures Lucifer seated on a smoky throne in the plain of Babylon, surrounded by innumerable little demons whom he sends out all over the world, 'no person, no place, no region excepted'. Lucifer's message is very simple. The demons are to ensnare all human beings in three stages, first through love of wealth, secondly through love of honour, and finally through overweening pride. It is not wealth or honour in themselves which are wrong, but the way in which we relate to them, becoming so possessed by them that possessions and honour become our gods, displacing God. Christ, who is pictured near Jerusalem with his friends around him, gives exactly the opposite message. His friends are to win people over to a love of spiritual poverty, which means desiring to have such an awareness and trust in the reality of God, present in every event, that nothing can shake us, even if we do lose our possessions. They are also to persuade others to desire insults, injury and abuse. This sounds very odd, as though encouraging others to fall into an unhealthy psychological state. We must not desire insults, injury and abuse in themselves, but if they come our way, as they usually do, they can serve a most useful purpose. For the pain we experience may be indicating the gulf that lies between our protestations that God is our rock, refuge and strength, and the reality, namely that it is my honour, my reputation with others which is, in fact, my rock, so that when these are removed, I feel devastated. If we can come before God in our distress, God can show us that we have been living on false security and that our only real security is in God. This is humility, 'from which', Ignatius says, 'all other virtues spring'.

I had made this meditation dozens of times, but now I was bringing it to bear on my everyday life in Stonyhurst. Why was I so anxious that my classes should do well in public examinations? Why were public examination successes given pride of place in the head-master's report at prize-giving on the state of the school, along with sporting successes? Why were prominent old boys, who had made a success in public life, invited to give out the prizes? Why were the better-qualified teachers normally given the brighter boys to teach? Was our value system in any way different from the value system of any other school, Christian or non-Christian? Did our religious belief and practice make any difference apart from the time we gave to these activities? Are our Christian creeds, in fact, statements about the whole of life, or are they concerned only with religious activity and practice, with the supernatural area of life?

I began to speculate on how the school would be if we were to allow the Sermon on the Mount and the Christian creed to be translated into its daily running. We are made in the image of God. As Christians, we believe that God's life is one of total sharing between Father, Son and Holy Spirit, so that no one Person of the Trinity possesses anything which does not belong equally to the other two. I remembered a phrase which I had come across in theology and which, at the time, I dismissed as just another abstraction, 'In God, persons are relations'. What a profound insight! We study theology in order to understand more of ourselves. As St Augustine put it, *'Noverim te, noverim me'*, 'That I may know you, that I may know myself'. Our notion, then, of personhood, is based on the false assumption that we first have something called personality with which we then relate to others. But if personality is a relationship, then we can only become persons in relation. Our being is in our relatedness. Perhaps that is why Jesus said, 'Unless you lose your life, you cannot find it'. The cultivation of 'me' is the death of me. The cultivation of a group, which ignores, or tries to suppress other groups, is the death of the group, whether the group be of Church or state.

How would Stonyhurst look if we tried to translate the Doctrine of the Trinity, of the Incarnation, of the Resurrection, of the Sermon on the Mount, into the daily running of the school? The school hierarchy would have to go for a start. 'The greatest among you must become the least of all and the first among you must become the servant of all.' Why shouldn't menial tasks also be done occasionally by the headmaster and heads of department? Where does power lie in the school? Who makes the decisions? Why should not the smallest and least academically gifted boy have the same share in decision making as the headmaster? The Spirit who lived in Jesus and raised him from the dead lives in all of us, so why should we show more respect to some than to others, listen more carefully to one than to another? And was not our whole educational system nurturing in our pupils a desire for possessions, power and success, rewarding those who responded well and showed promise, and punishing those who did not?

These thoughts and questions were both exciting and threatening, exciting because they opened up endless possibilities, threatening because any answers I found seemed utterly impractical and, if put into practice, would cause chaos and confusion. Is Jesus' teaching hopelessly idealistic? What would happen if we really did turn the other cheek, lent without asking for our money back, did good to those who hate us, loved our enemies, washed one another's feet, renounced our desire for power, status and control? I could see that there was much to be said for keeping God and religion in a separate compartment of our minds, because God running free is very threatening.

I owe an enormous debt of gratitude to Eric Kemmet, whose prank before the Easter Sunday military parade forced all these questions on me. I met him occasionally after he left school, especially while I was in Glasgow, where he lived as a journalist. Eric died of a heart attack while still in his forties, leaving a wife and two daughters. I felt honoured to be asked by Irene, his wife, to conduct his funeral service and to express publicly my appreciation and gratitude to him.

In 1962 Pope John XXIII opened the Second Vatican Council. In my last year at Frankfurt a visiting Jesuit from Rome – a man who, it was rumoured, had drafted many of the Encyclical letters of Pope Pius XII – gave us a talk on the proposed Vatican Council. He was sceptical about it, considered it inopportune and unlikely to effect much. 'The idea of the Council came into the old man's head as he was having a cup of coffee,' he said. That cup of coffee was to be explosive in its effects and the shock waves are still being felt today.

The scriptures are given not primarily to provide information about God's action in the history of the Jewish people, or to supply us with moral precepts for right living, but to help us recognise throughout that history that God is making history in us now. The Gospel story of Jesus calming the storm at sea illustrates what was happening at the Second Vatican Council. The boat is sinking, the disciples terrified; Jesus is asleep. What saved them was not their seamanship, their boat or their tackle, but their waking Jesus and his saying to the sea, 'Be calm, be still'. The bishops at the Council looked at the Ark of Peter in light of the Gospel and tradition, and reaffirmed the traditional message that faith in Christ, not particular structures, is the core of Christian belief. This may appear so obvious as not to need mention, yet it is precisely this Christ-centredness which has effected such a renewal in some and such turmoil in others, who seem to have been more attached to the external structures and ritual with which they were familiar than to the Spirit which these structures signified.

The most important document of the Second Vatican Council was the Constitution on the Church, entitled '*Lumen Gentium*', 'Light of the Nations'. A preliminary document prepared by the Roman Curia opened with a chapter on the hierarchy of the Church. The draft was rejected by the bishops and replaced with a new one in which the first chapter was entitled 'The Mystery of the Church'. Because the Church is mystery, therefore, it cannot be defined in precise terminology which is valid for all time. Of her nature she must be a pilgrim Church, a searching Church, constantly discovering her own identity, unable to predict in detail how she will develop or what she will become. The Church is a community whose life is the Holy Spirit. The final chapter of this document is on the universal call to holiness of all God's people. It was these seminal ideas which were to cause such turmoil. Because the Church was mystery, it was therefore impossible to define who was in and who was outside it in the way that many people wanted. The document recognised God's grace at work not only in other Christian denominations, but in all those people who follow the truth as their conscience reveals it to them – points which were elaborated in another decree on ecumenism. The role of the teaching authority in the Church is not to impose doctrines, but to express those beliefs to which Catholics already assent through the promptings of the Holy Spirit. The hierarchical structure, like every other structure in the Church, was therefore a means to an end rather than an end in itself: it cannot override individual conscience. Although the Council did not attempt to define the meaning and limits of papal primacy, it did emphasise that the teaching authority of the Church resided in the College of Bishops which is headed by the Pope. Just as the teaching of the magisterium is not something to be imposed on the rest of the Church, but must be an expression of the belief of the whole Church, so the Pope's role is not to tell the bishops what they are to teach, but to listen to them, and to speak, not as an individual, but as a member of the college of bishops, albeit their head. The decree on the liturgy allowed the Mass to be celebrated in the vernacular and with the celebrant facing the people instead of having his back to them. The Council also revised the readings both at Mass and in the Divine Office, so that Catholics were exposed to a much wider range of scripture readings.

The great majority of the bishops at the Council were not radical thinkers: most had been appointed because they seemed to be solid pillars of the institutional Church. The documents of the Council had to be approved virtually unanimously and many of the seminal statements, which were to open the Church more to the modern world, are set side by side with statements with which the more institutionally minded members could feel happy. Consequently, at the end of the Council one Scottish bishop could assure his Catholic flock that there was no need to worry as nothing had changed!

Following on from the Constitution on the Church, there was a document on The Church in the Modern World, called '*Gaudium et Spes*', 'Joy and Hope', dealing with the mission of the Church in its widest sense, which includes all human activity. This was an attempt, unique in conciliar documents, to bridge the gulf between the Church and the world. *Gaudium et Spes* sees the Church as being at the service of humanity, as distinct from earlier descriptions of the Church as '*Societas Perfecta*', the perfect society in an imperfect world. The document was to be of great importance, not so much for the analysis it offered and the solutions it proposed, as for the vision and hope it offered for the Church's universal mission.

As the Council's documents were publicised, there was a general mood of euphoria among most Catholics, a feeling of liberation and a naive hope that things could never be the same again. One writer on the Council, Robert Kaiser, summed up what had happened by elaborating on a sixteenth-century story. In 1523, the then Pope, Adrian V, a Dutchman, had been presented with a picture called 'The Barque of Peter' by a Florentine painter. The painting showed the ship raised above the sea by angels blowing eschatological trumpets. Immediately beneath the ship the sea was calm, but all around were angry waves. On the top deck sat the Pope with his papal guard around him. The sails were limp, but the papal flag fluttered above them. Out of the little portholes peeped the people of God, gazing at the arms, legs and heads of drowning heretics, schismatics and sinners. Around the rudder of the raised ship was a cluster of angels reading an illuminated text, 'Thou art Peter, and upon this rock I shall build my Church'. Pope Adrian was horrified at the gift, saying that this was not his ship. He wanted the ship to be on the waters, the sails filled, and he wanted to be saved along with all the heretics, schismatics and sinners. Shortly afterwards the Pope died. Some said he had been poisoned.

Before the Council, I had been meeting with a group of Catholic priests and Anglican vicars in Blackburn, near Stonyhurst. Our oldest member was Dean Linehan, a Catholic of generous heart but rigid theology, based more on the Catholic catechism than on scripture and tradition. He addressed us all as though he were taking an infants' religion class, but his obvious goodness and lavish teas did more for our ecumenical relations than our lengthy discussions. After the Vatican Council, I was invited by various Anglican and Methodist Churches to give talks on the Council. I soon began to realise that what divides us as Christians is not so much theology as culture, custom and non-cooperation, and all my subsequent experience has confirmed this. I gave what I thought a good summary of the document 'The Constitution on the Church' to a group of Methodists, and then invited questions. The first question was, 'What about bingo?', bingo being an activity in which many Catholic parishes engaged in order to raise funds, but, as it was a form of gambling, it was anathema to the Methodists. Most of the questions and comments which followed these talks were of similar nature, more concerned with peculiarities of practice than with the essential belief of Catholics.

A Catholic priest in nearby Whalley invited me to give a series of talks on the Council to a group of twelve of his interested parishioners, six women and six men. We met fortnightly for almost a year in a pub, where the landlord gave us a private room. The meeting began with the landlord taking orders. I would then speak for about half an hour and the rest of the meeting consisted of their questions and comments. At the first meeting I recommended a few books on the Council. At our next meeting someone brought copies of all the books, which they had borrowed from Preston County Library. I learned much from the people who came to these meetings. They read the books, thought about them, related what they read to everyday life and began to become enthusiastic about theology. I used to come away from those meetings feeling both sad and happy. I was sad because the Church, in Britain at least, was then so organised that the serious study of theology and spirituality was normally restricted to those preparing to be ordained clergy, and to some non-ordained men and women who were members of religious congregations. The vast majority of people had no theological education after school, and most did not pick up very much through Sunday sermons. Yet here was a group of men and women from a country parish eager to learn, intelligent and able to relate what they studied to everyday life. I was very happy to be with them, found the pub an ideal classroom, and felt great hope for the future of a Church in which those who were not professionally religious were given their rightful place, encouraged to reflect on faith and life, and to listen to one another's reflections.

Returning late from one of these meetings, I was struggling to complete the Divine Office, which every priest was bound to recite daily in full, omission of any one of the six parts of it being considered a grave sin. Until then I had struggled through the Office every day. That evening, with two parts unfinished, I put the book aside and went to bed, feeling not guilty, but free. It seems trivial, but for me it was a first step into freedom from the tyranny of external obligations.

Each Easter week, I used to take part in the national pilgrimage to Lourdes for children who are handicapped. The children were divided into small groups and lived for the week in one of the Lourdes hotels along with their helpers. These were exhausting weeks. Many of the children were in wheelchairs and we were with them all day, taking them round the sites of Lourdes, sacred and profane. Once the children were in bed and someone left in charge, the rest of us would retire to one of the many cafés. Parents were not normally allowed to be in the same group as their children, but an exception was made on one occasion for the father of a Down's syndrome child of exceptional energy who needed little sleep. His father never joined us in the evening, for it took him a long time to get John off to sleep. I persuaded him to let me take over one evening, so that he could join the others at a café. I tried every trick I knew to quieten John, but he kept on jumping around in the bed and pulling out the sheets. I started to tell him a story, making it up as I went along. On the previous day we had all been up in the mountains at Gavarnie and John had ridden a donkey. We started the story from there. John's donkey had wings and took off over the mountains, racing the eagles. I thought I heard John say something, but doubted my ears. We were just coming to land in a beautiful palace courtyard high in the mountains, having left the eagles far behind when I heard him speak again. This time it was unmistakable: 'Silly bugger,' he said! When his father returned, John was still wide awake and ready for more play.

The annual Lourdes pilgrimage was a wonderful experience for us all. We, the so-called helpers, soon came to realise that the children were, in fact, helping us. There are aspects of Lourdes which can deter the visitor from ever wanting to return: the commercialism of its pious supermarkets, selling plastic statues of Our Lady which shine in the dark, or shaped as holy water containers; the triumphalism of the massive Church buildings within the domain itself; and the clerical formality of some of the religious services. But the grotto by the Garve river, where St Bernadette had her visions, is a numinous place, especially in the late evening or early morning before the crowds gather. I found Lourdes a good image of the

Church itself, commercial Lourdes corresponding to the greed and exploitation which is to be found in it, triumphalist Lourdes corresponding to the power lust which can exist beneath clerical garb and pious utterances, the grotto corresponding to the numinous heart of the Church. There have been very few officially recognised miracles at Lourdes. I do not believe that is important. The miracle is that so many people can go to Lourdes weighed down by their physical, mental or spiritual illnesses, and come away with inner hope, assurance and peace of soul.

There were usually some children from Lancashire among the handicapped pilgrims. In my last years at Stonyhurst, I organised an annual holiday for children with handicaps at the beginning of the summer vacation. At the same time I ran a camping holiday for children in care of the Social Services, bringing the two groups together as far as possible. Stonyhurst boys and their sisters and girl friends were responsible for both groups. The presence of these children who were handicapped or in care had an enlivening effect on all who were involved in the week, and the college staff were most co-operative, especially the matron, Mary Featherstone, who willingly stayed on duty for an extra week and coped with all medical emergencies. Boys and college teaching staff were usually in awe of her. She was very strict, without ever being unkind, and had uncanny intuitive gifts both in medical diagnosis and crime detection. However, the children who were handicapped or in care had no such fear of her, nor did the college cleaning staff, in whom she always took a special interest. As a result of these camps I came to know her. She lived a most austere and isolated life, carrying responsibility for the health of over four hundred people, working long hours every day, and even into the night if anyone was seriously ill. Until her later years, when she was on a national nursing pay scale, her wages were a pittance. In spite of this she loved the college and had unerringly sound and wise opinions about all that was going on.

Although I enjoyed the teaching and the life at Stonyhurst and part of me would have been content to remain there, another part was growing increasingly restless. Dean Linehan had told me about nearby Blackburn Technical College with several thousand students and no chaplain, while Stonyhurst had a large staff of Jesuits for 350 pupils, selected mostly because their parents could afford the fees.

In my thinking about the nature of the Church and its meaning in the world, I was becoming increasingly frustrated with those in the school who did not seem to me to be concerned about these questions. This is a danger for all people who begin to hunger and thirst after justice and peace. In our enthusiasm for the cause, we can begin to despise those who do not see as we see, and we can begin to act in a way which only serves to create divisions and to alienate those who do not share our views. There are many forms of injustice and aggression. One of the most subtle and destructive forms, which can afflict well-meaning people, is the conviction that God is totally on our side, so that in God's name and for the sake of justice and peace, we begin to act unjustly and aggressively towards others.

After meeting with the Whalley parish group in the pub, I thought it would be good if British Jesuits could meet together to consider our future work in the light of the Second Vatican Council. I told the Jesuit provincial of this idea and he told me to go ahead and organise something. I did so, and among other speakers I invited Archbishop Thomas Roberts sj to lecture on authority in the Church. Archbishop Roberts had already been causing a stir by his writings, questioning Catholic teaching on contraception and on the morality of the nuclear deterrent. I was summoned one day by the provincial and told that this invitation was causing trouble among Jesuits, some being annoyed that a man who publicly criticised Church authority should be invited to speak on that very subject. I was asked to withdraw the invitation. I argued that this would cause great offence, that Archbishop Roberts was well qualified to speak on this important question, and that if he was to be asked to withdraw, then the provincial should do the asking. The provincial agreed that the invitation could not be withdrawn at this stage, but told me that I must consult him about any further invitations. There were no further problems about organising the conference. I had no idea then, however, that this conference was going to plunge me into the question of authority in the Church and threaten my future as a Jesuit.

The conference for Jesuits, held at Heythrop, was well attended and was appreciated, not least for Archbishop Roberts' contribution. While I was there, I chatted one evening with Heythrop's rector. He asked me about life at Stonyhurst and how I was finding it. I told him of my restlessness. He told me that the provincial had had a number of requests for Jesuits as university chaplains and asked if I would be interested. A few days later I got news that I was to move from Stonyhurst and go to Glasgow University in September 1967, as assistant to the Catholic chaplain.

I was delighted by the news, but also sorry to be leaving Stonyhurst where I had made so many friends and where a new headmaster, Fr Jock Earle, was introducing necessary changes and creating a less formal and more friendly atmosphere.

CHAPTER 8

✿✿✿

God for Whom There Are No 'Separated Brethren'

*He dedicated his life to defending the last bastions of Roman
Catholicism against the inroads of Christianity.* (J. B. Keane)

THE CATHOLIC CHAPLAINCY to the University of Glasgow, called
Turnbull Hall, after Bishop Turnbull, the last pre-Reformation Catholic
Bishop of Glasgow, was a large building of four floors, occupying one
end of a terrace. At the opposite end was the Orange Lodge. In
between were various university departments, including Soviet
Studies, Ecclesiastical History and the Church of Scotland's Divinity
Department. The scene was set for some practical ecumenism.

When I left Glasgow in 1942 for the Jesuit noviceship, my understanding of the Catholic Church and its mission was clear. It was the
one, true, holy, catholic and apostolic Church and its mission was to
enlighten the rest of the world and so ensure its eternal salvation.
When I returned in 1967, I no longer had the same clarity. Intellectu-
ally I knew that God was always greater than the Church, that God's
Spirit was at work in everyone, believer and unbeliever, and that the
Church was, of its nature, a pilgrim Church, a questioning and
learning Church. The unity of the Church was a divine command,
but the source of that unity must be God's Spirit. No one could
predict in detail the form a united Church would take: the form would
emerge as divided Christians became more open to the Spirit and to
one another, for the Spirit of God is a Spirit of love, of truth and of
openness. I knew, too, that the Second Vatican Council had been
called to reform the Church in the light of the scriptures and of
tradition, and that this reforming process had to be continuous. I

shared the euphoria of many Catholics after the Council at the prospect of living and serving in a Church which was shedding what one Council bishop had described as 'its legalism, triumphalism and clericalism', and which was now open not only to other Christian denominations, but to the whole world. In the next eight years I was to learn, at times painfully, the vast distance which separates intellectual knowledge from living truth.

Glasgow was a religiously divided city. A Sikh told me that when his children were registered for schooling in Glasgow, the education department declared them to be Protestant: not being Catholic, there was no alternative category! In the nineteenth century, vast numbers of Irish Catholics came over to Scotland to escape famine and find work. At first, they were well received and educated in Protestant schools. As their numbers grew, Catholics built their own schools and in 1967, over one third of the Glasgow school population was Catholic. For economic reasons, there was an attempt in the 1970s to build a school for Catholic and Protestant children. The only ecumenical element was the school boiler, everything else being separate, including a fence separating Catholic and Protestant playground areas. There was a long history of bitterness between the two denominations. Catholics, being the minority, were discriminated against in jobs and housing, were poorer and less well educated.

There was little official contact between the two Churches. In 1958, when I was allowed to visit Glasgow after ordination in Frankfurt because I said I was interested in Scottish theology, I made inquiries among the Jesuits with whom I was staying about their contact with Church of Scotland Ministers. They had none, so I went to the Church of Scotland office and asked to see their directory of clergy in Glasgow. I found the divinity faculty at Glasgow University, took a phone number at random and arranged to meet a lecturer, John Macquarrie, with whom I had two three-hour sessions, which ended with supper in the kitchen with his wife and himself. John Macquarrie was far better read in Catholic theology than I, yet he had never in his life spoken with a Catholic priest. He later became an Anglican, published many excellent books, and I was delighted to meet him again after fifteen years when Glasgow University gave him an honorary doctorate. He was then the Lady Margaret Professor of Divinity at Oxford.

In a chaplaincy file I found copies of letters exchanged in the late 1950s between the Archbishop of Glasgow and my predecessor as chaplain. The chaplain asked the Archbishop if Catholic students might attend a Church unity service in the university. The Archbishop granted the permission, provided the Catholics did not recite the Our Father together with the Protestants. This was not an idiosyncrasy of the Archbishop of Glasgow; he was merely giving the general ruling current at that time!

One day a woman in her late sixties came to my office and introduced herself as Mary, my first cousin. I had no recollection of ever having heard of her. She told me the story. Her father, Willie, was one of my mother's older step-brothers. Early this century Willie started going out with a Protestant girl. My grandfather issued an ultimatum: either Willie must leave the girl, or he must leave the house. Willie left the house, married the Protestant girl, and Mary was their daughter.

The problem of what was called 'mixed marriages' still existed in the 1960s. One student came to me in distress, threatened with expulsion from her Catholic home because she was carrying on a correspondence with a Protestant student from Aberdeen. When I visited her parents on her behalf, her father came quickly to the heart of the matter. 'Do you expect me to be content to return home on a Saturday afternoon after the match to find one of their supporters sitting in my house?' He was referring to Rangers, the Protestant football team, and to his own team, Celtic, which was Catholic. After the Vatican Council, a new cry was heard from the Celtic end during a match with Rangers, 'Get tore intae yir separated brethren, Celtic!' Ecumenism had reached Glasgow and this was the manner of its coming.

On the outskirts of Glasgow there was a housing estate where ecumenical relations, at least among the children, were excellent. In the course of their play they used to run in and out of the Catholic church. One Protestant child, attracted by the church, began accompanying his Catholic friends to Sunday Mass. One Sunday he went up to receive Holy Communion. On returning to his seat he received a hard dig in the ribs from his Catholic friend, who warned him, 'If you swallow that we'll bash you'. In my later problems over intercommunion, I always remembered that story.

My appointment as chaplain had been made by the Archbishop of Glasgow, so soon after arrival I visited him to be briefed on my role. His instructions were brief, 'Help them to keep the faith'. This general guideline was of little help: there were a few students who believed that the Church had gone Protestant at the Vatican Council, while others, flying high on the winds of change, found God in flower-power and love of everyone except those Catholics still in thrall to the Church's teaching authority. However, I shall always be grateful to the Archbishop for that instruction, for it has kept me asking the question 'What is faith? Is it something to be "kept"?' Fifteen years after leaving the chaplaincy, I was asked to write a reflection on my chaplaincy years. I wrote a biography of two fictitious students, Jonathan and Polly. Though the characters are fictitious, the imaginative exercise illustrates the problem of 'keeping the faith'.

Both Jonathan and Polly could be described as having 'kept the faith' at university and till death. They were practising Catholics, not only in remaining regular Mass-goers, but also in using their minds in the service of faith. Both were intelligent, lively and more than usually knowledgeable about Catholic teaching. It should now be apparent to any reader who has been a chaplain that Jonathan and Polly are fictions.

Jonathan got a First in English Literature, was an accomplished and witty debater, became president of the Students' Union and was a member of the Officers' Training Corps. He was proud of his catholicism, disrupting the OTC's annual military manoeuvres on one occasion by insisting on military transport to the nearest Catholic church on Sunday morning. He was a voracious reader in theology as well as English literature. A university colleague compared his mind to a munitions factory, which he stored through his reading with suitable ammunition to fire or lob at his opponents in defence of his Catholic position. He was a regular attender at the chaplaincy, but found the liturgy in English distasteful and kept his hands firmly in his pockets when it came to the moment when the congregation greet one another with the peace of Christ. He relished and enlivened chaplaincy lectures and discussion groups with his informative, witty and often barbed comments. He was accused at university, and even more in later life, of being racist, anti-semitic, bigoted and a social snob. He was not hurt by these accusations: he relished them, demolishing his critics by accusing them of affixing labels on anyone who stated truths they found unpalatable.

After a few successful years in journalism Jonathan became a Conservative Member of Parliament, retaining his seat throughout his career with an ever-increasing majority. He attained Cabinet office, eventually becoming Minister of Defence. In spite of his many political and business commitments, he still found time for journalism, especially in the Catholic press, reminding Catholics of their distinctive identity as members of a worldwide club and therefore of their duty to abide by its rules if they were to consider themselves genuine Catholics. The colleague at university who had compared his mind to a munitions factory described him as living in anticipatory obedience to every decree emanating from the Vatican.

Jonathan's Requiem Mass, celebrated in Latin at his own request, was presided over by Archbishop Bliss, the sanctuary filled with concelebrating clergy. In his address, the Archbishop declared Jonathan to be a champion of Catholicism, a model of rectitude, a beacon in the darkness of our times. He attributed his extraordinary gift of certainty and his adamant refusal to entertain doubts of any kind, to the depth of his Catholic faith. Jonathan's university colleague attended the funeral, commenting afterwards, 'He dedicated his life to defending the last bastions of Roman Catholicism against the inroads of Christianity'.

Polly, a contemporary of Jonathan's at university, was one of the few who could match him in wit, intelligence and knowledge of the Catholic faith. Some thought she was in love with him, but they soon drifted apart. Polly, too, had a great liking for the Latin Mass, loved Gregorian chant, and shuddered through chaplaincy folk Masses. She puzzled her contemporaries, because although she was so intelligent and outgoing, she remained attached to the devotions of her childhood, praying the rosary daily and often to be found in the chapel making the Stations of the Cross.

Polly had a fatal defect: she was always ready to listen and to see what was good in everyone and everything. This caused her severe inner conflict, and although outwardly she always appeared lively and assured, inwardly she was plagued with doubts, exacerbated by Jonathan's oft-repeated, 'If you are going to remain a Catholic, you can't just pick and choose what you want to believe, you have to keep the rules of the club'.

The Mass was the core of Polly's life. She understood it as the celebration of all creation, everyone and everything called to become the Body of Christ. While Jonathan kept his hands firmly in his pockets at the peace of Christ, Polly would reach out to everyone because the gesture expressed her being.

Polly was a post-graduate research chemist, choosing to specialise in the study of potato blight as her modest contribution to the problem of world hunger, and her response to Christ's call to feed the hungry. She discovered that her research project was being funded by a chemical firm engaged in the manufacture of nerve gas. She also discovered hunger on her doorstep among the families living in her tenement block. She felt she must resign from her research fellowship, but had no clear idea of what she should do instead. Her chaplain advised her to continue with the research, which could have a beneficial result even if the funding was contaminated. Her university friends told her she was being over-scrupulous, but as she persisted in giving her reasons for resigning, they became uncomfortable in her presence and began avoiding her company. Jonathan told her she was a damned fool, a stupid woman, ruled by her emotions and not by her head, and prophesied that she would come to no good. Polly listened, went through agony, but knew that she must resign from her fellowship. Her parents were horrified, for they had made great sacrifices for her education and were proud of her achievements so far. They were still more horrified and ashamed when Polly wrote to them saying she was now living in a squat and surviving on social benefit.

Life in a squat had a distressing effect on Polly. Formerly so placid, happy and full of life, she became increasingly angry as she felt the pain of rejection by her family and friends, and met with their unshakeable conviction that they were right and she was wrong. She suffered because of their insensitivity to her pain and their refusal to listen, and became very angry at the appalling squalor in which so many around her were condemned to live and at the cruelty they inflicted on themselves and others in their degradation. She offered her services to the local parish, an offer gladly accepted at first, but terminated on her return from a short prison sentence in Holloway gaol for breaking into and entering a nuclear base in order to pray there. Polly was thanked for her work so far, but told she was having a divisive effect on the parish.

She took a temporary job and acquired a council flat, which she shared with a variety of homeless people. This was the beginning of her life's work. Polly raised funds, negotiated with local authorities, and set up day and night centres for the homeless. She always insisted that the centres should be open to anyone in need, irrespective of their race, condition or religion. She called them basic communities, a decision which almost wrecked the project, because most sponsoring bodies could raise funds only if the projects were specifically Catholic, or Anglican, or at least Christian. The sponsoring bodies were always apologetic about this, but told Polly that she had to be realistic, accept that this was the way things were and, if she wanted the money to house the homeless, she would have to make compromises. Those who benefited from her day and night shelters and belonged to her basic communities were sometimes her most bitter critics because they projected their own frustration on to her.

Eventually the struggle became too much for Polly and she had to hand over the whole project to a wealthy Catholic organisation, which assured her that while it had no desire to turn anyone away, it must insist on a clear Catholic identity.

At the end of her life Polly was as penniless as the day she left university. She still did not know whether she was a Catholic in Jonathan's sense. She did know that God was always greater and that she had come to know God in the same way as the prophet

Jeremiah. 'You have seduced me, Yahweh, and I have let myself be seduced; you have overpowered me: you were the stronger. The word of Yahweh has meant for me insult, derision, all day long. I used to say, "I will not speak his name any more." Then there seemed to be a fire burning in my heart, imprisoned in my bones. The effort to restrain it wearied me, I could not bear it.' (c. 20) Polly had surrendered her life to God and she found God weeping in her heart, the God of compassion, who loves all that he has created.

I wrote this story fifteen years after leaving chaplaincy work, a distillation of memories. During the fermentation process I had no such clarity.

Soon after my arrival in Glasgow I heard of 'The Gorbals Group.' They were members of the Iona Community, founded by the Reverend George MacLeod, a maverick and prophetic minister of the Church of Scotland, who had set about restoring the ruins of the abbey on the isle of Iona, where St Columba had arrived in the sixth century. The Iona Community is a dispersed community of men and women, at first exclusively Presbyterian, but now ecumenical, who pledge themselves to a simple way of life and to the promotion of peace. The Gorbals Group of the Iona Community lived in separate flats, pooled their income, and met together every Thursday for three hours to pray and reflect on their work. I was invited to one of their meetings, held around the fire in the sitting room of one of the members. The scripture reading with which the meeting began was from Isaiah chapter 61. 'The Spirit of the Lord has been given me, for Yahweh has anointed me. He has sent me to bring good news to the poor, to bind hearts that were broken.' The group then reported on the intractable problems they faced in trying to live this message. The memory lingers because they were facing the problem which had been occupying me for years, the problem of bridging the gap between our religious language and the truth of things. To change the metaphor, this bicycle had a chain on it and the cyclists were struggling up a steep and ill-defined path.

The meeting ended with a Eucharist, a coffee table serving as altar. I felt at one with this group, but did not receive Communion because I felt bound by the Catholic Church's ruling which forbade Catholics to receive the Eucharist at the service of another denomination. The decision left me in a state of inner turmoil. I knew the reasons for this ban on intercommunion, namely that to celebrate the Eucharist together while our Churches remained divided would be hypocritical, but while I could appreciate this argument, acting on it did not bring inner peace.

The chapel in the chaplaincy had seating accommodation for two hundred. At the Sunday evening Masses the music was excellent, thanks to some very gifted students, and the congregation was encouraged to participate. The numbers attending grew and Catholics were bringing their Protestant friends, who would occasionally present themselves for Holy Communion. In spite of my ecumenical confusion, I knew that I could never refuse Communion to anyone who came forward. This decision caused me no inner turmoil, but was to lead to trouble later. After Mass on one Sunday evening, when there had been standing room only, one man said to me, 'You need to do something about the overcrowding'. 'What do you think should be done?' I asked. 'Tell the Catholics not to come' was his reply.

In the late Sixties and early Seventies, years of the counter-culture, large numbers of Catholic students were very critical of the Church, which they found too authoritarian. Many had given up going to Mass on Sundays and had either abandoned their faith or were thinking of doing so. Much of my time was spent in talking with individuals and groups about the faith and about the God they were thinking of abandoning. At first, I used to feel apprehensive about these conversations, thinking that if I failed to convince them about the error of their ways, I was failing to serve God and the Church. I went on a counselling course based on Carl Rogers' method and found this helpful, not only in counselling students, but for my own understanding of God.

Carl Rogers advocated an attitude of 'unconditional positive regard' in the listener, no matter who the client might be. I recognised the impossibility of achieving this ideal, for it demands a spirit of detachment from all our conditioning and prejudice, which no human being is likely to attain this side of death. But then I began to see God in this way, a God who is always for us, and this had an immediate effect on my prayer. God was no longer remote, no longer primarily interested in my failings. God was for me, and nothing I could do would change that disposition of God. Words can make the soul sing. Carl Rogers, the unbeliever, did this for me. Then I began to recognise this teaching in the scriptures, in Paul's 'nothing can separate me from the love of Christ' and in some Wisdom passages. The Book of Wisdom, a late book of the Old Testament, written in Greek to let the pagans know the nature of the God in whom the Jews believed, says of God, 'You overlook our sins, so that we can repent' and 'You spare all things because all things are yours, Lord, lover of life, you whose imperishable spirit is in all.' (Wisdom c. 11).

Rogers' method was based on the belief that the answer to all problems, the healing of all ills, lies within the afflicted person, so that the function of the counsellor is not to supply answers or remedies, but to enable the client to discover for themselves. This teaching took the strain out of my encounters with non-believers and with those who were in disagreement with the Church's teaching. I let them talk, struggling to remain full of unconditional positive regard and encouraging them to speak of the God whom they had rejected, or were about to reject. It was from these conversations that an indentikit picture of God formed in my imagination.

It was as though as little children our parents had taken us to meet 'good old uncle George', the family favourite, enormously wealthy, highly influential and loved by all. He had a white beard, gruff voice, and lived in a large, gloomy mansion. At the end of the visit he turns to us and says, 'I want to see you here regularly every Sunday, dears, and if you fail to come, let me show you what will happen to you'. He then leads us downstairs to the mansion's cellars. The heat becomes intense, the smell noxious, and we hear hideous screams. Uncle George opens a steel door revealing blazing furnaces into which little demons are hurling innumerable members of the people of God – men, women and children. He assures us that the furnace is our ultimate destination if we do not visit him regularly, and leads us back to our parents. We clutch at both in terror and are taken back home. On the way, mummy leans over and says. 'Don't you love Uncle George with all your heart and soul, mind and strength?' Remembering the furnaces, we answer, 'Yes, I do'. We obey Uncle George's orders: in our heart we consider him a monster, but dare not admit this even to ourselves.

This image is a caricature, but it illustrates one form of the many deformed images of God which can dominate our lives and have, in fact, nothing to do with God. Such distorted images can be implanted in our minds by parents, teachers, preachers. We become what we worship. If we worship a God who is primarily a God of judgement, whose main interest lies in our failings and in inflicting suitable punishment, we become like that to ourselves and to others. We become people of the law, hardliners, intolerant, self-righteous, con-demnatory, practising a Christless Christianity and calling it orthodoxy. Those students who were struggling with their faith in God and in the Church, and who thought they had lost it, were on the journey from Jonathan's type of faith towards Polly's faith. They were moving from infantile acceptance of what they had been told to a critical assessment of it, a necessary step for true growth in faith in God who pervades all things.

Conversations with students, whether individually or in groups, whether on the existence of God, the Church's doctrinal teaching, sexual morality, or the just war theory, ceased to be a strain once I had accepted the principle of 'unconditional positive regard', and became instead a source of interest and of learning for me and for them.

It is very often only in retrospect that I can see the significance of particular past events. One day a Polish woman from the Soviet Studies Department called in to see me. She was Catholic, her husband atheist, and she wanted to have her child baptised in the Turnbull Hall chapel. She warned me before the ceremony that hardly any of those who would be attending were Christians. I found prep-aration of the service difficult. How was I to explain the ceremony to a congregation of unbelievers? Then I asked myself what I thought I was doing in the ceremony of baptism. I knew the theological answers, that I was incorporating the child into the life of God, Father,

Son and Holy Spirit, and cleansing it of original sin, which, no doubt, pleased the baby's mother, but what did the ceremony say about the rest of the congregation and their unbaptised children? Were they doomed to outer darkness after death because they were not baptised into the life of God? Then I realised a truth which has been developing in me ever since and which has enormous implications for every aspect of life. The sacraments of the Church are celebrations of our awareness of God's continuous action on every person, including the atheist and the atheist's children. This was another thought which made my soul sing, but my song was not always in harmony with the local church to which I belonged.

The first discordant note came in autumn 1968, when Pope Paul VI issued his Encyclical, *Humanae Vitae*, which included the statement that artificial contraception is intrinsically wrong, 'intrinsically' meaning that it is wrong under all possible imaginable circumstances. I had always found the phrase 'intrinsically wrong' difficult to understand. To put a knife into someone, even to take another's life, was not considered 'intrinsically' wrong in Catholic moral teaching, for a surgeon can operate, and the official Church teaches the morality of capital punishment and of waging a just war. None of the arguments from scripture or the Church's tradition which were brought to bear in support of the intrinsic wrongness of artificial contraception seemed convincing. Before issuing the Encyclical, Pope Paul VI had consulted a group of advisers, clerical and lay, the great majority of whom had advised a change in the traditional teaching. All papal encyclicals appear first in Latin. In the Latin text, Paul VI had called contraception *'intrinsece inhonestum'*, avoiding the Latin word *'malum'*, meaning evil or wrong. This important nuance was lost in the English translation. Paul VI was also careful to explain that an encyclical letter did not present infallible teaching: it was therefore open to change.

Before the Encyclical appeared I had discussed the problem of contraception with many Catholic married people and with others. Two conversations in particular troubled me. One was held with a woman who accepted the teaching of the Church that artificial contraception was wrong, while her husband did not. It was her final sentence which struck, 'I am beginning to hate my husband.' My other conversation was with a priest who had upheld the Catholic teaching on contraception to a couple who were afraid of having another child because of the wife's health. A year later the priest met the husband and asked after his wife. 'She died in childbirth' was the shattering reply.

When the Encyclical appeared, I thought that I should let the Archbishop of Glasgow know of my difficulties, for he had appointed me, and my job included teaching ethics to undergraduate medical students. In a letter, I explained my problem with the phrase 'intrinsically wrong', said that I had no intention of preaching or teaching against the Encyclical, but that if anyone were to ask me whether I believed that artificial contraception was intrinsically wrong, I should have to tell the truth, which was that I did not so believe.

The archbishop's secretary rang me later and arranged an appointment. The archbishop expressed his astonishment that I, a Jesuit priest, bound by a vow of obedience, could have any problem in accepting the Encyclical, while his own diocesan clergy did not. At the end of the interview he promised me his prayers and for several weeks I heard no more. Then I had a visit from the Jesuit provincial's deputy, the provincial being abroad at the time. The deputy looked more than usually solemn. He told me that the archbishop wanted me to leave the chaplaincy after Christmas and that in the meantime I must say nothing on the subject of *Humanae Vitae*, nor on my dismissal. I was benumbed by the news. When the provincial returned to London, I went to see him. He came up to Glasgow, visited the archbishop, then told me I was to be allowed to stay on at the chaplaincy.

Four years later, in June 1972, I had a phone call from the Jesuit provincial telling me that the archbishop had again dismissed me from the chaplaincy, but had given no reasons for the dismissal. I tried to get an interview with the archbishop, but was refused. The voice of early training urged me to be obedient and humble, say nothing, and leave the chaplaincy, but another voice objected strongly, for to act in this way was to collude in a decision which I knew to be unjust. The archbishop had the right to dismiss me, but

I and the people with whom I worked had the right to know the reasons. I told the Sunday Mass congregations of my dismissal. The press took up the case and some university staff tried to interview the archbishop, but without success. At the end of the week the Jesuit provincial did have an interview with him.

The only information which I received on the reasons for my dismissal came from a Lancashire student, a Protestant, whom I had been seeing. He appeared in the chaplaincy a few days after my dismissal and said 'I hear you've been in a bit of trouble. Can you give me the archbishop's address, for I want to write to him?' I gave the address with a caution that whatever he wrote should be respectful. The student returned an hour later to say that he had talked with the archbishop in person and asked him why I had been sacked. The archbishop told him that in the Catholic Church there was a rotation system in all clerical appointments and that it was my turn to rotate! Having told me this the student asked, 'Do you think he was having me on?'

A week after I had been dismissed the Jesuit provincial told me that I had again been reinstated and I remained at the chaplaincy for another three years until 1975. Three months after my reinstatement, after the archbishop had retired, his successor told me that the reason for my dismissal was twofold: I had given Holy Communion to Protestants, and because of my views on Catholic schools. This explanation made me even more angry, for I had never ignored the Catholic ruling forbidding intercommunion and had frequently explained the thinking behind it, nor had I ever issued an invitation to receive Holy Communion to those who were not Catholic. I did, however, give Holy Communion to whoever came forward to receive and shall always continue to do so. As to my views on Catholic schools, I had never spoken against the principle of Catholic schooling, but had often said that in particular circumstances and in particular localities, Catholic schooling could reinforce Catholic tribalism and nurture a Christless catholicism, which was destructive of faith.

The two dismissals threw me into confusion when they occurred, but in retrospect they taught me more about the nature of the Church than I ever learned while studying theology.

I am told that the Chinese character for 'crisis' contains two signs, one meaning danger, the other opportunity. At the time I was aware of the danger of disillusionment, of leaving the Jesuits, the priesthood and the Catholic Church. During the second dismissal, when my mind was in turmoil, I had a sudden experience of great peace and of reassurance that all would be well, and I felt encouraged to hang on.

The two crises brought the Gospels alive in a new way, especially in terms of a clearer understanding of Jesus' temptations in the desert. Jesus was tempted; the Church must also be tempted. Jesus, the sinless one, resisted the temptations; the Church is not sinless, and therefore one should not be scandalised by the sinfulness and injustice one finds there. There is sinfulness and injustice in me and in every member of the Church, which affects its very structures, so the Church itself is in need of continuous reformation. Jesus' temptations in the desert are portrayed as temptations to exercise power and control over people. The Roman Emperors controlled their subjects by giving them bread and circuses, and by declaring themselves to be divine, so as to control the religious instincts of their subjects. Jesus was tempted to turn stones into bread, to leap from the Temple pinnacle, and finally to take over control of all the kingdoms of the world, if he would only kneel and worship Satan. Jesus rejects all these temptations to power and control by appealing to God. 'Human beings do not live by bread alone', 'Thou shalt not tempt the Lord thy God' and 'God alone shalt thou worship, God alone shalt thou adore'.

The temptation narrative goes to the heart of all religion: religion is about relationship with God, a relationship of worship and adoration. This relationship has to be expressed in cultic form of some kind. The danger is that the cultic form, the religious organisation, becomes the focus of worship, so that God and the worship of God are reduced to a series of religious observances controlled by those in authority. Deep in human nature is the desire to control others, to dominate, to take over from God. The most striking characteristic of Jesus' life is his relationship to God. The first words, which are also the only words recorded as spoken by him before he began his public life, are on his being found by his parents in the Temple, having been missing for three days. 'Did you not know that I must be about my Father's affairs?' In his agony in the garden he prays, 'Father, if it be possible, let this chalice pass from me, but not my will, but yours be done.' And in his dying he prays, 'Into thy hands I commend my spirit'.

In the Gospels, the word 'Church' appears very rarely. Jesus speaks of 'the Kingdom of God', 'the reign of God', but to his disciples, arguing as to which of them will be greatest in the coming kingdom, he gives very clear instructions on the nature of authority. 'The rulers of the pagans lord it over their subjects, and their great men love their influence to be felt. With you it must not be so. The greatest among you must become the least of all, and the first among you must be the servant of all, for the Son of Man came, not to be served, but to serve, and to give his life as a ransom for many', a teaching which permeates the Gospels and is the core of Jesus' teaching in the Sermon on the Mount.

With hindsight I can be genuinely grateful for my two dismissals from the chaplaincy. At the time the events confused and benumbed me, then made me feel angry, resentful and disillusioned, but the lasting effect has been to reveal a God who is greater, more attractive and more surprising, a Church which is more mysterious, more provisional in all its structures, more exciting and inclusive and to be found in all kinds of surprising places, a Church in which the centre is often to be found on the perimeter and the perimeter at the centre.

While writing this I have thought often of the archbishop who dismissed me. Even at the time of the dismissals I never felt any personal dislike, for he was normally a most affable man, capable of great kindness and generosity, with a sense of humour and without any trace of malice. He was a canon lawyer with such a dedication to the institutional element in the Church that when he believed it was being damaged, he was ruthless in its defence. I could not share his vision of the Church, but his opposition, expressed in good faith, forced me to question my own vision, and for that I am grateful. I visited him later when he was in retirement and he was as affable as ever.

When I recall the eight years I worked in Glasgow, the first memories are not of dismissals and theology, but of hillsides and mountains with a straggling line of walkers, of nights and early mornings spent in song and laughter in what had once been the ballroom of Inverailort Castle, which the owner, Mrs Cameron Head, kindly gave over to student and other groups. My memories of Turnbull Hall are of the music at crowded Sunday evening Masses, of occasional all-night vigils when alternate hours were spent in the silence of the chapel and in the lounge, where the theme of the vigil was explored in music, poetry and discussion. Another memory is of Christmas Day Mass when I used to invite all my relatives and all their relatives. On one occasion, the gathering included forty-three children under the age of nine. There were always groups around the chaplaincy, usually having tea with Harry and Cathy Campbell, who acted as caretaker and secretary, and lived with their three children in the basement.

Every encounter with another human being is like entering a magnetic field, which either energises or enervates. In Glasgow I moved in a magnetic field that was almost always energising. The strange thing about memory is that it seems to be able to store the energy of those encounters, so that more than twenty years on and many hundreds of miles away, those memories can still actively energise. Every encounter affects us permanently for better or worse, and though there is an essential part of us which is affected by what happens at a given time, the encounter is also beyond time, is eternal. We are essentially linked with each other, whether conscious of the link or not. I am grateful for Glasgow's magnetic field and nothing can separate me from it.

There was one series of encounters during this time in Glasgow which had nothing directly to do with the chaplaincy, but which has affected me in all my subsequent work. In 1968 I joined The Samaritans and did night duty once a month for the next six years. The organisation had been founded by an Anglican clergyman, Chad Varah. Finding himself in a parish with very little to do, he put an advertisement in the local newspaper, offering to chat with anyone in distress, and giving his phone number. He was swamped with calls and The Samaritans became the worldwide organisation from which millions of people have benefited.

The Samaritans is an excellent counter-witness to our contemporary tyranny of knowledge, for its members are ordinary people, unqualified in psychology or psychiatry, but trained in the art of listening. They are warned against giving advice or making judgements about their callers, although they may give factual information if asked. Members are chosen irrespective of their religious persuasion or lack of it, and are cautioned against any form of proselytising.

It was a strange experience to sit in the office of The Samaritans in the still of night, hear the telephone ring, then engage in conversation with some anonymous person, lonely or in distress. It was also encouraging to receive such frequent confirmation of Carl Rogers' claim that the answer to problems lies within the person who has them: usually the caller, having been allowed to talk, was calmer by the end of the call. At first, I made no conscious link between The Samaritans and retreat-giving and spiritual direction, but it was this link which was to influence my work in spirituality over the next twenty-five years.

Two memories of individuals always come to mind when I remember my years in Glasgow. On one Thursday following Ash Wednesday, a man rushed into my office. He introduced himself as Patrick Joseph Aloysius Dolan, told me he had just been released from Barlinnie prison, had not received the ashes on his forehead on Ash Wednesday, but would like to have them now. We had the ceremony immediately, using cigarette ash. This was the first of many visits. Patrick Joseph Aloysius was an alcoholic, constantly in trouble, usually financial, but he had a childlike simplicity and trust in God. Life had treated him roughly since infancy, but he never showed any bitterness or trace of self-pity. He seemed to be blissfully unaware of Catholic sexual morality. At one time he was living with a woman, but was worried because she would not accompany him to Mass on Sundays. He had no illusions about himself and never justified himself: he brought to life Jesus' parable about the Pharisee and the tax-gatherer who go up to the Temple to pray. The Pharisee thanks God that he is such a virtuous man, observing all the rules and regulations, and that he is not like the tax-gatherer who observes none. The tax-gatherer prays, 'Lord, have mercy on me, a sinner'. Jesus says that it was the tax-gatherer who went out of there in a right relationship with God. Patrick Joseph's life was lamentable and tragic in the world's eyes, but God's goodness shone through his ravaged mind and body. Although I was irritated by some of his peremptory visits, I always felt the better for having seen him and understood more easily why Jesus enjoyed the company of sinners.

The other individual was very different. Her name was Stella, whom I had first met when I visited the Gorbals Group of the Iona Community. As a Red Cross nurse, she was among the first British people to witness the horrors of Belsen concentration camp in 1945. She later wrote of this as her road to Damascus. Stella stayed on in the Belsen neighbourhood looking after displaced children and later she became a Church of Scotland missioner in Pakistan. On returning to Scotland in 1968, she was appointed by the joint Churches to work with immigrant Asian families living in Glasgow. Her small house, known as the international flat, was usually crowded with people from India, Asia, Pakistan and Africa, frequently those who would not normally associate with one another. If invited to a meal at Stella's, it was advisable to eat whatever was provided immediately, for more visitors would be sure to arrive and those already present were expected to contribute from their own plates to make a meal for the newcomers. Stella had great compassion and generosity and assumed everyone else shared these dispositions. Her mind was always full of ideas for improving race relations. Consequently, she frequently dropped into Turnbull Hall, wanting help for her latest scheme and she accused me of running away whenever I caught sight of her! Twice a year she had to go before a Church Board to give an account of her work. These meetings would reduce her to a state of dithering incoherence, but afterwards she would be helpless with laughter as she recalled the meeting. Like Patrick Joseph, she had no illusions about herself and no trace of self-pity. When Stella died of cancer in 1982, her funeral was attended by a large congregation of many faiths. A Sikh gave the address. He compared Stella to water which is life-giving, cleansing, refreshing, and assumes the shape of whatever contains it. 'Stella,' said the Sikh, 'was to me a Sikh, to my Muslim friends a Muslim, a Hindu to Hindus.' He ended by saying, 'I have never understood what Christians meant when they said Jesus died for our sins, but I know that Stella died for ours.'

God, where are you? I saw God in Stella. I never told her so while she was alive for I know how she would have reacted, starting with a laugh, then declaring with complete sincerity that she was light years away from being Christlike. She acknowledged her own weakness, but she did not make much of it for she never took herself too seriously, laughed easily, and knew, like her patron, St Paul, that when she was weak she was strong.

CHAPTER 9

꧁

God of Catholics, Protestants
and Pagans

*When Jerome Nadal, one of the sixteenth-century Jesuits, was
asked, 'For whom are these Spiritual Exercises suitable?', he
replied, 'For Catholics, for Protestants and for pagans'.*

IN MY FIRST YEAR at Turnbull Hall, a beautiful and forceful medical
student called Laura, who was engaged to a Catholic, came to my
office and said, 'Tell me about the Catholic God'. 'There is no such
thing as the Catholic God,' I said, 'There is only one God of all things
and of all peoples, a God who is mystery, who can never be defined,
who transcends all our categories.' 'You sound like an agnostic,' she
replied, 'yet your Church does not seem at all agnostic. It appears to
know infallibly, through the Pope, exactly who God is, God's likes
and dislikes. God likes Catholics who go to Mass on Sundays, avoid
contraception and believe the Pope. If you are as agnostic as you
sound, you should not be a Catholic priest.' 'Nonsense,' I replied, not
yet having done the counselling course, 'If I do not acknowledge that
God is mystery, then I should not be a Catholic priest.' Laura had the
last word. 'I don't think you know who you are.' Her remark did not
trouble me at the time, for I then knew that I was a Catholic, a priest
and a Jesuit, but it acted like a depth charge, exploding several years
later.

Chaplaincy experience raised many questions. What is faith? What
does it mean to be a Catholic, a priest, a Jesuit? I had been meeting
and working with people of other Christian denominations, of other
religions and of no religion, who appeared to me to be loving, open
to truth, compassionate and thoughtful. I had also met Christians

committed to their own Church, champions of their respective orthodoxies, who seemed to be short on human qualities, were bigoted, narrow-minded and wedded to a system rather than to people. I had seen many examples of Lucretius' remark, 'To such evils can religion lead'.

For me, one of the most worrying questions concerned the Spiritual Exercises of St Ignatius, the inspiration of Jesuit life. I had heard countless sermons and lectures on the value and wisdom of the Exercises and on their wonderful results in the lives of so many people, including canonised saints. I knew something of their value, especially through reading Karl Rahner, who revealed depths of meaning of which I had been unaware. But I was still uneasy about the manner in which the Exercises were normally given, with four long lectures a day: thirty days for the full Exercises, eight days for a cut-down version. Still more worrying was the way in which the themes of the Exercises were often expounded from pulpits, instilling fear and exhorting to loyalty and conformity to the law, observances and teaching of the Catholic Church.

I had read James Joyce's *Portrait of the Artist as a Young Man*, with its horrific description of a Jesuit sermon on hell, heard when he was a schoolboy. I had heard similar sermons myself. Shortly after reading Joyce, I came across a book on brainwashing, in which the author devoted a chapter to the Spiritual Exercises as an illustration of brainwashing techniques. Brainwashing succeeds when the victim is reduced to a state of paralytic fear, then offered a means of escape to which the victim will cling, as though their very life depended on their assent to the prescriptions offered by the brainwasher.

The characteristic of Jesuit life was obedience, as the archbishop had reminded me when I told him I could not accept the intrinsic wrongness of artificial contraception. Criticism of papal utterances was considered a failure in obedience. One Scottish Catholic news-paper, on my second dismissal, headed its account 'The Disobedient Jesuit'. If the Spiritual Exercises were being used as instruments of conformity, buttresses of an authoritarian, hierarchical structure, then could I remain a Jesuit?

In the summer of 1974, while I was still at the chaplaincy, I made an eight-day retreat on a deserted island called Eileach an Naoimh, which means 'the rocky island of the saints'. It is the southernmost of a group of three small islands known as the Gavellachs, 'jewels of the sea', in the Firth of Lorne, south of Mull and about eight miles from the mainland. According to legend, this was the island where Columba took refuge when Iona became too much for him. On the island, which now belongs to the National Trust, there are eighth-century Celtic remains, including a chapel, whose walls still stand to a height of six feet, a twin beehive cell, and a very small underground cell near the chapel. The island is about a mile in length and a quarter of a mile across, with high cliffs running its length on the west side.

I pitched my tent between the chapel and the underground cell. The island felt very peaceful and I fell asleep to the sound of the sea. On the first morning, I awoke to the patter of rain on the tent. It was still raining as I sat breakfasting on the steps leading to the underground cell, the island enveloped in mist. My thoughts matched the weather as I contemplated eight days of rain and no way of escape. As I was sitting, wrapped in gloom, the mist began to clear, the sun broke through, and the grey surroundings were transformed into a scene of such intense beauty that I sat gazing at it instead of getting down to my first prayer period of the day. My spirits rose from gloom to gladness and the beauty took hold of me. Gazing at it, whether sitting or walking, became the pattern of my days. Prayer was no longer something I had to get down to: it happened in me. Unlike previous retreats I did not work through the key meditations of the Spiritual Exercises, but I just prayed as I felt prompted to pray and knew God's goodness at a deeper level of my being. Each day I celebrated the Eucharist within the walls of the eighth-century chapel, using as altar an upturned fishbox which I found on the shore. The congregation were the sheep and the gulls, the rocks and the seals, the whole of creation.

At the end of eight days I felt as though all my senses had been cleansed and as though I had discovered for the first time in my life that God really is the God of unconditional positive regard, present in all things, the God who is always for us.

God of Catholics, Protestants and Pagans

It was this retreat, together with the questions arising from previous experience, which led me to ask the Jesuit provincial if I could move from being a university chaplain to working on spirituality. I wanted to explore further the meaning of Christian faith, the nature of prayer and its relationship to everyday life, the Spiritual Exercises of St Ignatius as they were originally given. I also wanted to continue working with people of other Christian denominations. The provincial asked me to join a group, just recently formed, called The Way Community. The initiator of this group was Fr James Walsh sj, founder and editor of a spirituality periodical *The Way*. The group included four other Jesuits and two religious sisters and had been formed for the study and promotion of the Spiritual Exercises.

I left the chaplaincy in April 1975 and had planned to spend a few months in Rome, studying the history of the Spiritual Exercises and how they had been given in St Ignatius' time, and also in meeting some of the Jesuits who were now recovering the art of giving the Exercises individually. Knowing that in July and August the weather would be very hot and that most of the people I wanted to meet would be out of Rome, an idle thought came to me: 'Why not walk to Rome, arriving at the beginning of September?' The idle thought eventually became a decision and the ten weeks on the road from Weybridge to Rome were the most valuable ten weeks I have ever spent.

Before deciding to ask to work on spirituality, I had some other idle thoughts about the future which I quickly dismissed. One was of living as a hermit near one of the Scottish nuclear bases. I abhorred the presence of nuclear weapons in the beauty of the West of Scotland, but knew the uselessness of any verbal protest I might make and therefore felt prompted to protest with my whole being. Another thought was of living in what they call in Glasgow 'a single end', a room in some poor part of the city where I could know what it was like to live among the poor. I did not take these thoughts seriously, but dismissed them as wild and impractical. In reflecting on them now, I see two tendencies in me: one is to behave correctly, to be ordinary, to conform and do what is expected of me because I need approval; the other tendency is wild, unpredictable, unstable, fanciful.

Upbringing and education, both religious and secular, have put such emphasis on the common-sense side that I have not listened sufficiently carefully to the other, for God is not predictable and does not seem to share our reverence for common sense. Perhaps I should not have lived in a tent by Faslane, or in a single end, but I should have given these fantasies more attention, reflection and prayer.

When in mid June 1975 I set out from Weybridge to walk to Rome, I thought I knew clearly why I was doing so. I wanted to learn more about the Spiritual Exercises of St Ignatius, how they were originally given, why, and with what effect. It was only after I had completed the walk that I realised there was a deeper motive for undertaking it.

Recently I heard a polar explorer state that all who go in for long and arduous journeys are suffering from a degree of madness: unable to cope with their own inner problems, they externalise the conflict into a physical journey. To call them 'mad' is an exaggeration, but I believe that in all who undertake long journeys there is usually a deeper motivation than our conscious minds can grasp. In every human mind, if we dare to look, there is confusion, uncertainty, bewilderment. This is not a sign of madness: it is recognition of the mystery and complexity of our being. Some ignore or repress the confusion, live ordered, if not very interesting lives, and try to impose the same order on others. Others face the inner chaos, perhaps have a temporary breakdown, and often become very creative people. There are others, perhaps most of us, who cannot cope with the inner complexity, and so they externalise it in some form of neurotic behaviour. Long-distance walking is a very healthy way of externalising the inner complexity.

Pilgrimage has been called 'the poor person's substitute for mysticism'. Unable to cope with the inner complexity, but longing for some resolution of it, the pilgrim chooses some holy spot, symbol of the answer to their inner longing, and then walks towards it. The outward physical journey can clarify the inner struggle. I set out for Rome with many questions swirling around in my mind, questions about the nature of God, of the Church, the Spiritual Exercises, Jesuit life, not least Laura's comment 'I don't think you know who you are'.

The walk to Rome did not answer all my questions, but it did leave me with a very clear answer to 'Who are you?'. The answer still brings me great peace, and if I had gained nothing else from the walk, this answer alone would have made it worthwhile.

The answer was, 'I am happy not to know who I am'. Answers are so obvious once we have found them. God is mystery. In God we live and move and have our being. We are made in the image of God and just as we cannot clearly define God, so we cannot clearly define ourselves. St Augustine prayed, *'Noverim te, noverim me'*, 'That I may know you, that I may know myself', but he knew that the knowing is a process of endless exploration. As everything in creation is essentially related, a clear and complete knowledge of ourselves would be possible only if we knew all things. Faith is entrusting ourselves to this mystery in which we are living, trusting that love is at the heart of it, so that it is safe to explore; unsafe to rest in what we consider our present certainties. Those who rest in unshakeable certainties no longer live in faith, although they often pride themselves on being the only people who have true faith. Faith brings a certainty which enables us to move with sureness in all the uncertainty, confusion, disappointment and disillusion of life. Nothing so masks the face of God as our security in our own certainties. With faith in God we see everything as provisional, and we are always open to new possibilities.

Another question which had troubled me for years, especially when I clashed with authority in Glasgow, was, 'Am I really a Catholic? Do I genuinely believe the articles of the Creed?' In particular, did I really believe in Christ's resurrection from the dead and in our own resurrection after death? Was the Gospel account of the empty tomb true? What would happen to our faith if Jesus' body were to be discovered in such a way that there could be no doubt as to its identity?

I was greatly helped by one article I read in which the author stated that Christian apologists would do better to stop attempting to prove that we shall have material bodies after death, and should concentrate instead on the unlikelihood of our having a material body now. Focusing on the mystery in which we now live was helpful.

The source of most of my difficulty with belief in the resurrection, whether of Christ or of all humankind, was the fact that I was thinking of Christ's resurrection as an external past event, and the general resurrection as an external future event. Struggling with this doctrine brought me to a clearer understanding of the meaning of doctrine in general. The scriptures and Church doctrine are given to us, not primarily as a record of past events, but as a means of helping us to recognise God at work in our own lives now. If it is true that Christ is risen and that we, too, are to rise again, then that truth is given in order to help us to live now. If Christ is risen and his Spirit, as St Paul says, is now given to us, then death is not the end, for we have within us a Spirit which nothing can destroy, not even death itself. Therefore the resurrection is a source of endless help and reassurance. If we live by that Spirit, then no crisis, no loss, no failure can ever shatter us. Belief in the resurrection is not simply a hope for the future, but also a power in the present, which enables us to move from self-preoccupation to selflessness, from timidity to courage, from despair to hope, from sadness to joy. My earlier difficulties with the doctrine of the resurrection disappeared in much the same way as my problem with self-identity. I had been worried at my own lack of faith in the resurrection because I could neither think nor imagine what resurrection would be like. Now, in Rome, I was no longer worried. I still cannot imagine or think what resurrection will be like, but that does not matter. When the Corinthians asked St Paul what kind of bodies we would have after death, he told them not to ask stupid questions. What is important is whether we believe that the Spirit of the risen Christ is given to us now, and that we live according to that Spirit.

When I recall studying the Spiritual Exercises while in Rome, I notice another strange aspect of memory. There were various points which struck me as I studied. It is only now, twenty years later, that I realise how significant they were, and how they were to affect me over the next twenty years. It is as though our subconscious and unconscious intelligence is not as time and space bound as the conscious mind. Consequently, our subconscious can grasp the future significance of an idea or of an incident far more quickly than the conscious mind. The indication to the conscious mind that the sub-conscious is at work, burrowing, as it were, into the future, is that the idea or incident not only registers in our consciousness at the time as being interesting or exciting, but that the memory lingers and recurs, as though knocking at the door of consciousness and demanding entry.

One of the phrases which struck me at the time, and which has been persistently knocking at the door ever since, was a quotation from Jerome Nadal, a contemporary of St Ignatius. When asked, 'For whom are these Spiritual Exercises suited?' he answered, 'For Catholics, for Protestants and for pagans'. In Nadal's world, pagans would have meant Muslims. One of the earliest Jesuit houses outside Italy was in Dubrovnik, then under Turkish control, and presumably chosen in order to make contact with Muslims.

In Britain, the full Spiritual Exercises of thirty days, and even the eight-day retreat, were limited to Catholic priests and to men and women of religious congregations. They were not normally given to Catholic lay people, and certainly not to Protestants and pagans.

I was also interested to read in more detail of the Inquisition's uneasiness with the Spiritual Exercises and the opposition they encountered from some theologians and clergy. Ignatius was accused of being an illuminist – that is, one who claimed to be taught directly by the Holy Spirit, thus bypassing the official Church. The Exercises were considered dangerously free and likely to upset Church order. Four centuries later the same objection can still occasionally be heard.

I was already familiar with the text of the Spiritual Exercises, having listened to many preached retreats, but in Rome I took time to study the text, and began to see the importance of passages which previously I had read only cursorily.

Ignatius prefaces his Spiritual Exercises with a few preliminary observations, called annotations, which are primarily meant as guidelines for the giver of the Exercises, whom I shall call the guide. These annotations include some advice for the person making the Exercises, whom I shall call the pilgrim. Contrary to all my experience of the Exercises, with four lengthy talks delivered daily by the guide,

Ignatius tells the guide to be as brief as possible in giving the pilgrim prayer material for the day. As some of the sixteenth-century pilgrims may not have been able to read, and as the Bible was available only in Latin, the guide would have had to read the translated text to the pilgrim. The reason for this advice was, in Ignatius' words, 'When one in meditating takes the solid foundation of the facts, and goes over it and reflects on it for himself, he may find something that makes them a little clearer or better understood . . . Now this produces greater spiritual relish and fruit than if the one giving the Exercises had explained and developed the meaning at great length. For it is not much knowledge that fills and satisfies the soul, but the inner understanding and relish of the truth.' (s. 2). This is a key principle, not only in retreat-giving, but in all teaching and instruction.

All his preliminary observations assume that the Exercises are being given individually, so Ignatius advises that they be adapted to the capacity, energy, ability and willingness of the pilgrim. They are not presented as a ready-made obstacle course which all pilgrims must complete. He writes, too, of the difficulties and darkness the pilgrim may encounter, and how the guide is to treat them with gentleness and kindness. He also cautions the guide to be careful with the enthusiastic pilgrim, lest such a one should rush into making a promise or vow. He tells the guide not to get in the way, but to be 'like a balance at equilibrium, without leaning to one side or the other', so that God may 'deal directly with the creature, and the creature directly with his Creator and Lord'. This is not the advice which one brainwasher is likely to give another!

When the Exercises were first given, they became very popular and the early Jesuits were in great demand. In spite of the pressure on them, they did not rush around giving the Exercises to all comers. They spent time getting to know their pilgrim, did not start on the Exercises until they considered the person to be ready, and they probably gave the full Exercises to very few. Ignatius himself kept Francis Xavier and Pater Faber, two of his first companions, waiting for years before giving them the Exercises. In recent years, since the Spiritual Exercises have become popular among Catholic and

Protestant lay people, I have come to appreciate the wisdom of those early Jesuits.

There is a letter, written by a Jesuit novice master to the Jesuit general at the beginning of the seventeenth century, in which the novice master complains of having so many novices that he cannot possibly give them the full Spiritual Exercises individually. He then tells the general of the advantages to be gained by the novices if they make the retreat as a group. The group method will better ensure that the novices really do give the full time to prayer, and knowing that they have to report to their fellow novices afterwards will encourage them to pray more intensely! The general replies to the novice master that to give the Exercises to a group, rather than to individuals, would be contrary to Jesuit tradition. He tells the novice master that he may shorten the length of the retreat, but that he must continue to give the Exercises individually. However, such was the demand that other retreat-givers abandoned the individual retreat and gave the Exercises to groups, sometimes to over a hundred people together. So began the custom which persisted until the late 1960s and is still not uncommon today. The reluctance to revert to the original method is not just because it is labour-intensive and time-consuming: the deeper reason is fear, for if the Exercises are properly given, the guide has no control over the pilgrim, who may be uncomfortably challenging.

The effect of the Exercises when given by the early Jesuits was astonishing, freeing pilgrims from fear and releasing springs of creativity in them. The sudden expansion of the Society of Jesus throughout Europe, Asia, India, and North and South America, and the originality they showed in missionary method, sprang from their experience of the Spiritual Exercises. It is astonishing that this original method was so soon forgotten. Instead of being a means of helping pilgrims to discover for themselves, they were delivered in the form of lengthy talks to large groups. Far from freeing individuals to make their own discoveries, they became a means of ensuring conformity, hence the brainwashing accusation.

From Rome I returned to London at the end of November 1975 to join The Way Community, who were living in a wing of Southwell

God, Where Are You?

House, Hampstead, the rest of the house being occupied by a community of Jesuit scholastics, who were studying in London. I already
knew all but one of The Way Community members: James Walsh
initiated the community, Jock Earle had been headmaster at Stonyhurst, Billy Hewett and Michael Ivens had taught there with me, Felix
McGowan had been on the Mount St Mary's staff while I was a pupil
there, and Kathleen McGhee, a Notre Dame sister, had been working
in Glasgow while I was at the chaplaincy. Mary Grant, a Sacred Heart
sister, was the only member whom I did not know. The Way was a
completely new form of community living as far as I was concerned,
being a mixed community of men and women, free to discover the
structures which would best help us to pursue our task, the study
and giving of the Spiritual Exercises. Apart from Glasgow, it was by
far the most enjoyable community I had ever been in. We cooked
our own meals and spent hours in informal conversation, besides our
more formal meetings, prayed together and had time to get on with
our own study or writing.

Although I enjoyed the company and this form of life, I felt uneasy.
In 1974, the Jesuits had held their 32nd General Congregation, which
included a decree, No.4, stating that to be a Jesuit was 'to engage,
under the standard of the Cross, in the crucial struggle of our time,
the struggle for faith and that struggle for justice which it includes . . .'
Similarly, solidarity with men and women who live a life of hardship
and who are victims of oppression cannot be the choice of a few
Jesuits only. It should be a characteristic of our communities and
institutions as well.' Ever since Albert Camus had sent me back to
the Old Testament prophets, I had felt uneasy about the security
which Jesuit life afforded. I did not have to worry about having a roof
over my head, or where the next meal was to come from. I knew
the theoretical answer, namely that it was up to me to live in poverty
within that security, but it is very difficult to do so, and even if one
succeeds, the fact that the security exists cuts one off from living like
the poor. It can also engender middle-class attitudes and values,
which can blind us to the plight of the poor and deafen us to
their cries.

My other source of uneasiness lay in our Way planning sessions.

Our work seemed to be directed exclusively to working with Catholic priests and religious. I had no idea as to how we were to open up the Exercises to other Catholics, Protestants and pagans, but our deliberations seemed to ignore the question.

In January 1976, Michael Ivens and I received a letter from the Jesuit provincial asking us to take over the running of the tertianship at St Beuno's from September 1976, so we spent much of our time reflecting on the style of tertianship needed in light of the Second Vatican Council and the Jesuit 32nd General Congregation. To continue my study of the Spiritual Exercises and to plan for the tertianship, I went to the USA and Canada in March 1976.

In the USA I stayed at a Jesuit noviceship and retreat centre in Pennsylvania. In charge of the retreat centre was Fr George Schemel, one of the Americans who had been greatly influenced by Fr Paul Kennedy, and who had developed the individually given retreat. He also trained others, including lay people, in the giving of the Exercises. I went there to observe, to study, and also to continue the writing which I had begun and which was eventually published as *In Search of a Way*, reflections on the walk to Rome. I also studied a three-volume work by the French theologian Louis Bouyer on the history of Christian spirituality. Earlier reading of books on spirituality I had found to be either boring or troubling, as the authors described states of prayer which corresponded to no experience of mine. In Bouyer's synopsis I found phrases from ancient authors which I recognised as true from my own experience. I was particularly delighted to read a phrase by Evagrius, from the fourth century, 'Sin is forgetfulness of God's goodness', for that was the truth I had learned on my first retreat on the island of Eileach an Naoimh. Now that I was learning a little more of the Spiritual Exercises, I began to appreciate Ignatius' ability to get to the heart of things, for whatever I read, whether of the Fathers of the Desert, or Benedictine, Dominican, Franciscan or Carmelite spirituality, I was able to relate it to the movement of the Exercises, and see the different spiritualities as complementary rather than as opposed to one another.

In May I travelled to Guelph, Ontario, to have my first experience of giving the full Exercises in a thirty-day retreat. John English, a

Canadian protégé of Fr Paul Kennedy, had set up a centre in Guelph where the Exercises were studied, and given individually. He had gathered a team of Jesuits who, besides giving eight-day individual retreats, ran several six-week courses each year, which consisted of a few days of preparation followed by the full thirty-day retreat, and ending with a week's reflection on the experience. Those attending the course were all Catholic priests or religious, mostly from the United States and Canada. The team giving the retreat had a wealth of experience in giving the Exercises individually, their retreatants including most of the bishops of the Canadian hierarchy. The Jesuit team at Guelph met regularly to evaluate their work and to reflect on the Exercises in light of their experience of giving them. I felt privileged to be allowed to work with them, for in Britain, apart from Paul Kennedy at St Beuno's, who gave the Exercises individually to a few religious, the individually given retreat was still unknown.

Giving the full Exercises to individuals was an invaluable experience and John English was refreshingly down-to-earth, clear and flexible, whenever I consulted him. As Benjie Winterborn in Manchester had given me ideas for chaplaincy work, John English gave me ideas which I was to find helpful two years later, when I was asked to develop St Beuno's as a retreat centre.

On reflection, I think I ought to have made the full Exercises at Guelph rather than have given them, because I had had no experience of being individually directed. Although I valued the Guelph experience, and delighted in John English's view of the Exercises as a way to inner freedom, my own experience of giving the Exercises left me with questions about the gulf there is between theory and practice. Catholic religious life, even in apostolically active orders and congregations, tended to be monastic in lifestyle and spirituality, with a great emphasis on loyalty and fidelity to the Rule, to superiors and to obedience. Personal feelings were not considered important, attending to them was a sign of softness, and discussing them with others was not encouraged. Consequently, many religious lived a very private inner life and were often very fearful, a fear masked by the appearance of cheerfulness, a cheerful demeanour being part of the Rule, as God loves a cheerful giver! The second Vatican

Council's visionary document on the Constitution of the Church with its appeal to all religious to return to the inspiration of their founders, and its emphasis on freedom of conscience, together with the cultural upheaval of the Sixties, had caused a revolution in priestly and religious life, and large numbers of men and women were leaving their religious congregations.

True inner change takes decades, whether in an individual or in a body of people. One cannot get in touch again with feelings which have been ignored for years simply because superiors now say that feelings are important. I realised this in the first retreat I gave. As I went through the Exercises with one person, and encouraged him to talk of his feelings and thoughts in prayer and during the day, his account was always the same, whether he was praying on sin and repentance, the life of Christ, or on the passion and death of Jesus. All his experience was described as 'beautiful', 'wonderful', 'neat', 'delightful'. I was feeling increasingly uneasy, but I did not know how to read my own feelings at this stage. It was only towards the end of the retreat that he began to talk about his real feelings, which were neither neat, beautiful, nor delightful. He was the elder in a family of two. His younger sister had a learning disability and was a burden to her parents. Conscious of this, and unwilling to burden them further, he had always pretended that all was well with him and with life, hiding the truth from himself, and trying to hide it from God, a state of affairs which had manifested itself in cancer. Through that experience I began to appreciate the wisdom of the early Jesuits in not rushing to give the Spiritual Exercises to people until they had come to know them. If the pilgrim is not in touch with his or her own feelings, then making the Spiritual Exercises can be a profitless occupation, and they are unlikely to effect any lasting change in the individual.

Each evening during the retreat, the guides would meet together to report, in general terms and while preserving confidentiality, on how the retreat was going. In every meditation Ignatius includes a petition, prefacing it with, 'I will pray for what I desire', then adding 'here it will be to pray for a deep and intense sorrow and tears for my sins', or 'for an intimate knowledge of our Lord, who has become man for me, that I may love him more and follow him more closely'. I felt uneasy at many of these sessions, for the reports tended to centre on the question of the petition, and whether the pilgrims really were receiving what they asked for. Some of the guides seemed to have no doubt that these graces were being received and I wondered how they could be so certain, for I was not at all certain with any of my six pilgrims. Later, experience taught me the wisdom which lay hidden in my own uneasiness, for the guide should never try to become a grace-diviner. There is also the danger that if intent on whether or not a particular grace has been given, the guide may fail to notice what really is going on in the pilgrim. A further danger is that an anxious-to-please pilgrim will pick up the guide's anxiety that the grace prayed for should be received, and will then convince themselves that they have received it in order to please the guide. I was beginning to see that the giving of the Spiritual Exercises individually is a much more delicate and complex process than I had thought.

I returned from Canada in July for a two-week Way Community meeting which I had thought was to be a planning session for future work. On arrival I discovered that we had been joined by a Jesuit psychiatrist and a Jesuit psychologist, who were to help us communicate with one another. I had not noted any difficulty in communicating so far. These sensitivity or human-encounter groups were becoming fashionable among religious who were trying to renew themselves in the 1960s and 1970s. The sessions were useful in their insistence that we communicate from our guts and not from our heads, and in encouraging us to be more in touch with our feelings, but such meetings can do lasting damage if they are not handled with extreme care and sensitivity. Michael Ivens later compared our sessions to being introduced to a game and encouraged to play in utter freedom: naively joining in, one soon discovered that there were very strict rules which, if transgressed, caused you to be clobbered and held up to ridicule by one or other of the facilitators. One of the gravest transgressions was to question their method. Any criticism was considered by the facilitators to be evidence of some personal quirk of the critic. The facilitators were thus rendered invulnerable and the critics very vulnerable. The other grave trans-gression was to theorise in any way about the process of the encounter group. This was labelled escape from feelings into the head. The facilitators liked to keep feeling and thinking clearly separate.

These sessions were useful in encouraging us to communicate from our feelings, and such communication did deepen our under-standing. I was able, for the first time in my life, to share my feelings about Marie's and Margot's deaths with a group, but some of the interventions of the facilitators were unhelpful and eroded the sense of mutual trust which we had before the encounter group began. At the time, I could not pinpoint my uneasiness. The facilitators had no problem in diagnosis: my uneasiness was fear of my own feelings. While this was true, for I had unconsciously repressed feelings for years, I think my uneasiness was rather with the hidden control which the facilitators were exercising, and also with the sharp, dangerous and false distinction which they seemed to be making between feeling and thought. Feelings are important and must be listened to, for they are intelligent, often more intelligent than our conscious minds. If we do not follow von Hugel's advice, 'where your heart is, let your brain be also', then we can fail to pick up the messages our feelings are communicating. Emotion and reason are not opposites, but complementary.

In September 1976, Michael Ivens and I moved to St Beuno's to begin our first tertianship. I felt anxious, for I was so full of questions and doubts on the nature of Jesuit life that I did not feel competent to be instructing other Jesuits in their final year of training. Returning to St Beuno's did not help. Apart from the addition of central heating throughout the house, it seemed little changed since I had left it thirty years earlier. The resident community consisted mostly of elderly Jesuits, eight of them being Jesuit brothers. They were all dressed in Jesuit gowns and Roman collars, a dress to which I had been accustomed for years, but had donned only rarely in recent years.

There are times and circumstances when the wearing of religious or clerical dress can be helpful for the work we are doing, but when the dress becomes a counter-witness, it no longer serves any useful apostolic purpose. It may seem a trivial point to fuss about, but for me the black suit and Roman collar symbolised a whole conglomerate of attitudes which I thought were destructive. The dress was distinctive, setting us apart from others. Advocates of clerical dress would maintain that this was precisely its purpose: to remind ourselves and let others know, too, that we are set apart, consecrated to God, in the world but not of it. 'We should be proud of our uniform', as I had heard one retreat-giver say. Clerical titles reinforced the apartness, the higher the title the greater the distance, going from Reverend to Very Reverend, Lordship, Grace, Eminence, titles against which Jesus warned his followers. 'He put aside his divinity and became a slave out of love for us', 'Call no one Rabbi, . . . call no one father, . . . call no one teacher.' St Ignatius prescribed common dress for the early Jesuits, specifically excluding any special form of dress. Clerical dress now raised questions for me about the power structures in the Church, for the dress seemed to signify conformity to a mode of life which was tightly controlled and in which the virtues of loyalty and fidelity to the system were more emphasised than openness to truth and justice. In mid-Seventies Britain, religious and clergy were not notably concerned with political and social questions: the few who were concerned were frequently considered oddities, and their vocation sometimes suspect. The setting-apart function of clerical dress reflected the setting apart in our spirituality of the sacred from the secular, the holy from the profane, the natural from the supernatural. Consequently, the sacraments, instead of being understood and celebrated as signs of God's continuous love for all creation and for every human being, became sacred rituals which, as it were, confined God's activity to formal religious services.

The black suit and Roman collar are very effective in keeping most clergy apart from the rest of the world, for people then tend to address them accordingly, switching to deferential religious mode and talking politely on Church matters. Driving from London to Scotland one day and wearing a sports shirt, I picked up a hitch-hiker. My passenger was a Geordie, who was also a Celtic supporter, and he entertained me with kick-by-kick accounts of games he had attended, every noun qualified by the same effing adjective. Eventually he asked me if I had been to London on business, then what the business was. When I told him I was a Jesuit priest, his first words were 'Sorry, Father', and he then bored me for the rest of the trip with stories of his early days as an altar server.

There are obvious advantages of easy identification in having some form of distinctive dress, but the black suit is a curious choice, shared with the secret police and fascist organisations, the colour which inspires fear. I chatted with one priest who was very attached to his clerical garb, wearing it on all occasions. He always wore it because he did not believe he had any self-worth, and so his only usefulness was in fulfilling a role. In his case, wearing a uniform was a flight from himself. Later, as I gave retreats to individuals, I was fascinated to notice how their dress and their inner disposition matched. Some priests and religious, who began the retreat in collar or veil, would discard the uniform as they began to experience greater inner freedom and self-assurance.

Michael Ivens and I were left free to design the tertianship as we thought best within the very general parameters laid down for all Jesuit tertianships. The course lasted nine months and we knew it must not be modelled on our own very monastic tertianship experience. The Spiritual Exercises, the inspiration of Jesuit life, provide a spirituality for people living in the world, to help them become 'contemplatives in action', as distinct from contemplatives within monastery or convent walls. The tertianship was to be, according to Ignatius, a *schola affectus*, a time for getting in touch with our inner feelings and emotions. We devised a programme which centred on the experience of the full Spiritual Exercises, the preliminary weeks of the course being a preparation for the thirty-day retreat, and the remainder of the course being an earthing of that experience in the form of a four-month experiment in an inner-city area, where tertians could experience Christ poor and, in the words of the 32nd General Congregation, 'learn from the poor what we can do to help them'. There was also study of the Jesuit Constitutions, which are an application of the Spiritual Exercises to this particular form of religious life, study of Jesuit history, more detailed study of the text of the Exercises, and training in giving the Exercises to individuals.

From the mid Sixties, the numbers joining the Jesuits had been decreasing and the number leaving increasing, so there were only fifteen making the tertianship in 1976, half the number who had made it in 1959. Also, men were no longer coming to the tertianship immediately after theology, as had been the case, but were now coming after a few years of experience in some form of pastoral work. One of our tertians came to his final year of training after twenty-five years as a Jesuit! In the first two years of my involvement in the tertianship, the majority were from the British Province, but with a sprinkling of others from the USA, Austria, Spain, Africa, Japan, Yugoslavia and Czechoslovakia. In my third and final year there was only one man from the British Province, while all the rest were from various other countries.

We began the tertianship with an exercise in faith sharing. The group of fifteen were encouraged to scan their lives with the question, 'What has God meant for me?' or, if they preferred, 'What have been the key events in my life?'. They would then share their experience with the rest of the group, in so far as they were willing. Michael Ivens and I also shared in this exercise, which was our first experience in communicating in a group at this level. Those who shared their story first tended to be brief, those who followed taking much longer, so that the exercise lasted for several days. It was always a most moving experience, illustrating the very different ways in which God leads each one, and the uniqueness of each. Sometimes it was harrowing to listen to an individual's childhood history and religious upbringing. As the exercise progressed, trust grew among the group, so that people could share more easily. We had a rule that the sessions were listening sessions only, not for discussion, so no one could question another except on a point of information. Such faith sharing reveals the superficiality of so much of our human communication, for normally we exchange conventional greetings, limit our speech to things external to ourselves, and rarely communicate what matters most to us, in case we are considered to be oddities.

In preparation for the thirty-day retreat we also ran courses on

human development, enabling people to get in touch with their feelings, to express them to others, in order to understand more clearly
their cause and where the feelings might be directing us. The Spiritual
Exercises assume this ability in the pilgrim, otherwise what Ignatius
calls 'the movement of the spirits' will not occur and there will be
no possibility of discerning the will of God in our lives; the daily
session with the retreat guide then becomes a profitless exercise.
After the thirty-day retreat we had five days for individual and group
evaluation of the experience which, for many, was as important as
the retreat itself. Study of the text of the Spiritual Exercises and a
course in the art of spiritual direction came afterwards. These later
courses could be of value only in so far as they built upon the personal experience of participants who had themselves made the full
Exercises individually.

After the retreat evaluation there were lectures on the Jesuit Constitutions and Jesuit history in which we always tried to relate both
subjects to our present world. It is said that there is no better way of
learning than having to teach, and in spite of my sense of inadequacy
for the work, I appreciated this opportunity to deepen my own knowledge of things Jesuit and to see more clearly how far the Jesuit
training I had received differed from the innovative and flexible spirit
of the Spiritual Exercises and the Jesuit Constitutions.

After Christmas, the next four months were spent in experiments
in living in an inner-city area, their purpose being to earth the retreat
experience. Two criteria in the Jesuit Constitutions for the choice
of ministries had particularly struck me. Ignatius had written, '*Quo
universalius, eo divinius*', 'The more universal a work is, the more it
is divine'. The majority of Jesuits in Britain were engaged in work in
all-Catholic environments – schools, retreat houses, parishes – which
could not, without very tortuous reasoning, be considered universal.
Christ's mission is universal. 'In Him all created things have their
being'. When his disciples acted as though they were an exclusive
group, he rebuked them and said, 'Whoever is not against us is for
us'. Therefore the experiments should offer the tertians the opportunity to work in a more general environment than most parishes
could provide. Another interesting criterion for ministry was Ignatius'

comment that if a work was of God, then there would be a disproportion between the resources invested in the work and its results.
This fascinated me, for I had already observed as a general principle
in Church activity that the more money invested in a project and the
more time and energy spent in preliminary planning meetings, the
less effective the project was likely to be. This was confirmed by one
of the tertians, Augustin Duc Thu, a Vietnamese, who had been in
Vietnam until a year before the fall of Saigon. He told me that before
the Vietnam war, the Catholic Church was very powerful with strong
resources in money, buildings and personnel. After the Second
Vatican Council there were many meetings and renewal courses
throughout the country. 'But,' he said, 'nothing happened'. Then
came the war and the Communists. The Church lost almost everything: then things began to happen and converts to Roman
Catholicism poured in. Before he left Vietnam, Augustin's job was
the instruction of converts, and he had about three hundred to look
after. In 1974, the 32nd Jesuit General Congregation had declared
justice to be integral to faith and had encouraged all Jesuits to make
work with the poor their preferential option.

It was on these principles that the experiments were designed.
They were also to be experiments in living together in small groups,
so that people could share experience, reflect and pray together. In
the late 1970s, this was something new for most British Jesuits who
had spent most of their Jesuit lives in large institutions with a clear
timetable for each day.

I had previously visited people in London and Liverpool who were
involved in some form of community activity and were willing to
introduce tertians to their work. I had also found cheap accommodation and begged for or borrowed minimal furnishings. When I
explained to people what we were about, I met with extraordinary
generosity and co-operation. Tertians worked with drug addicts,
alcoholics, homeless people, in hostels, inner-city schools, in hos-
pices for the dying, with youth clubs, and a few were given an
introduction to sign language and worked with the deaf. For the first
two years of the tertianship, the groups were admirable in the way
they adapted to what was for them a novel and very demanding

lifestyle: individually and as groups they reflected on the experience in light of the Spiritual Exercises.

In these first two years of working with tertians, I felt both encouraged by the experience and hopeful for the future of the Society of Jesus. St Ignatius was a man of his time, who lived in a world in which society, both ecclesiastical and secular, was essentially hierarchical, and he probably could not conceive of any other way of organising society. His vision of the Church was of an ordered society, Christ's kingdom on earth, united under the Pope. But he was also a mystic with an awareness of God's presence in all things and of the unity of all things in God, and it is this awareness and his response to it which is at the heart of his Spiritual Exercises: hence his respect for the individual, his essential flexibility and adaptability, both in the Exercises and in the Jesuit Constitutions, where he lays down general principles, but constantly reminds the reader that these principles are to be applied in a spirit of love, and to be adapted to particular circumstances of place and person. Through working with the tertians I was beginning to see the Exercises as a way of finding freedom in the Spirit.

In the summer months, when there was no tertianship, I tried to start individually given retreats for lay people, irrespective of denomination. I was warned beforehand that such a project was unrealistic, for laity would neither have the time nor the capacity to spend eight days in silence, praying for several hours each day. The authorities at St Beuno's would not allow the house to be used for this novel form of retreat, so I found other places. In the first summer we had twenty-six people making an eight-day retreat, and the following year we had over a hundred. These retreats were also most encouraging and gave me great hope. Most who came soon found the silence congenial, and once they were introduced to some new methods of prayer, and encouraged to experiment to find the method which was best for them, they had little difficulty in praying for several hours each day. There was a great variety in age, occupation and religious outlook among them, and I began to see the truth of the remark of Ignatius' early companion, Jerome Nadal, that the Exercises are suitable for Catholics, Protestants and pagans, for they are a means of getting in touch with our own experience, provided they are given individually and the retreat-giver is not afraid of allowing the pilgrim to be free.

In my first year at St Beuno's I completed my first book, *In Search of a Way*, but I then ran into difficulty with the censors. There was a rule among Jesuits that we may not publish books unless they are first submitted to censors, whom the Jesuit provincial appoints. Now the rule has been changed, and the author can choose his own Jesuit censor. Of the four censors appointed to read my book, three were against publishing and only one was in favour. I asked that the book should be submitted to other censors. Eventually it was published with only one very minor change, but the censorship process took longer than it took me to write the final draft. I am not against Jesuit censorship: it can be very helpful to have one's work criticised, and it prevents an author from presenting a personal view or prejudice as though it were Church teaching. But in this case I felt frustrated, for I was not allowed to present certain facts in case they might displease ecclesiastical authority. This seemed to me to be putting loyalty to the system before loyalty to the truth. Many things are likely to give offence. We are all prickly, and it is hard to write anything interesting which is not going to offend someone. If the avoidance of offence is made the ultimate criterion, then we are doomed to produce only anodyne books and to remove the Cross from Christian life. When we are all accepted as nice, harmless people who disturb no one, we have betrayed the Gospel. The good in the process was that I was allowed to put my case, which was eventually listened to, and the Jesuit provincial allowed the book to be published.

After the experience of the first eight-day retreat for laity, I wrote to the provincial about the use we were making of St Beuno's, which had over fifty rooms, was most beautifully situated on a hill overlooking the Clwyd valley, yet was occupied for most of the year by fewer than twenty elderly Jesuits. Under the new form of tertianship, tertians were only in the house for about four months of the year. I was thinking of St Beuno's in comparison with Wernersville and Guelph, centres where the Exercises were being studied and given, and where training was offered so that others, including laity, could be enabled both to make them and to give them to others. In September 1978 the provincial appointed me superior of St Beuno's to develop it as a spirituality centre, while continuing to run the tertianship with Michael Ivens.

CHAPTER 10

୪୬ଲ

God of Communists
and Bishops

I have had to learn the lesson that reactions at a microscopic level can have macroscopic results. (Hugh Montefiore)

CHILDHOOD MEMORIES, having longer to linger, become more clearly etched in the mind, like fossils in rock. More recent memories swim around in the consciousness in shoals, and while more access-ible, their significance is more difficult to assess. In this and the following chapters I shall look at those memories which still evoke feelings, whether pleasant or painful, and which have consciously affected me ever since.

After being asked in September 1978 to develop St Beuno's as a spirituality centre, I learned one important lesson: never to take on a job without asking for a very clear briefing beforehand. To start a spirituality centre one must have a competent staff and the money to get started. Michael Ivens and I still had a tertianship to run, as in the two previous years. Although Patrick Purnell, a contemporary from schooldays, joined us to take on what is called in Jesuit houses the job of minister, responsible for the daily administration, the task left him with little time for retreat work. Not only did we have no extra money to launch the project, but because the house had now changed status and was no longer a house of Jesuit studies, the subsidy, which had previously supported it, was withdrawn. While it is true that St Ignatius had stated in the Jesuit Constitutions that a disproportion between the resources invested in a project and the good results obtained indicates God's blessing, he did not mean that to ensure the success of a project those in authority should withdraw resources so that the project might flourish!

As it was impossible to get started with neither staff nor money, all we could do was dream of what St Beuno's might become if we had both. Because members of most Catholic religious congregations are allowed to make an annual retreat, and because St Beuno's was so beautifully situated, we foresaw that all our time and energy could be taken in giving such retreats, leaving no space for Protestants, pagans, or even Catholic laity. We decided that we should have to introduce a points system among retreat-givers, graded from −1 for RC religious and priests, +1 for Catholic laity, +3 for other denominations, rising to +8 for a card-carrying Communist or a bishop. We had several Communists before the first bishop arrived!

Besides coping with absence of staff, shortage of money, and the work of the tertianship, I was responsible for a large community of elderly Jesuits at St Beuno's, three of whom were in three different hospitals in autumn 1978. Few in the house could drive a car, so I had to do hospital visiting, too. All three died within four months. At the time, the hospital visiting and care of the sick was a burden, but the memory of some of those old men lingers, while I have forgotten many of the details of my busyness. There was one in particular, known in his day as a martinet, very strict and very rigid. In his old age and helplessness, he recovered a childlike simplicity and talked of his past hurts, but without resentment. He was a man of natural tenderness, which he had overridden out of a sense of duty. With him and with others, I began to know that they were unlikely to die while they were anxious. Past training had left many of them prone to scrupulosity, especially in face of death. I used to read them Psalm 131, 'Yahweh, my heart has no lofty ambitions and my eyes do not look too high. It is not for me to consider great affairs or marvels beyond my scope. It is enough for me to keep my soul tranquil and quiet, like a child in its mother's arms, like a child that has been fed. Israel, rely on Yahweh, now and forever.' Very slowly, the psalm I was reciting to them began to sink deeper into my own consciousness.

It was unfortunate that the tertianship of 1978–79 was of a very different nationality mix from that of previous years. Of the eleven Jesuits, seven were American, one British, one Japanese, one Polish, one African. Had I been more detached from feelings of responsibility for the group, it would have been a fascinating and amusing study in the problems of inculturation. While the Americans were individually charming, able, and full of good will, as a body they had difficulty in appreciating any culture other than their own. Some were not unaffected by the values of the me-generation, so that their ideas of spiritual and religious development tended to be individualist, more influenced by current psychological ideas than by the Gospel. A few did not take easily to the themes of justice and peace, or to the inner-city experiments which the two previous years had entered into so wholeheartedly. The final part of the tertianship, an assessment and evaluation of the whole course and an eight-day retreat, was a very painful experience. Although I did not see it at the time, I realise with hindsight that I was a large part of their problem. Because I was so harassed with other responsibilities, I did not give enough time to planning the experiments in detail, nor did I consult them sufficiently in the planning.

This memory and the feelings associated with it still linger, for the reluctance of some of the tertians to engage in the inner-city experiments, and their apparent unawareness of the essential connection between faith and justice, led me into areas of my own consciousness which may have had nothing to do with the group. For years my own life of faith had enclosed me in what I then understood as a Jesuit mould, a unit of the Roman Catholic Church which, for many years, I identified with God's kingdom on earth. As I began to know God as always greater, God of all things and of all peoples, I became impatient and intolerant of religious attitudes and actions which did not appear to recognise a God beyond all boundaries. I had not yet learned that people cannot be changed by words, or by any form of coercion, and that the only thing we can change is our way of perceiving reality. Faith is about perceiving God in all things, and it is this kind of perception which can move mountains.

There are two memories from those years which can always lift my spirits when I recall them. One was my room in the tower at the top of the house, a small room with a window which opened on to a view of the Clwyd valley. On a clear day I could see the mountains of Snowdonia to the west, the Llandudno peninsula and the sea towards the north. I used to gaze out of this window when I was tired, and the view became for me a symbol of God. Sometimes the valley was enveloped in thick mist, or there was a glowering sky; at other times the sky was a mass of bright clouds. The valley was constantly changing not only with the seasons, but also with the light. Most beautiful were some of the winter days when the valley glistened with a sprinkling of frost and the mountains of Snowdonia were snow-covered. At moments I could recover a feeling I had first experienced when walking in the Highlands, that I and what I saw were somehow one, so that the fields and hedgerows, the streams and hills were praying with me and in me. I was not looking at a view, but was part of everything I saw, so I could hand over all my worries and anxieties to the valley, which did not change or seem at all troubled: it simply accepted them and took me to itself. I felt caught up in something much greater than I, and this put any worries into perspective.

There was one other room in the tower, which was empty for the first two years I was there. One stormy Sunday afternoon when the gulls were flying inland, I saw a gull scampering along the road, unable to fly. I picked it up, my first meeting at close quarters with a gull and my first experience of a gull's bite. Its wings did not appear to be broken, so I placed it in a cabbage patch in the garden, reckoning it would there have food at hand until it recovered. Then I remembered the many cats which used to forage in the garden. I decided to strip the room next door and I brought in the gull together with a supply of food and water. For days it stood in a corner of the room, the food untouched. I worried for the gull, but also for the room lest the smell of captive gull become permanent. I phoned a vet and explained my problem. The vet was full of breezy reassurance. Gulls could suffer exhaustion for days. She recommended as remedy beaten-up egg laced with brandy, to be fed into its mouth with a syringe. Having prepared all that was necessary, I moved into action, but though exhausted, the gull could still scuttle along the floor in

avoiding action and when caught refused to open its beak. I summoned Michael Ivens and one of the tertians. Michael held it, the
tertian opened its beak and I squirted in the potion. The result was
almost immediate. The gull began to eat for the first time, to flutter
its wings and fly from the floor to the water-filled wash-basin. On a
Saturday afternoon, six days after first finding it, Michael and I took
it to the garden and threw it into the air. It opened its wings and
glided for a few yards before coming to rest, making no effort to
escape when we picked it up again, perhaps hoping for more egg
and brandy before final take-off. Next day I went to its room. The
gull was standing by the open window moving from foot to foot.
Then it opened its wings and flew off, never to appear again.

Later, when I told this story to someone, they said, 'What a marvell-
ous symbol of what St Beuno's could become: a place to which
people can come innerly exhausted, recover their strength, then fly
back into ordinary life.' Years later, when I lived among aboriginal
people for a few weeks, I realised that they would have understood
the gull story immediately as a message of encouragement for the
future of the house.

The other cluster of memories centres on Beuno, a Labrador dog.
I knew from past experience that if St Beuno's was to become a
retreat centre, then it was essential that those arriving, for a retreat
or course, should feel welcomed and at home. The more at ease they
could feel before beginning the retreat, the more likely they were to
be at home in their own experience. Therefore it was important
that the house should be as informal as possible, and notices and
regulations should be kept to a minimum. This was not easy to effect,
because one of the results of institutional religious training is that
the institutionalised do not feel at ease unless secure within a framework of detailed regulations and rules. There were, for example,
seven notices in the room reserved for washing up cups, one notice
being on top of a dustbin and reading 'Not in here, please'!

Some friends in the area offered to give us a Labrador pup. In my
imagination, this dog, which I had decided to call Beuno, would add
to the homely atmosphere, because they are an affectionate breed. I

imagined that Beuno might even be trained to accompany people to
their rooms on arrival.

I collected Beuno when he was six weeks old and studied a book
on dog training. He was a pure bred, his grandfather having won
prizes, and the kennels assured me I could expect great things of
him. They were right, but the benefits were not what they expected
and Beuno was never destined to win prizes at Crufts; his genius lay
in other directions. I let him out of the car and he followed obediently
behind me as I took him round his territory of the garden. He was
quickly house-trained and grew rapidly. Animals have a difficult time
in religious houses as they divide communities into admirers and
haters. For this reason, and because he had an endless appetite for
play, sometimes leaping on me in the middle of the night, I kept
Beuno in a kennel outside most of the time. When he was sufficiently
trained to be quiet for short periods, I took him with me occasionally
if I went to watch the TV news. As members of the community
entered, he would get up to greet those he liked, wag his tail at those
he acknowledged, and remain motionless when his enemies came in.
When I took him up to my tower room one evening, he disappeared,
returning seconds later with a packet of cigarettes in his mouth which
he had collected from one of the rooms.

I thought I was training Beuno: later I realised he was training me.
Every morning I let him out of his kennel and walked him to the
kitchen, where I would find a bone or some bacon rind. On being
loosed from his kennel, his behaviour was deplorable, leaping on me
with dirty paws, ignoring the command to sit, then running off if he
picked up some interesting scent. He always returned, occasionally
bearing in his mouth a scarf or glove, and on one occasion a nun's
veil. I discovered later that she was a very little nun. I had succeeded
in training him not to go into the kitchen and when I emerged with
bone or bacon rind, I would meet a reformed Beuno, sitting motionless outside like his prize-winning grandfather, the only movement
being the saliva dripping from his sad mouth. He would then follow
me through the house, ignoring people with gloves, scarves or veils,
his eyes fixed on my hand. On reaching my office, he was trained to
sit in the far corner while I stood by the door. We had a few moments

of stillness before I said 'to heel' and gave him the bone. Later, I realised what a wonderful illustration Beuno gave of the true meaning of detachment. Such was his attachment to the bone or bacon rind that in the strength of that attachment he was able to let go his attachment to people's scarves, gloves and veils. The key to the spiritual journey is desire. It is only if we have a strong enough desire for the things of God, to hunger and thirst after justice, to long for peace, to be able to love and be loved and to be wedded to truth, that we can let go of attachments which divert us from these things. Beuno taught me that there can be no healthy detachment without a stronger attachment, and so taught me to pray with the psalmist, 'Show me Your face', 'Show me Your attractiveness, otherwise my search for detachment will become egoism'.

Besides teaching me about detachment, Beuno also taught me the virtue of living in the present moment, for on walks everything seemed to interest him and he obviously did not discriminate between smells by our criteria of pleasant and unpleasant. To him all smells, however repulsive to human nostrils, were of interest, some more interesting than others. The Latin poet Terence had written, *'Humani nil a me alienum puto'*, 'I consider nothing human to be foreign to me'. Beuno went a step further: nothing that exists was foreign to him. In my attempts to train him and his refusal to submit, I used to get impatient and smack his snout with a folded newspaper, a punishment he would forget within seconds, being as affectionate as ever. So he taught me, too, about forgiveness. When Michael Ivens, Patrick Purnell and I used to meet of an evening for planning sessions, Beuno would join us, forming a quaternity. Occasionally we dressed him up with a Roman collar round his neck and spectacles on his nose, adding a touch of solemnity to our deliberations.

As we had not the staff to put on a set programme of individually given retreats and long-term courses, we contented ourselves with a few weekend courses, usually some kind of introduction to prayer. We also put on courses for people who could not normally come to retreat houses; we had a weekend for lapsed Catholics, another for the divorced and separated, and a mid-week course for unemployed people in the Kirkby area of Liverpool.

The weekend for the lapsed Catholics was one of the most striking. About a dozen people came, all genuinely lapsed, apart from one young man who somehow thought he was coming on a course about religious vocation. The course was put on not to win the lapsed back to a practice of their religion but to enable us to learn from them their reasons for abandoning the practice of their religion. Most had been away from the Catholic Church for many years, since well before the Second Vatican Council. We invited them to talk about the advantages and disadvantages they had found in abandoning Catholic practice. With most it was the authoritarian nature of the Church, especially in sexual matters, which had caused them to lapse, for others the teaching they had been given seemed to bear little or no relevance to life as they experienced it. The sad thing was that most had so identified worship of God with the practices of the Catholic Church, that having abandoned the Church, they felt they had no right to pray. It was this lack of prayer and depth in their lives which they found to be the disadvantage in lapsing. It came as a great relief to some of them to know that they could still pray to God while not belonging to the Catholic Church. It also helped some of them to see that if their experience had been the whole truth of the Catholic Church, then they were right to abandon it.

On the Sunday, I told them that I would be celebrating Mass, which they were under no obligation to attend, but I did not want them to feel excluded so if they wanted to come they were welcome. They all came. For most of them it was their first experience of Mass in English and according to the post-Vatican-Council rite. We celebrated in a common room, seated round a table. Their reaction was strange. Although they had not been to Mass for years, they did not like the changes. I think it was threatening to some of them. They could cope with a liturgy in Latin, celebrated formally, the priest with his back to the people, a solemn transcendent action. Mass celebrated in the new rite was too near the ordinary, too immanent. Whereas they could abandon the transcendent celebration without feeling much affected, the immanent nature of the new rite was threateningly close and uncomfortable.

The weekend with the divorced and separated had a similar function, namely to give them an opportunity to meet together and share with one another the advantages and disadvantages of their present state. It was also to give those of us running the course the opportunity to listen. On the first evening, after introductions, people were invited to share with one another. I became alarmed at the depth of grief and intensity of pain in the group, and was at a loss to know how to cope. This was fortunate, for they coped with one another much more effectively than I could ever have done. This was further confirmation of the enormous untapped spiritual wealth in the Church which our present heavily clerical structures prevent us from developing.

The midweek course for unemployed from Kirkby was run on the same lines, allowing them to share with one another what it was like to be unemployed. In spite of our attempts to make the place as homely as possible with a minimum of rules and regulations, this group, on entering the front door and seeing the large corridors and religious pictures on the wall, began to try to walk on tiptoe and to speak in whispers for, as one of them said, it was like coming into church. They soon thawed and talked easily. One of the most striking sessions was on the Exodus story. We invited them to sit in groups of three with a lighted candle in the centre and to pretend they were in the wilderness, making for the promised land. They could relate this to their own experience without difficulty. Just as the Israelites in the desert longed for the leeks, garlic, cucumbers and meat they had enjoyed in their slavery in Egypt, so they reminisced on the good old days when they could afford to go to the pub with their friends and maybe have enough to take the family on a holiday. Their open sharing and mutual support raised them out of their hopelessness and they began to plan together what they might do in Kirkby with the skills they had, even if they were unable to find paid employment. The remarkable thing was that almost all of them found employment within a short time, although this was not the purpose, nor the hope, of the course. Because they were no longer demoralised, they were more ready to go out and look for work. I know that this could never solve the unemployment question, but the worst affliction in unemployment is the demoralisation which it can cause in the individual.

We were just getting some kind of programme together for St Beuno's when Patrick Purnell, who had been working on Catechetics in Scotland before coming to St Beuno's, was invited to become national director of Catechetics in England. Fintan Creaven came to take his place. Without him we could never have got started. Although new to the work, he was naturally suited for it and he never shirked a challenge.

Once the tertianship was over, I was free to give more time to St Beuno's. On one weekend I invited about twenty people engaged in spirituality work, Jesuit and non-Jesuit, men and women, to a brainstorming session on possible ways of developing St Beuno's as a spirituality centre. There was no fixed agenda and participants were not expected to produce a clear plan, but encouraged to offer ideas, however impractical. Although most of the suggestions made *were* impractical, given our financial and staff limitations, the meeting was most useful, for out of the ferment of suggestions we could concentrate on those which seemed more immediately feasible. Suggestions included the need for St Beuno's to become a centre where scholarly study of the Spiritual Exercises could be undertaken, eight-day and thirty-day individually given retreats offered, and training courses in retreat-giving and spiritual direction provided. Alongside all this there could be weekend and mid-week courses on prayer, human development and holiness, on affectivity, sexuality, and justice as integral to faith.

For the next three years we concentrated on offering eight-day individually given retreats and very occasional thirty-day retreats, and on putting on some weekend and mid-week courses, always including on our programmes an invitation to people of any Christian denomination or none. As there were, at first, only Fintan and myself on the full-time staff, we invited retreat-givers and lecturers from outside for particular events. Slowly the numbers applying for retreats and courses began to increase and Jerome Nadal would have been pleased with the variety, for it included Protestants and pagans!

In the late 1970s, there were no formal training courses in Britain on individual retreat-giving and spiritual direction. We had to learn by trial and error. While not recommending that anyone should embark on this kind of work without training, it is true that no matter how good a training course may be, the real learning comes from practising the art.

In retreat-giving and spiritual direction the conversation normally, but not always, begins with the pilgrim trying to express in words, or sometimes through drawings or paintings, their felt experience and thoughts during and after prayer. From this starting point they then begin to make connections with other events in their lives, frequently going back to early childhood. It is as though the prayer acts as a kind of torch: in its light the pilgrim can begin to see connections between outer events and inner states of mind, which previously appeared to be unrelated. To be with someone as they do this is a great privilege and has its awesome moments. It is also a great delight to be with someone who, having perhaps stuttered and stammered for a while as they try to put their experience into words, suddenly pauses, looks up with surprise and says, 'Now I see'. I have learned far more from listening to pilgrims than I could ever learn from books or lectures. Once a truth is experienced, it can seem so obvious as not to be worth repeating. To some readers, what I write in the next few pages will already be familiar, but I write it because these familiar truths still retain a freshness for me.

One truth which becomes very obvious in individual retreat-giving is the close relationship between an individual's prayer, provided they have learned to pray with the heart as distinct from gabbling set prayers, and every other facet of their existence. It follows from this that the basic principles of retreat-giving and spiritual direction, and the guidelines which St Ignatius gives for what he calls 'Discerning the spirits' have application not only in retreats and in time of prayer, but in every aspect of life. Once seen, the truth of this is obvious: but it is equally obvious that we do not necessarily recognise this identification of prayer and life in practice, even if we are engaged in spirituality work. The split between life and prayer is reflected, too, in much teaching on prayer, suggesting that all true prayer should be without images, ideas, memories, which are all lumped together as distractions. This thinking then influences the way people understand religious life, so that the more that religious, even the apostolically active ones, can be separated from 'the world', and kept in a state of suspended animation, the closer they are considered to be to God. All this assumes God to be not, as Augustine said, 'closer to me than I am to myself', but infinitely distant.

Everything that happens in prayer, whether joy and delight, agitation and sadness, or doubts and darkness, mirrors what is happening in life, especially when people learn to pray using their imagination. One pilgrim, for example, tried to imagine the scene in Luke c. 2, where Jesus is presented in the temple. On the first few attempts, the pilgrim could get no further than the temple steps. While sitting there, painful memories returned of childhood rejection. Eventually the pilgrim managed to get into the Temple, saw the little group of Mary, Joseph and the child in Simeon's arms, and heard Simeon's words, 'This child is a sign that will be rejected'. The immediate effect was great joy that she shared rejection with the Christ child. Later she began to see how this childhood experience of rejection had blighted all her subsequent relationships, rendering her fearful of any close relationship which might lead to further rejection. Through the experience given in that prayer, she not only understood her own past behaviour more clearly, but knew God was present to her in her feeling of rejection. Consequently, she became less fearful of rejection by others.

The inability to use imagination in prayer often reflects a general fear of risk, an inner rigidity, an inability to relate to other people. I write 'often', because the inability to use imagination can sometimes come from thinking that all imagination must be visual. People with little visual imagination may be very imaginative thinkers. A pilgrim who arrived at St Beuno's as we were introducing women retreat-givers for the first time illustrated the fact that what happens in the retreat situation reflects what is going on, not only in the individual, but in life in general. At her first session with the guide, the pilgrim was sitting upright, her body language eloquent of disapproval. Her opening sentence to the nervous guide was, 'I have come a long way and spent a lot of money both on the journey and on my stay here, and I paid to have a Jesuit'! The encounter ended happily eight days later. But this pilgrim's reaction was not simply about retreat-giving – it reflected her own and much of society's perception about women's place and role in life.

Similarly, I soon learned that people's reaction to the way liturgy is conducted indicates far more than their reaction to a religious service. Attitudes to liturgy reflect attitudes to life: those who prefer to keep their distance from most other people and who disapprove of most things and of most human beings, are usually uncomfortable with any informality in religious services. Since the Second Vatican Council, the Mass, formerly celebrated in Latin throughout the world, may now be celebrated in the vernacular. This has caused a split among Catholics, a minority favouring the Latin Mass as it had been celebrated since the sixteenth-century Council of Trent. Aesthetically, this older rite has much to commend it, but some of those who advocate return to the Tridentine rite are not always influenced simply by the beauty of the older rite. They are often people who prefer to keep God at a safe distance, a God who does not interfere with their belief in capital punishment, just war, in the absolute right to private property, and who believe in a hierarchical society in which people know and keep their place.

In retreat-giving I began to see, too, how dangerous rigid divisions can be between psychology and spirituality. One very intelligent and gifted woman made the full Spiritual Exercises in a thirty-day residential retreat. I met her three years later, when she was still suffering the after-effects. Towards the beginning of the retreat, disturbing childhood memories came back to her. Her guide told her to ignore them and get on with making the Exercises, but the pilgrim could find no peace. The guide had apparently made a clear distinction in his own mind between matters that he considered spiritual and those which were psychological. It is the same human psyche at work, whether in a therapy or in a spiritual direction session, and God is at work in both. If some thoughts, memories or imaginings are constantly recurring in prayer, then they must be acknowledged and allowed to come into the prayer. It may be that they indicate profound psychological disturbance, which may require professional treatment, but pilgrims must be allowed to discover this for themselves and be encouraged to trust that God is at work in the psychological disturbance, hovering over the chaos and creating out of it. If too clear a distinction is made between the psychological and the spiritual, the danger is that spiritual direction and retreat-giving will be restricted to nice, well-balanced, wholesome people, which excludes all but a tiny minority of humankind, and the nice are likely to be the least creative.

In daily conversation with retreatants, it became clear that what exhausts, agitates and wears out a person is not so much the external circumstances of their lives, but an inner drivenness, what Dr Frank Lake, the Anglican priest who was also a psychiatrist, called 'a hardening of the oughteries'. In retreats, these 'oughteries' come more clearly to consciousness. Listening to them I became more conscious of my own inner 'oughts' and of the inherent ambiguity in the phrase, 'the will of God'. If 'oughts' remain unexamined, so that we do not distinguish between those which are arising from within our spirit and the 'oughts' which are external to us, imposed by others, the phrase 'the will of God' can become a merciless bully. The individual can thus remain locked in these external 'oughts' from which there can be no escape as long as they are assumed to be God's will. Beginning to see that God's will is our freedom, that God's will is that we should discover what we really want, is a wonderful liberation, but it is also frightening because it reveals to us more clearly that we prefer security to freedom, and it reveals how we cling to our 'oughts' because we are afraid of the cost of thinking and acting out of our own individuality.

Another point that became very clear in giving these retreats was that God does not seem to attach as much importance to denominational differences as do the members of those denominations, especially the clergy. After a time I found I was usually unaware of a person's denomination and saw clearly that the real division among Christians does not lie in the denomination to which they may belong, but in the way in which they relate to God and the world. There are often much bigger divisions between people of the same denomination than between individuals of different denominations. Denominational differences are part of the external 'oughts' which keep us apart. The differences are rarely theological, but more usually result from cultural conditioning, which impoverishes all who are caught up in it. I began to see that in these retreats we were getting to the heart of ecumenism.

In giving retreats to people from a variety of backgrounds and religious affiliation, I noticed something which was to influence me in future work. Irrespective of their religious denomination or practice of prayer, I found that those who were actively engaged in some form of justice and peace work, whatever form it might take, tended to develop spiritually more quickly and more deeply than those who were not so engaged. I first noticed this in giving retreats to assistants in the L'Arche communities, founded in the 1960s by Jean Vanier. In these communities, which now exist worldwide, assistants live and work with people with learning disabilities. There were many others, people working and living in inner-city areas, working with the unemployed, with drug addicts, people in the caring professions, workers for racial harmony, those involved in human rights, women's rights, and active members of peace organisations. The reason soon became obvious. God is the God of justice, of peace, and it was in the doing of those things that these people were meeting God. Because of the difficulties, frustrations and opposition they met with in their work, often from their own families, they experienced depths of pain unknown to them before. In their pain, they became more aware of their own fragility and of their need of prayer.

Having had plenty of practice in noticing how reflection on prayer experience can reveal patterns of thought and behaviour which pervade every aspect of our life, I discovered by chance that reflection on any incident in our lives can reveal these same patterns. Having given so many retreats to other people, I made a retreat myself at St Beuno's. One day during the retreat I went to have a bath and found two nail brushes on the bath rack, one a bright blue nylon brush, the other a dirty wooden one with worn-down bristles and a dirty-looking layer of soap of the ages covering the remaining bristles. My immediate thought was to get rid of the worn-out brush. In the course of the bath, the dirty nail brush fell into the water. Being on retreat and with time on my hands, I picked it up and began looking at it more closely, rubbed the wood with my finger and saw this beautiful piece of speckled wood. I cleaned the bristles and admired the craftmanship, the way in which the bristles were neatly bound together and fitted into the wood. I no longer wanted to throw it out, useless as it was as a nail brush.

The event was trivial in itself, but for me it mirrored my own pattern of perception, the inbuilt tendency to compare things one with the other, to divide reality into good and bad, useful and useless, and I began to see how damaging this was, for it prevented me from seeing things as they are. I realised that this tendency to compare affects all our perception; the way we regard people of other races, classes, nations, religions and denominations, the way in which men think of women and women of men. We have to make judgements, and we have to discriminate, but we do not need to judge and dis-criminate in terms of bad and good, useful and useless, rejecting what we consider bad or useless. I remembered meeting a youngster who showed me his class photograph. He first pointed out himself, then gave me a run down on the others. 'There's Freddie, he's very bright and top of the class. That's Tom, he is not very bright but a bit of a swot so he comes about the middle. This is John. He is dumb, bottom of the class.' Everyone was graded in this child's mind according to their class marks. We turn this same habit of comparing on to ourselves, rejecting those aspects in which we do not measure up to other people's expectations, repressing them or ignoring them, and consequently living uneasily with or even disliking ourselves. Once I had become aware of this habit of comparing, I began to see more and more clearly how deeply conditioned we are, seeing what we want to see and trying to impose our mental pattern on creation instead of allowing creation to teach us. That is why gawking is such a useful exercise, looking at things and letting them speak to us, as distinct from quickly categorising everything we see into our own very narrow filing system. Contemplation is praying without a mental filing system.

In the Spiritual Exercises Ignatius, in his introductory notes, says that the full Exercises can be given to people in the course of everyday life. The retreatant reserves time each day for private prayer and meets every now and again, perhaps once a week, with a retreat-giver. The full Exercises made in this way may last for six to nine months. Because the note in the text is No. 19, this type of retreat has become known as a nineteenth-annotation retreat. The early Jesuits probably gave the full Exercises to very few people, but they would give the first part of them, on sin and repentance, to many. If the Exercises are to be made widely available, then they must be given in this form, for no matter how many retreat houses there may be, and how limitless the finances for running them, only a tiny percentage of people can be reached.

As an increasing number of people were coming to St Beuno's, we began to reflect on the direction it should take. One day, Michael Ivens said to me, 'Do you realise that having escaped from teaching in a private school, you are now building up another one; only the more affluent and privileged can come on retreat to a place like this.' This line of thinking led us to plan special courses at St Beuno's for people who were already engaged in retreat work and spiritual direction and for those who were about to embark on this work. We hoped that through these courses we could train people who would then be able to give retreats in daily life. We reckoned that three months would be a suitable length of time for these courses. The core would be the full thirty-day retreat, preceded by a two-week period of preparation in which those participating would be encouraged to undertake faith-sharing in groups, experiment with various methods of prayer, get in touch with their feelings, and generally relax before beginning the retreat itself. The retreat would then be followed by a period of reflection and evaluation, both individually and in groups. There would also be a variety of short courses on the history of Christian spirituality, and on the centrality of justice to faith, ending with a two-week workshop on spiritual direction and retreat-giving, in which the participants would each give a three-day retreat to one other under supervision. We presented this plan to the provincial and by 1982 had a team of five Jesuits ready to start the three-month courses.

An Anglican priest from the Kimberley diocese of South Africa came to St Beuno's to make an eight-day retreat. After his return, I received a letter from the Bishop of Kimberley, Graham Chadwick, inviting me to spend three months giving a spirituality course to his clergy. I replied that I would gladly come, give a couple of eight-day retreats and a two-week workshop on spiritual direction and retreat-giving, but that I was incapable of giving a three-month course on my own. In January 1982, a few months before we were due to start our own three-month course, I flew to South Africa for the first time. By the time I arrived there, Graham Chadwick had already returned to the UK. He had run into trouble with the authorities because he was asking too many questions about the fate of detainees in his diocese and had been banished from Kimberley. He then tried to run his diocese from a distance, realised this was unfair to his people, and eventually resigned.

On my first Sunday in Johannesburg I went to Mass in a nearby church. There was a large congregation, white and coloured. The celebrant was a sad-looking man who preached on the dangers of the charismatic movement, of Lutheranism and of Calvinism. He then led the prayers of intercession, praying for 'Our boys at the front', busily engaged at that time in subjugating Namibia. The congregation answered 'Lord, graciously hear us' without any signs of dissent. In my conversations with whites, few seemed preoccupied with the apartheid question. The more I saw of South Africa, of the appalling conditions under which blacks lived in the townships, and the more I heard of the atrocities committed against them, the more astonishing I found the reactions of so many whites, who professed Christianity yet lived under this regime, preoccupied more with the state of the economy than with the plight of 80 per cent of the population. It was only later that I looked at my reaction to all this and asked myself how much I knew about the oppression of the poor, both black and white, in Britain, and to what extent I was really concerned about it.

In 1983 the South African situation looked hopeless for the blacks, held down by a regime which possessed great wealth, bristled with modern arms and still had influential friends and allies in high places in Britain and the USA. I met Beyers Naudé, the prominent Afrikaner Minister of the Dutch Reformed Church, who had renounced the apartheid dogma, founded the Christian Institute, was investigated by the police and had been under house arrest for years. He was not burning with indignation and rage, as I had expected, but seemed wonderfully calm and confident, and had retained a sense of humour. I knew that there was an appeal before the government from many prominent South Africans to end his house arrest. I asked him whether he felt hopeful of the appeal's success. He laughed and said, 'No hope at all. I know the Minister for Security well. He was a deacon in my first parish!' Bishop Desmond Tutu had the same calm confidence in face of an apparently hopeless situation.

While in South Africa I gave two eight-day retreats and a two-week workshop on the basic principles of spiritual direction and retreat-giving to people from a variety of Christian denominations, although most were either Anglican or Catholic. I also gave a few lectures and spent two weeks running a parish in a coloured township not far from Soweto. I had tried to find a parish in Soweto itself, but at that time no white person was allowed to stay overnight in a black township. Various memories of those three months recur.

One of the retreatants was an English Anglican religious sister from Lesotho, who told me the story of her vocation to religious life. She was at a private school in England during the war. The school chaplain took the sixth form up to London for a day's culture, so they visited a museum in the morning and went to a concert in the afternoon. When they reached Waterloo station in the evening to catch the train back to school, the air-raid sirens went and the girls were hurried down to a shelter, normally the preserve of men living rough. This girl got into conversation with a tramp who spent the spring and summer months walking the length and breadth of Britain. He seemed very happy and content and it was this conversation which led her to question her own life and future and by what values she wanted to live. Another retreatant was English, a priest from the Anglican Community of the Resurrection at Mirfield in York-shire. In appearance he was small and appeared timid. The appearance was deceptive: he had been a paratrooper during the war. Shortly after this retreat he was arrested, imprisoned, and spent some time in ankle chains, manufactured in Birmingham. He was arrested because he refused to give information on a student who had come to him and whom the police wanted to question.

In the presbytery of the township parish there was a black woman who came in daily to clean. When not cleaning she would sit in perfect stillness on a chair in the hallway. She had a thin, very lined face and her expression bore the suffering of her people. I tried hard to get her to talk, but for the first week she answered in monosyllables. One day she did speak, quietly but with burning resentment against the government, whom she referred to as 'The Dutch', who had driven her family out of their own home. She spoke, too, of the daily humiliations to which she, as a black, was subjected by these same Dutch.

That evening I had been invited to preach at a student Mass in a parish church in Johannesburg. Just before Mass began, a very well-dressed man came to the sacristy, introduced himself as a medical doctor, and told me that he was preaching at all Masses. He preached on the evils of abortion, giving a mixture of statistics and emotive utterances on the mass murder carried out daily in South Africa through the practice of abortion. He said never a word about the murders of the living, of the daily oppression of the many blacks by a few whites, or of the poverty, homelessness and hopelessness to which millions were condemned by this ruthless regime. It was a relief when the sermon was over and I invited the congregation to make prayers of intercession. Many of the students spoke, praying to be delivered from pharisaism in all its forms, and begging God that Christians should also attend to the problems of poverty, unemployment, homelessness, lack of education, which all contributed to the abortion problem.

While in Cape Town I did some work with university students and on two occasions I walked up Table Mountain and thought Cape Town geographically the most beautiful city I had ever seen. The contrast between the physical beauty and the political ugliness was strikingly visible on the way up Table Mountain with its view over Robben Island, the prison of so many politically active Africans, Nelson Mandela among them.

I returned to St Beuno's a few days before our first three-month course. On this first course a large number of countries were represented; there were a number of Anglicans and a few lay people. The variety and mixture increased in subsequent courses. We limited the numbers to thirty-six, leaving six rooms available for people who wanted to make eight-day retreats during the period of the three-month course.

When I returned from South Africa, I met with Bishop Graham Chadwick who, by an amazing coincidence, was now living four miles away from St Beuno's and was on the staff of St Asaph Cathedral. I told him about the three-month courses and he applied for the one at the beginning of 1983.

In the four three-month courses in which I was involved, a good community spirit developed among the participants, but each time this was threatened during the latter part by a three-day course on questions relating to faith and justice, on racism, sexism, militarism, capitalism and socialism. This was yet another instance of the split nature of our spirituality. Some of the participants had lived among the poor of the Third World, knew oppression, exploitation and injustice at first hand: others, including some from Third World countries, had never had this exposure, but lived a more sheltered type of life, administering the sacraments and living a spirituality which was more concerned with the next life than with this. Some of the women were passionately feminist, and they did a service to the men in helping us to become a little more aware of our chauvinism, which was so ingrained that we were not even aware of it. An inherent danger in Christian spirituality is its inability to deal honestly with conflict, and the tendency to avoid it, ignore it, or smother it in smooth phrases. When strong feelings erupt, either in an individual or in groups, it is not only a sign of life, but it also indicates that there is something important which needs to be looked at. It is as though the timeless subconscious is giving an early-warning signal to our conscious minds. By ignoring or trying to smother these feelings we may be ignoring the promptings of God inviting us to change.

We were surprised at the popularity of this three-month course, for applications were coming in from all over the world. My uneasiness lay in the fact that most of the applicants were Catholic religious from overseas. One year we had twenty-three different countries represented among thirty-six applicants. The courses were useful and enjoyable, but not all who came were, in fact, suited or inclined to work subsequently in retreat-giving and spiritual direction, in spite of references assuring us that they were. Also, because the great majority were from overseas, the courses were not producing many people for work in this country.

Between three-month courses we had one remarkable mid-week course. An executive member of the Communist Party in UK at that time was a Catholic, and she had come to St Beuno's to make a thirty-day retreat. Later she organised meetings between Christians and Communists, and one of these meetings was held at St Beuno's. Participants included Tony Chater, editor of the *Morning Star*. For years I had prayed at the end of every Mass for the conversion of Russia, which meant their conversion from Communism. The first Communist I had ever met was Jimmy Reid, who led the famous strike of the Upper Clyde shipworkers in the late 1960s, and who later became Rector of Glasgow University. His inaugural speech as rector was one of the best expositions I have ever heard on Jesus' Sermon on the Mount. Later, at St Beuno's, another Communist member came to make an eight-day retreat and she gave me her story. Her father was a Communist and local councillor in Clydebank. Her mother used to hide any spare food or clothing in case her father would take it and give it away to people in need. The daughter, who was making the retreat, was educated by the Notre Dame Sisters in Dumbarton and was preparing to joint the Notre Dame Congregation, until she went to Mass one Sunday just before the local council elections. The priest spoke against her father in his sermon, telling the congregation that they must not vote for him. That was the end of her Notre Dame vocation and she became a party member. During the St Beuno's week I met many more party members, some of them practising Catholics, whose dedication to the creation of a more just society left me hoping that they would also pray for my conversion.

In autumn 1983, I received an invitation to work permanently in South Africa in two separate jobs. One job, chaplain to the Catholic University students in South Africa, was only part time; it did not involve day-to-day chaplaincy work, but I was to help the Catholic Society in preparing and holding their regional and national meetings. The other job was to be Secretary for Ecumenism to the South African Bishops' Conference. When I asked what this job entailed, I was told that it would involve making contact with Christians of other denominations, with members of other religions, and with people of no religion. The broad brief was very attractive and challenging.

Before the invitation arrived I was already thinking of asking for a move from St Beuno's. The place was established as an Ignatian spirituality centre and now had a competent staff. In the Glasgow University years and while working at St Beuno's I had become increasingly preoccupied with the question of our nuclear defence policy. I did not want to join the Campaign for Nuclear Disarmament, important and valuable as it was, or any of the other active peace organisations. Instead, I wanted time to work, reflect and pray about the spiritual meaning of nuclear defence. The Romans had a saying, 'To preserve peace, prepare for war', a principle which still governs the defence policy of most nations and one which the Church does not clearly oppose. In Britain, the vast majority of Christians and of Christian leaders supported a policy of nuclear deterrence as a means to preserving peace, a policy which I had never questioned until Easter Sunday 1961, when Eric Kemmet's prank at Stonyhurst forced the question on me. The more I reflected on Jesus' Sermon on the Mount, the more uneasy I became. Christ's peace is based on love, not on the power to crush opposition into our way of thinking and being. For years I struggled with the question until I saw that if I was to support nuclear deterrence, then I must conclude that Jesus' teaching, however sublime, is, in fact, impractical given our present circumstances. This proved difficult in conversation with Jesus in prayer: 'Dear Lord and God, while I admire the sublimity of your teaching in the Sermon on the Mount, I think you overlooked the practical difficulties which we were to face in the latter half of the twentieth century!'

As I struggled with this question, I began to see that it was opening up a whole host of questions on the roots and nature of violence, the relationship between the outer and the inner world, the meaning of spirituality, how it permeates all our activity, and the way in which we constantly try to keep spirituality from interfering with everyday life. As Bishop Hugh Montefiore has written, 'I have had to learn the lesson that reactions at a microscopic level can have macroscopic results'.

I had met many people active in peace and justice, men and women whose dedication to the cause of justice was admirable, but who did not consider themselves to be spiritual people. Many of them would not have called themselves religious, yet these men and women seemed to me to show more obvious signs of having the mind and heart of Christ than many professed religious and clergy. Most of these committed individuals were unlikely to come to retreat houses or spirituality centres. I wanted to work with such people, irrespective of denomination, and therefore to work outside of a retreat house, so that I could be free to go to any peace and justice groups who were interested in exploring the spiritual dimension of their work and in integrating that work with their Christian faith. When the invitation came to go to South Africa, I told the provincial that although it attracted me in many ways, I felt more drawn to working in this country on the spirituality of justice and peace. He spoke of the needs in South Africa and asked me to go. Although I preferred to stay in Britain, South Africa also attracted me, so I did not find it difficult to agree.

CHAPTER 11

eᴠᴏᴏᴠ

God of Surprises

The churches' ecumenical response, while good in itself, is far too
slow when compared with the universal wild rush to the abyss.

(Alexander Solzhenitsyn)

I LEFT ST BEUNO'S in December 1983, having already applied for a
visa for South Africa where I was to start work in June 1984. I relished
the prospect of six months free of responsibility with time to reflect
on and clarify the seven years I had spent at St Beuno's. Individual
retreat-giving is a very different process from teaching or lecturing,
for the retreat-giver is more deeply affected, more exposed to what
is going on in the depths of the retreatant. The experience had left
me with an image of my own subconscious, as though it was
swarming with little lizards which would fleetingly appear in consciousness and were hard to catch, yet which affected my moods,
feelings, perceptions, thoughts, energy levels. I hoped to catch some
of the lizards.

The sky was a cloudless delicate blue, snow-clad Snowdonia was
clearly visible, the valley sparkled with a thin covering of snow the
day I left St Beuno's for my new temporary home in the Friary, a
former Franciscan church in inner-city Liverpool, where a group of
Jesuits were setting up a Centre for Peace and Justice. While I was
glad to be free of responsibility, it was a wrench to leave.

I have never lived in a place which so affected me as St Beuno's,
where I had experienced both great delight and depths of gloom. I
do not believe those swings of mood were wholly subjective. Places
and buildings are affected by those who dwell in them. St Beuno's

had always been a house of prayer since it was built in 1848. It was as though the very walls had been affected by the inner light and darkness, the peace and the turmoil of its inhabitants, so that unsuspecting visitors can find themselves affected by feelings they cannot account for.

I had sometimes prayed to be delivered from what seemed to be a place of darkness and turmoil, but I had also had glimpses of God's presence, which far outweighed any sadness or gloom. For me St Beuno's has the same feel of God's presence as Eileach an Naoihm and Iona. Sometimes I could be in the house or grounds and feel in reality the delight which I felt in my dream the night before I left Glasgow for the noviceship forty years earlier, when I was in a light-filled room which looked out on a beautiful garden.

We speak of God's coming, but there can be no coming of a God who is always fully present. We can become conscious of God's presence, can focus our attention in prayer and become more aware of the reality of God, sometimes dramatically, more often quietly. I find God a quiet giver and rarely notice the gift at the time. God's gifts are like little seeds which fall noiselessly. It is only much later that I become aware of them. I received such a gift one day shortly before I left St Beuno's. I hardly noticed it at the time, but the memory has lingered and still gives life whenever I recall it.

While walking in the Clwyd valley, I noticed a ruined building in the far corner of a field and went to have a look. It was a fifteenth century chapel of Our Lady. Outside the south wall was a beautifully carved circular well, the force of the hidden spring visible in the current of clear water at its centre. The edges of the well were covered in slime and dead leaves. I stood staring at it. In the strong sunlight I could see little motes of soil dancing to the force of the spring in the well's centre. The image lingers. Now I see a little dancing mote of soil as representing my conscious mind. When dancing in the sunlight to the movement of the clear water the little mote says to itself, 'Life is wonderful. I am bathed in light, safe in God's hands, praise the Lord.' Then, through the movement of the water the little mote drifts towards the sludge and is now saying, 'I am trapped in darkness. This is reality. What I previously experienced was illusion. It is hopeless. There is no escape.' The gift was an awareness of the limitations of my conscious mind, of how little I perceive of the reality in which I live, of my connectedness with everything in creation and of all creation existing in God's presence. The gift was not just a thought, but an assurance, beyond my conscious thinking and feeling, that God is always there, even when I feel hopelessly trapped in darkness. When I remember this image of the well, I can better understand St Paul's words: 'Nothing therefore can come between us and the love of Christ, even if we are troubled or worried, or being persecuted, or lacking food or clothes, or being threatened or even attacked. . . . For I am certain of this: neither death nor life, no angel, no prince, nothing still to come, not any power, or height or depth, nor any created thing, can ever come between us and the love of God made visible in Christ Jesus our Lord.' (Romans c.8)

This gift was still at the seedling stage when I entered the Friary in Liverpool and it did not dispel the dread I felt at an unknown future. I was shown my room. The predominant colour was dark brown and the windows were obscurely glazed. I opened them to see the view. Outside was a junk yard, beyond was a road flanked by derelict buildings, the only brightness breaking the encircling gloom being the broken glass sparkling on the roadway. In the distance was the spire of Liverpool's Catholic Cathedral, known locally as 'The Mersey Funnel'. I felt the gulf between my professed desire to be poor with Christ poor and the reality of my feelings of revulsion at my new home in the inner city. However, although based in Liverpool, I was to spend very little time there.

In January 1984, I went to Manresa House, a Jesuit retreat house in Dollymount, Dublin, to make a thirty-day retreat, for I had never yet made the full Spiritual Exercises with an individual retreat-giver. There were many things I wanted to look at in this retreat, many lizards to catch, many unresolved questions swirling round within me, some so unresolved that I could not even formulate them.

Uppermost was the whole question of integrity, which included the relationship within myself between my role as Jesuit priest, clerical member of a hierarchical Church, and Gerard W. Hughes, human being. I had been pondering this question for years and while running the tertianship had formulated an answer which helped to some extent. I realised that I was not primarily a priest or a Jesuit. Primarily, I am a human being and only remain priest and Jesuit because for me, with my temperament, upbringing and inclination, this seems a good way of being human. I was also helped by a remark of one of the tertians when we were discussing the nature of priesthood. He said that he believed priesthood was not primarily about role, or function, but essentially it was about the quality of our relationships. However, these answers still left many questions unresolved. Did I remain a Catholic priest and Jesuit simply because early conditioning had pointed me in that direction, and did I now have the courage or the imagination to choose an alternative? How far was I really committed to the Society of Jesus as I had experienced it? In Britain it often seemed to be characterised by a spirit of timidity and respectability, more tolerant of the ultra-conservative than of the mildly radical. The English Dominicans seemed much more exciting and radical, although they were rapidly dwindling in numbers. And how far was I really living the spirit of the vows I had taken of poverty, chastity and obedience? I also wanted to prepare myself for the break from family, friends and country in order to start work in South Africa. I felt that I needed not a thirty-day retreat, but a Buddhist three-year retreat, to sort out the questions facing me.

I tried not to concentrate on any one of these questions, prayed to be open and detached, and decided only to look at any particular question if it kept popping up in prayer. There were no great traumas during the thirty days, neither ecstasies nor depths of despondency. About the prayer time itself, there was little I could say to my retreat-giver at the end of each day. I finished the retreat without any new intellectual answers to the many questions with which I had begun, but with something much more valuable, a sense of assurance that it was all right to have these questions and a readiness to live with them. The image of the well was teaching me to keep myself detached from inner moods and feelings and not to identify myself with them. Instead of saying, 'I am confused, uncertain, sad, or in darkness', I could say, 'There is a sense of confusion, uncertainty, darkness in me today', but whatever it might be, it did not disturb a deeper sense of peace, which prevailed through all the passing moods and feelings. Those recurring phrases of the Bible, 'Do not be afraid' and 'I am with you' spoke to a depth of my soul deeper than any conscious thought or feeling. I felt ready to go to South Africa, although I still felt much more drawn to working with justice and peace people in this country.

Each day, and often at night, I used to walk the strand of Bull Island near Manresa. I loved the blustery days with an angry sea and the sight of Dublin Bay at night, the phosphorescent wave crests breaking on the shore. The sea is a symbol of God. As I walked by its edge, I was walking in a presence greater than I, longing to be taken up in it. It was as though these wild surroundings were breathing life into me, which, of course, they were – a feeling which intensified when I recalled that statement, I think from Francis of Sales, that in death we are like raindrops falling into the ocean. When the raindrop has fallen, then it becomes the ocean. As I walked by the sea the longing to be set free from self-imprison-ment, to be taken up in something much greater, became urgent, a painful delight.

After the retreat, I had asked if I might spend the rest of the time, before I was due to depart in June for South Africa, on the Isle of Skye, to do some writing. I had heard that there was a church in the town of Portree, which included a room, but no resident priest. I chose Skye because of its remoteness, its mountains and magnificent scenery.. The priest at Glenfinnan welcomed my services. He had to travel over 150 miles whenever he said Mass on Skye, monthly in the winter and weekly in the summer.

Before going, I tried to imagine Skye, the church and the room. In my imagination the church stood on a hillside, its room was spacious, flooded in light, looking out over the Cuillin mountains and the sea. The window had a large ledge on which all kinds of seabirds perched.

In mid March, I was driven from Fort William to the Catholic church in Portree by a priest who was on his way to the island of South Uist, by way of Skye. It was snowing hard and several times we were caught in snow drifts. I then had to get out, shovel away snow, run after the car and jump in again, the melting snow soaking through my clothing. It was dark when we reached Portree. The church of my imagining was, in fact, a corrugated-iron-roofed building set in a council estate on the outskirts of the town. The room of my dreaming was dark and narrow, with two tiny oblong windows high on the wall. To look out of them I had to stand. They looked out on to a steep bank about 20 feet away which obscured the daylight. The room had a bed, a cooker, a heater and a tiny wobbly table, which served as desk and dining table. Next door was a toilet with shower. This was my home for the next five months.

I had arrived on a Saturday evening. On Monday morning a bull-dozer, a cement-mixer and three men arrived, each with a transistor radio permanently tuned to Radio 2. They began to build a house 30 feet away from my room. This was one of the reasons for calling the book I eventually wrote there *God of Surprises*, but there were other surprises to confirm my choice. Within a few days of arrival I heard the sound of tinkling glass in the church, and collected the large stone which had been hurled through the window. Another stone arrived a few days later and a third came through the narrow window of my room. Skye did not take kindly to Roman Catholics, above all RC priests, the island being staunchly Presbyterian. The Presbyterian Church was itself divided into three branches, each stauncher than the other. The stone throwing occurred just as classes finished at the nearby High School. I paid a visit to the headmaster, who was very courteous. I explained my problem, said that I would be delighted to meet his pupils, and that if any of them were interested in the phenomenon of a Catholic priest, they were welcome to come and visit. He declined my invitation to meet with his pupils but said he would have a word with his staff. There were no further stones and I met with nothing but kindness during my stay, especially from the Catholic community.

As there was no letter-box in the church, I had to go and collect mail from Portree Post Office. Daily I went, hoping for a letter from the South African Embassy with my permit visa. It was not until the end of May, within a few weeks of my planned departure, that a one-sentence letter arrived, telling me that I would not be granted a visa.

When I informed the Jesuit superior in South Africa, he told me that the Bishops' Conference was negotiating with government officials on my behalf and that I should hold on: September would be early enough for my arrival. It was in July that I heard the result of the negotiations. I would be permitted to go to South Africa for a year to prepare a South African to do my job. As I reckoned I would need about three years to get into the job myself, I knew I could not train anyone else. The Jesuit provincial in London agreed, and instead allowed me to plan future work with people active in justice and peace in the UK. So that was a further reason for calling the book *God of Surprises*.

One of my problems in starting to write was my own vagueness about the subject matter. I wanted to write about some of the questions which preoccupied me as a Catholic, a priest and a Jesuit, hoping that the writing might also be of interest to other bewildered and disillusioned Catholics, whom I was constantly meeting. Another problem was mental inertia, so I kept on finding good reasons for not starting just yet. I would find shopping or cleaning to do, letters to write, or else I would decide to clear my mind by going for a walk. When I did eventually get started, with pen poised, there was the further problem of the opening sentence. My first day's attempt produced nothing but frustration and several sheets of scored-out first paragraphs. I then made a wise decision. I decided to sit myself down at the typewriter each day and to write whatever came to mind, giving no attention to style, coherence of thought, grammar, syntax or spelling. I set myself to write three to four thousand words daily. The noise of the builders and their transistors forced me to concentrate and after six weeks at the typewriter I had a vast number of typed sheets and three possible books, one on the spiritual journey, the second a modern version of the Spiritual Exercises, and the third a faith autobiography. Often I grew disheartened and felt that I was writing banalities. If I did write what really mattered to me, I could hear the voice of critics asking me about my sources, or accusing me of being totally subjective, asking what right I had to foist my private prejudices on others in the name of religion. Through this process I came to recognise one of the lizards which scuttled around in the depths, a devastating self-criticism and self-deprecation, which could reduce me to frustrated silence. By the end of June, I had a mass of material and a clearer idea of what I wanted to write, but it took me until March 1985 to put it into coherent shape.

As I had no form of transport, I hired a bicycle and walked or cycled for two hours every day in all weathers, taking a full day off every week. I came to know the north end of the island well, grew accustomed to Skye's wet and windy weather, and climbed most of its hills, apart from the Cuillins.

I made many friends on Skye, especially among the Catholic community. There was a retired optician living in Portree, Roger Grey, a Presbyterian elder, whom I had met previously on Iona. Roger had been in the army during the war, was afflicted with a most severe stammer in consequence, and came out of the army with a passionate dedication to peace. He never allowed his affliction to prevent him from talking publicly on peace, and he had addressed the General Assembly of the Church of Scotland. His little garden by the sea had a lawn cut in such a way that the daisies displayed the Campaign for Nuclear Disarmament sign for all who passed by. He had such vigour and energy, always arousing interest, challenging and repelling the lethargic, that to be with him was like being caught up in a powerful magnetic field, but his intensity was modified by a robust humour. Years before I met him, he had broken his leg climbing the Cuillins and spent the night hanging from a rope till rescue came at dawn. He told me it had been the most wonderful experience of his life as, dangling on his rope, he watched a glorious dawn. He wanted to invite me to preach in his church in Portree, but not even Roger could overcome the fears of his fellow elders. He often came to Mass on Sundays, and on one weekday brought a group of his friends, so that I found myself celebrating Mass with a 100 per cent Protestant congregation. A few years later, Roger died of a heart attack while addressing a group on Iona about Peace.

'Remember' is a fascinating word; re-member, as though it means putting the separated members back together again, whether of a group or of the human body. Remembering can be painful, but it is the cost of recovering wholeness, and even if painful, it is also life-giving. When I remember Roger, and people like him, I do not just recall past facts, but feel an energy charge, as though he has given me a living source of energy which I can draw on whenever I think of him. A modern nuclear physicist has stated that there are no such things as ultimate particles: 'in each particle exists every other particle'. As human beings we live consciously as separate individuals, more or less – usually less – aware of our dependence on each other. But the reality is that for better or worse we are far more at one with each other than we realise.

I was very sorry to have to leave Skye after five months. The friends I had met and the kindness I had received made me reflect on the disadvantages of Jesuit life. In the Constitutions, Ignatius had written, 'It is our vocation to travel to various places'. He and his early companions pledged themselves to go wherever the need was greatest and to move on as soon as they had found others who could answer that particular need. One of the early Jesuits commented that one individual had spent rather a long time in a particular place, having stayed there for four months! I see the value of a wandering ministry, but it has serious disadvantages. The danger of constant uprooting is that one becomes rootless. In spirituality work, especially in giving individual retreats, one shares with another at a depth which, perhaps, they have never reached with any other individual, even within their own family. After a week we say goodbye. It becomes impossible to continue the contact with so many. I felt a great longing to be able to settle down in one place, in some small community, knowing everyone in it and known by them. The wandering can lead to superficiality in relationships and to a deep loneliness.

Loneliness can be dangerous: it also provides a wonderful opportunity, for it is a necessary element of the inner journey. It is as though in loneliness our path is blocked by a strong steel door. We may hit at it, kick against it in rage and frustration, damaging and destroying ourselves, or we may accept that we are blocked and knock gently on the door. The door opens and we enter the inner chamber of our being. There loneliness is transformed into aloneness, which has a very different feel, a feeling of at-one-ness, which banishes the pain of loneliness and makes of solitude a nurture;

then, no parting from another ever feels final, for we have entered the inner sanctuary where we, and all creation, are held in being and at one.

After I knew that South Africa was no longer possible, St Beuno's invited me back to join the staff for the autumn three-month course, an invitation I gladly accepted, for it would give me time to work on *God of Surprises*, and also time to think about and plan future work.

Before going to St Beuno's for the three-month course in autumn 1984, I went to London and worked for a while in the Pax Christi office in Holland Park. Pax Christi began after the Second World War to bring about reconciliation between Germany and the Allied countries, but it soon developed into a much wider peace organis-ation and is now international. Although I knew I wanted to work on what I then called the spirituality of peace and justice, I had no idea of how to set about it and hoped that contact with peace activists might give me some ideas. I got in touch with Bruce Kent, then chairman of the Campaign for Nuclear Disarmament, told him what I was about and asked his advice. He gathered a group of people from different denominations and different peace organisations, invited me to meet with them and to ask for their suggestions. They suggested that I spend some time in London working as an office boy in various peace offices, in order to learn more of their organis-ation and how they tried to influence public opinion.

I had already decided to spend six weeks at the beginning of January 1985 in Portadown, Northern Ireland, where a community of Irish Jesuits were living in a housing estate, working on peace, justice and reconciliation. I hoped that by living with them and observing their work, I might have some clearer ideas on how to proceed in Britain.

The Jesuits had only recently arrived in Northern Ireland. They had been offering to work there for many years, but the offer had been declined. In Portadown a community of four, three priests and a brother, lived in a council house in the middle of a very Republican estate. The Superior, Fr Paddy Doyle, who had been Provincial of the Irish Jesuits, was engaged in retreat work, spiritual direction and general pastoral work, especially in the Maze prison and in local hospitals. Brian Lennon was editor of a magazine on social justice questions, which was produced in Dublin, but Brian elected to live in the North. Declan Deane was responsible for the Northern Ireland branch of the Dublin School of Ecumenics, and Brother Dave Byrne, besides managing the house, was a qualified social worker. There was a fifth non-resident member of the community, Henry Grant, who was at Queen's University studying the roots of the Northern Ireland conflict. I came to observe and learn what I could of the problems they had to face and the way they faced them. It was a most valuable six weeks.

One of the most attractive features of living in Portadown was the homeliness of the house and of the area. People would drop in any time to pass the time of day, use the phone or ask for information. There was a spare room which was used for meetings of various groups and Brian invited me to attend some of these. Meetings were conducted in a fashion I had never encountered before. Everyone spoke at once, they slanged and contradicted one another, broke all the rules on how to conduct a meeting, yet ended in excellent humour and with clear decisions. I still do not understand the process!

Another most striking feature was the friendliness of the neighbours. Because I was living with the Jesuits, I was accepted in spite of my English accent. There was hardly a family on the street which did not have a member in prison, just out of prison, or who had been killed. Their stories of what they had suffered from the military and the police were horrific. I hated the violence of the IRA and thought their campaign misguided, but I could understand why they received such support, because they were seen by many as the only defenders, not only against sectarian attacks from Protestants, but also from the military and the police. After my six weeks in Portadown, I shared their deep anger when I heard the smooth voices of British politicians condemning the evil acts of 'the terrorists' without any acknowledgement of the violence inflicted on defenceless people by the forces of law and order. But the people knew the truth of things, and that is why loud condemnations of 'terrorists' only increased support for the Provisional IRA.

I had interviews with two members of the Orange Order. One was a married woman, working for peace in the middle of an area of Protestant paramilitaries. She had become a kind of mother confessor to some of them, who confided in her the conflict of conscience they suffered in their organisation. This role did not defend her from attack against herself and her children by extremists, angry because she had spoken out against their atrocities. I was amazed at her calmness and hope in spite of the horrific and dangerous situation in which she, and her children, were placed. The other member was a man no longer living in Belfast because it was too dangerous for him. He had been prominent in the Orange Order, but eventually left it because he was scandalised at the behaviour not only of paramilitaries, but also of some churchmen. He chatted to me about his early life and his longing to convert Ireland to Protestantism. The better to equip himself for this task, he went to Bible college in England. I laughed as I pictured this earnest young man planning to convert the Irish Catholic clergy to the true cause. Then I remembered my own youth, the prayers for the conversion of Scotland, England and Wales, and my belief that salvation could only be found within the Roman Catholic Church.

Both interviews illustrated the damage we do by thinking and reacting to people not as individuals, but as members of a particular group. It is an act of violence against the integrity of the individual, and like all acts of violence, it infects the victims and forces them into violent reaction. There can be no lasting peace in any situation as long as the opposing sides continue to think of one another in general categories. Protestant men and women expressed the same longings for peace and justice as so many Catholic men and women, but because they lived in separate camps with no easy way of meeting one another, the mutual longing of both groups for peace and reconciliation could not be effective. The first step to peace is to try to create the conditions under which the antagonists can meet in some neutral place, not to discuss their differences, but simply to meet. Many had tried to do this in Northern Ireland, but in the end they usually had to meet either in mainland Britain or in the South.

But the friendships forged could not then be continued without risk to their lives when they returned to the North.

On two Sundays, I was able to get into the Maze prison to say Mass, two Masses in different parts of the prison on each Sunday. It was snowing heavily on my first Sunday, the ground hard frozen. It was a shock as we got out of the car to see the tall wire perimeter fence with its searchlights and gun emplacements, just like a scene out of Solzhenitsyn's *One Day in the Life of Ivan Denisovich*. At the first checkpoint I had to hand over everything in my pockets. I was then photographed with an instamatic camera and given one photograph for myself while the other was given to the warder, who then escorted me through many other checkpoints until we reached the place where Mass was to be celebrated. It was a large room with barred iron doors, the warders standing outside. This weekly Sunday Mass was the only opportunity in the week when prisoners from different sections of the Maze could meet together. Some came for a chat rather than for Mass, but they sat together in a corner and did not distract the others.

Had I been blindfolded and taken to this room, then asked, when the blindfold was removed, where do you think you are, I would have guessed from looking at the many young intelligent faces, that I was with university or polytechnic students, or possibly in a seminary or noviceship of a religious order, although there were also a few older men. We had one hour for the service, which had to finish promptly; besides the Mass, some might want to go to Confession. I decided to give them fifteen minutes to chat before Mass began. I was feeling apprehensive, but the feeling did not last long because they seemed delighted to chat to a stranger, even if he did come from Britain. One of the first to greet me was a Glaswegian, who had already been inside for many years. When I asked him when he hoped to get out, he answered, 'I'm just a bloody hostage', and I was to meet a number who were in for indefinite periods with no idea of when they might be released. I spoke to another young, very fit and healthy-looking man with bright, intelligent eyes. He told me he had been on the blanket protest for two years. I had read about this attempt by the prisoners to be given political status. They refused to wear prison clothing or to emerge from their cells, breaking the cell windows, because they preferred the cold to the enclosed stench of their excrement, which they plastered on the walls. The protest succeeded in that they were permitted to wear their own clothes. 'What effect did it have on you?' I asked. 'It was a profound spiritual experience,' he said. 'I enjoy everything now. This tea tastes wonderful.' The lukewarm tea was served in paper cups. He went on to deplore the lowering of morale which had occurred in the prison after the blanket protest and also the hunger strike. I asked another, an older and quieter man, what effect the Maze prison had had on him. 'I've learned a lot,' he said, 'I can now read the Bible in Gaelic.'

When Mass began, a few took up their places in a corner of the room and chatted quietly. The majority sat around the altar, more still and concentrated than an average congregation. For me it was a strange experience, as though I was caught up in two different and opposing forces, the gentle drawing power of God and the power of destructive violence. I could not sift my feelings at the time. I was conscious of the conflict, but not of its ingredients. Our whole past life is in every moment we experience. As I reflected on this experience later, I began to see more clearly some of the elements in the conflict. It included a sympathy for these men, for it is always sad to meet people who are locked up, no matter what their offence may have been. There was also a sympathy for their cause, but not their methods, for my own grandparents were from Ireland, on my mother's side from the North. I also knew something of the injustices committed against these people, of the beatings and torture, which were excused by investigative government commissions as having been reasonable. However mistakenly, these men saw themselves as being in a war situation and were ready to risk their lives in the cause. They saw themselves as prisoners of war and were men of dedication and of courage. But there was also a feeling of discomfort. We were celebrating the Eucharist, remembering God's action in Christ when he took the bread, broke it, and said, 'This is me, given for you. Do this in my memory.' Was it not my duty to state at the beginning of the celebration that unless in our hearts we renounce violence against another human being, then we should not take part in this celebration? But if the congregation believed they were fighting in a just cause, what right had I to make this announcement? The Church still held to a just war theory and, although as a private individual I do not believe that any modern war can ever be justified, in celebrating the Eucharist I am not acting as a private individual but as a representative of the Church. They were all the old problems of the conflict between role and person, of the relationship between sacramental ritual and daily living, of non-violent resistance to evil being at the heart of the Gospel. All these were being touched in that first celebration in the Maze prison.

I returned to the Maze the following Sunday. In the meantime I had tried to imagine myself as a prisoner and how it would feel to attend Mass and listen to a strange priest from England, who probably had not a clue on the reason for the armed struggle and no idea of what it means to be locked up indefinitely with generally hostile warders. I invited them at the beginning of Mass to make their own comments on the scripture readings, even if it was just to repeat a phrase that they liked or disliked. Unfortunately, the readings on that particular Sunday included the Letter of Peter in which he exhorts his people to obey the legitimate authorities. This was the phrase they seized on, beginning with a few disapproving comments on Pope John Paul II, whom they found too authoritarian. They then moved on to the question of authority in general, asking what one was to do when the authorities acted unjustly. I refused to answer any questions, so that they could answer their own. In the middle of the congregation there was one striking-looking man with the build of a middle-weight boxer, who spoke well and vehemently. He stated that when the authorities were acting unjustly and non-violent protests were ineffective, there must be resort to violence. I threw this statement back to the congregation. There was silence. I said, 'I take it then that you are agreed on the need to resort to violence when legitimate forms of protest are ineffective'. An older man then spoke. 'Not at all,' he said, 'we are not agreed. Some of us are for, some against, some in the middle.' The vehement young man was just starting on another speech when I looked at my watch and saw that if we were to finish Mass within the hour, we could afford no more contributions. I silenced him as politely as I could. At the end of Mass, with about a minute to spare, I went to him and apologised for having to stop him. 'Not at all,' he said, 'I was just so grateful that we were given the chance to speak our minds.'

I keep remembering those visits to the Maze and I know that if those men are ever to change their minds about violence, a precondition is that they must be allowed to speak their minds and be listened to. The Thatcher doctrine of having no truck with 'terrorists' always struck me as greatest folly. When an individual is silenced, for whatever reason, whether the silence is enforced from without or is imposed from within the individual, resentment builds up, defences are strengthened, and the possibility of change is lessened. With hijackers and kidnappers it is essential to keep communications open for as long as possible. Enforced silencing is a form of violence and violence, of its nature, both spirals and is imitative. Besides, when 'terrorists' become sufficiently destructive, the authorities are forced to negotiate.

While in Portadown, I had a phone call one day telling me that the director of the film *The Killing Fields*, Roland Joffé, was planning to make a film called *The Mission*, an account of the Jesuit expulsion from Paraguay in the eighteenth century. In Paraguay the Jesuits had set up a state for the Indians, protecting them from marauding Spanish and Portuguese slave traders. In *The Killing Fields*, Joffé had found a native Cambodian, who was not a professional actor, to take the principal role, and he was trying to find a Jesuit to do the same for *The Mission*. The caller asked if I would be interested in meeting with the casting director, Susie Figgis, who would come to Belfast. I met Susie at the airport. She gave me the script, chatted briefly about the film, but spent most of the time on her own atheism. She asked me to read the script and come to London to meet Roland Joffé. The theme of the film interested me, for it centred on the conscience conflict of the central character, 'Gabriel', between loyalty to the Indians and obedience to Church authority. Joffé told me of his own very mixed religious background and said that he saw *The Mission* as a commentary on what was then going on in South America, where many priests are still caught up in this same conflict between their own consciences and Church authorities, which may be in league with unjust and repressive governments.

I was then invited to audition for the part of Gabriel, in the form of an hour's role-play with Robert de Niro. He acted as a violent prisoner on death row whom I had to visit as the prison chaplain. I tried all my counselling techniques on a withdrawn de Niro and the only clear statement I could get out of him at first was 'Oh, shit'. The director would occasionally interrupt to move the situation on. I had to have a second session after de Niro had supposedly attacked someone else in the prison. Then Joffé asked me about the things that enrage me, and he played the part of coercive authority to which I had to react. At the end of the one-and-a-half-hour session, he told me that he still had to do auditions in the USA, but would let me know the result in a few weeks' time. Six weeks later he rang to say he had decided to employ a professional actor, Jeremy Irons. That was the beginning and end of my film career. A friend, having seen the film, said to me, 'Thank God you didn't get the part. Jeremy Irons was splendid!' Two Jesuits, Fr Dan Berrigan, the well-known American peace protester and writer, and Fr Anthony Lawn from Britain, were eventually given parts in the film.

I loved living in that small Jesuit community in Portadown. The superior, Fr Paddy Doyle, had been a nuclear scientist before becoming a Jesuit, and in the early 1940s had been engaged in research work on the atomic bomb. As a Jesuit, he had developed a very cosmic understanding of Christ, and believed that all creation is to be divinised. I always felt better after a discussion with him. While of a highly speculative nature, he was also very down-to-earth and spent much of his time working with hospital patients, with prisoners and their families, and he felt for the people among whom he was living. He was aware of the injustices which many of them were suffering, yet he was never bitter nor did he show any signs of being downcast by the impossible situation in Northern Ireland.

In March 1985 I left Portadown to return to Liverpool to begin work with people in Britain involved in work for justice and peace.

CHAPTER 12

ఴఄ

God of Love and
Wrath

*Everything that happens within us, every thought, every act of will,
has cosmic repercussions, and affects all creation, for better, for
worse, for richer, for poorer.*

I BEGAN MY WORK on justice and peace spirituality by becoming
an office boy at the Campaign for Nuclear Disarmament, at Christian
CND and at Pax Christi, spending two weeks in each office. The
office work at CND was monotonous, mostly filling up envelopes with
information for their 100,000 members. The only brain-taxing work
was at Pax Christi where they were in chronic financial straits. Their
economies included buying up stamps cheaply because they were of
a denomination no longer in use, so that each letter sent out was an
exercise in mental arithmetic. In each of the offices the company,
mostly volunteers, was a most encouraging mix of old and young,
professional and unemployed, atheist and religious, but all united in
a horror of nuclear deterrence. There may have been rows and tensions in the offices, but I saw only good humour and tolerance among
people who were often working in very cramped conditions.

At Christian CND, I was asked to scan all the Christian weekly
papers for articles on peace. It was a sobering experience, for the
peace issue was obviously of no great concern to the majority of
the editors nor, apparently, to most readers of Christian weeklies.

On Easter Monday 1985, I joined a peace protest at Molesworth
which, like Greenham Common, was a site for US Cruise missiles.
That memory will always linger and ten years later it still disturbs.
Many thousands joined the protest, including a large number of

elderly ex-service men. Set in beautiful rural East Anglia was this hideous site, protected by a perimeter fence of razor-like barbed wire, designed to tear the flesh of any intruder. Protesters walked around it, mostly in silence, some placing daffodils on the fence, technically a criminal offence. This was the spot from which the blazing furnaces could be hurled at our enemies in order to defend our national values.

The thoughts and feelings which arose from this visit to Molesworth caused a kind of nuclear devastation within. I know so many good, intelligent and religious people, admirable in their personal lives, who accept our nuclear deterrence policy as a necessary means of national defence in our fallen world and can argue their case rationally and calmly. The question caused me inner turmoil and went far beyond the rightness or wrongness of nuclear deterrence to the nature of God, in whom all creation has its being. Is God the God of compassion who loves all that is created, who is present in all things and in all people? Can we be making our home in this God while planning to defend ourselves with weapons which can possibly destroy all human life on earth? Was my inner turmoil a sign of inner imbalance? How is it that good individuals, many of them religious believers, can act as a nation in ways which are utterly destructive of other peoples, and ultimately of themselves? As a nation, one of our most profitable industries is our arms trade, exporting worldwide, often to tyrannical governments, who use these weapons against their own people. Most of our scientific research is linked to the arms trade. Promotion of this trade is called 'Backing Britain'.

While in London, I searched for literature on the theology and spirituality of peace, but apart from the writings of the American Cistercian Thomas Merton, I could find very little. Even among those actively committed to peace there seemed to be little interest in examining the roots of violence and in tracing the roots to their starting point in our own minds and hearts. We need to look at the way we perceive reality, especially other human beings, and our tendency to project outwards what we cannot tolerate within ourselves, thus creating enemies around us and feeling self-righteous in defending ourselves against them.

Having worked in peace offices, I was invited to write in their periodicals, introducing what I then called 'peace spirituality' and offering to work with any peace/justice groups, irrespective of religious affiliation, who might be interested in linking their commitment to peace to their life of faith, prayer and worship. I was amazed at the immediate response, and this is the work in which I have been mainly engaged since 1985, travelling around the country giving lectures, weekend workshops, mid-week courses and eight-day individually given retreats.

I soon realised that 'spirituality of peace and justice' is a misnomer, suggesting that there are Christian spiritualities which can ignore these questions. God is the God of justice, of truth and of peace, as the Old Testament prophets make clear in their message which lies at the heart of the Bible. The idolatry they rail against is every form of worship which ignores this truth.

> I hate and despise your feasts,
> I take no pleasure in your solemn festivals.
> When you offer me holocausts,
> I reject your oblations,
> Let me have no more of the din of your chanting,
> no more of your strumming on harps.
> But let justice flow like water,
> and integrity like an unfailing stream. (Amos c. 5)

After I had travelled around the country for a year meeting different peace and justice groups, an old Catechism question kept recurring in memory: 'What are the marks of the one true Church?' The Catechism answer was, 'She is one, holy, catholic and apostolic'. There were further questions and answers on the meaning of each mark, the general message being that these characteristics could only be found within the Roman Catholic Church. Slowly I understood why the question was recurring: I was beginning to see these marks in the groups I was meeting, which included people of a variety of Christian denominations and of none. This raised very fundamental questions about the nature of the Church and its mission.

Although peace and justice groups are as likely as any other human grouping to disintegrate because they cannot practise peace and justice among themselves, yet in all the groups I encountered, there was a remarkable spirit of unity. They did not keep talking or singing about it: they showed it unselfconsciously in their behaviour. When we met for a day course, participants laid out their lunch on a table and everyone shared. This was in contrast to some of the other groups I worked with who were not active in peace and justice, but interested in prayer: they tended to sit with their lunch on their laps! There was also a lightness and spontaneous good humour among these groups, although they were engaged in active peace protest which would bring some of them to prison. In spite of the seriousness and risk of their commitment, they did not take themselves too seriously. Many of them were no longer church-goers, yet in their work for peace and justice they showed a unity of mind, heart and purpose, which I had rarely encountered in church groups.

The unity of the Church must be a unity of the Spirit, which is not the unity of conformity. The Spirit of God is a Spirit of truth, justice and peace, a Spirit of unity which embraces all creation. God is always greater than any Church, any religion. These little groups, consisting of a variety of Christian denominations, and of people who claimed to belong to no denomination, bore witness to the unity of God by their own unity in working for peace.

If I had said to any of these groups, 'You are holy', they would have laughed. For many of them their idea of holiness had nothing to do with the work for peace and justice in which they were engaged, but was derived from statues and holy pictures, of people with halos and sweet smiles, cradling a crucifix and rapt in constant prayer. The fact that they lived simply, gave time, energy and money to the cause of peace, struggled to be tolerant and forgiving with themselves and others, and felt the need of prayer, did not strike most of them as having anything to do with holiness. One woman, middle class, a justice of the peace and mother of five, came for a retreat after spending six years at Greenham Common. She had frequently been imprisoned for praying within the perimeter, gaining access with a pair of wire-cutters, and she fasted while in prison. Her sentences were normally of one week, but on one occasion she fasted for the duration of a thirty-day sentence. At Greenham, she kept night vigils when she would confront the missile carriers as they left the camp. i asked her why she wanted to make a retreat. 'I want to put my spiritual life in order,' she replied. I wished I had such a spiritual life to put in order. Her retreat was a time for reflecting on her own remarkable life experience, recognising God in her appreciation of the preciousness of every human being, an appreciation which had drawn her to nursing, then to midwifery, and finally to protest with her whole being against nuclear missiles. When engaged in such work, she raged against her opponents, and rage did not seem to her to be compatible with holiness!

In scripture, God is described as holy. The word holy is used both to describe the otherness of God, the transcendence of God, always greater, always beyond the grasp of our minds and imaginings, but also to describe God's relationship to creation, and this relationship is one of compassion, for 'God loves all that He has created'. It is because God is the God of compassion that God is also described as the God of wrath, who utters fearsome threats against those who kill, oppress, exploit, or even fail to notice the needs of others. In human beings, the quality of holiness is manifest in their spirit of compassion, which embraces all life.

These peace groups felt for their brothers and sisters in Communist countries and in the southern hemisphere, and many of them felt for the rivers, plants and trees, for the fish and the animals of the earth. They had a horror of every form of exploitation, of racism, sexism, militarism in all its forms. They were catholic in the literal sense of that word which, in its Greek origin, means universal. From their commitment to peace and justice they could easily grasp the meaning of the phrase 'the sacramentality of all creation', and Celtic spirituality, which finds God in the ordinary, spoke to them. Although their membership was composed of many different Christian denominations and those who subscribed to none, their ideal was catholic, reflecting the catholicity of God.

Apostolic literally means 'sent'. Most of the peace people I encountered did not set out to preach and did not consider themselves to be engaged in evangelism. However, when they learned to reflect on their experience and to ask what it was that kept them going in spite of the opposition they met, the frustration they felt, the contempt with which they were regarded by others, sometimes including their own families and friends, they began to see that they, too, were 'sent'. Many of them wanted, at times, to abandon their commitment because of the personal cost, but found themselves unable to do so. When they read the prophet Jeremiah's complaints to God, 'You have seduced me, Yahweh', 'Why have you inflicted on me this incurable wound?', they recognised the echo of that cry in their own hearts.

In their churches and parishes these peace people were often considered trouble-makers, a disturbing influence, unprayerful, fringe people. While working with one peace group over a weekend, I offered my services in the local church on Sunday. On learning that I was working with a peace group, the parish priest said he would first have to obtain the local bishop's permission if I was to preach in his church! In other churches where I was invited to preach, some people walked out when I invited the congregation to look at our nuclear deterrence policy and our arms trade in light of the Gospel. In most churches they remained in their pews, but many would comment afterwards that they had never before heard these issues being mentioned from the pulpit. These and many similar events crystallised into an image.

Imagine a ring at your doorbell one evening. On answering it, you find there on the doorstep the risen Lord himself. Somehow, you know without any shadow of doubt that it is he. What do you do now? Leave him on the doorstep, tell him to come back on Sunday? Presumably, you welcome him in, and summon as many as possible to meet him. You then find yourself making ridiculous statements to the Lord of all creation, 'Do make yourself at home, and stay as long as you like'. Jesus accepts your invitation.

Now take a two-week leap in imagination. How is it at home now? The Letter to the Hebrews says, 'Jesus Christ, yesterday, today and the same forever'. In the Gospel Jesus once said, 'I have not come to bring peace but the sword, I have come to set son against father, daughter against mother, daughter-in-law against mother-in-law'. So how has it been over family meals during the last two weeks, and what has Jesus said or asked to cause such division within the family?

As you have invited Jesus to make himself at home, he is now inviting his friends to call. Who were his friends in the Gospel, and what kind of people are arriving at your door? What are the neighbours saying, and what is happening to local property values?

You feel it wrong to keep Jesus all to yourself, so you invite him to give a talk at your local church. In the Gospels he gave a little talk to the chief priests, scribes and pharisees, in the course of which he assured them that the tax-gatherers and the prostitutes would enter the Kingdom of God before they did. He gives substantially the same message to the elect of St Jude's parish church and there is uproar, the parish subsequently losing its principal benefactors.

You return home again with Jesus, who has caused trouble at home, trouble with your neighbours, and trouble with your parish. Jesus has become an embarrassment. The easiest solution would be to ask him to leave, but one can hardly do this to the Lord of all creation. You look around the house with care, find a suitable cupboard, clear it out, clean and decorate it, sparing no expense, and have good strong locks fitted on the door. You place Jesus inside, turn the lock, place a lamp and flowers in front, and each time you pass, you bow in deep reverence. You now have Jesus where you want him and he does not interfere any more!

This image of Jesus in the cupboard crystallised the questions which were constantly arising through work with justice and peace groups, causing a kind of inner spiritual vertigo. As I developed this image, so much of our religious activity appeared cupboard-centred, with different Christian denominations intent on their own cupboard, establishing its validity as containing the one true risen Lord, and jealously preserving it from any who might think otherwise.

My mind reeled. It was as though I could hear Christ cry out, 'O my people, what have you done to me? I came to set you free, but you have imprisoned me. I came to show you God whose life is given for all, who longs to draw all creation to himself, but you have made me a God as self-righteous as yourselves, a God of punishment and condemnation, as wedded to worldly power and prestige as you are. You lament over your dwindling church congregations, about disbelief, the death of God in human hearts, and yet you are blind to the truth that you may be a contributory cause. You claim to serve me, but you use me and my name in the service of your own narrow, divisive and destructive interests.'

Involvement in issues of peace and justice was forcing fundamental questions, which had been lying quietly dormant, to the surface of my mind. I knew from past experience the value of long-distance walking as a method of unravelling the mind's twisted strands of thought and feeling. Ever since walking to Rome in 1975 I had dreamed of walking to Jerusalem. In the summer of 1983 I had walked from Skelmorlie, in Ayrshire, to Hull as a first step of the journey and had hoped to do the rest after leaving St Beuno's in December 1983. However, the invitation to begin work in South Africa in June 1984 did not leave me sufficient time. I did not relish walking through a European winter in January and February, so I abandoned the idea. Three years later, spiritual vertigo made it seem more attractive. I could visit some European peace groups on the way and see whether they offered any spiritual training to their activists. If the walk was sponsored, I could also raise funds for the impoverished Pax Christi, enabling them to buy normal stamps! At the end of February 1987, I set out from Birmingham, where I was now living, took a train to Hull and the ferry to Rotterdam to begin the European leg of the journey. When I reached Munich at the end of March, it was still snowing after the coldest European winter in years. The walk did not banish the questions, but it did begin to alter the way I saw them and gave me some uncomfortable insights into my own spiritual vertigo.

It is difficult to describe this spiritual vertigo. The starting point was the question of nuclear deterrence. Dorothy Day, an American peace campaigner and founder of *The Catholic Worker* newspaper and of homes for the homeless, once asked, 'What is the difference between throwing blazing furnaces at innocent people and throwing innocent people into blazing furnaces?', yet the question did not appear to be of major concern to most Christians. Because many intelligent and good Christians, whom I admired, defended the morality of the nuclear deterrent. I began to doubt my own judgement, and to feel that I could be mistaken in what I was seeing with utmost clarity, namely that the nuclear deterrent could never be justified. This doubt then joined forces with all the other doubts of my life. Because I could no longer trust my own judgement, I could trust nothing and no one in the future, including myself. All that I had tried to do, all I had longed for, the whole direction of my life seemed meaningless. I hung on to God with my lips, mouthing 'You are my rock, my refuge, my salvation', but my being felt untouched, and the words seemed a mockery. The only scriptural phrase which spoke to me was the ending of Psalm 88, 'You have turned my neighbours and friends against me, and now darkness is my one companion left'. Gerard Manley Hopkins, who had been so unintelligible to me in my youth, became all too intelligible:

> O the mind, mind has mountains; cliffs of fall,
> Frightful, sheer, no-man-fathomed.

Besides mountains, the mind also has layers. It is as though our mind is a mansion with many rooms, our consciousness able to move from room to room, acting appropriately in each. My mind had discovered the basement with its rotting foundations, which would eventually cause the whole edifice to crumble. I could not then visit the other rooms, whether dining room, study, prayer room or bedroom, without knowing that everything was about to disintegrate. I carried on normally as far as I could, but without energy, interest or zest. My mind felt powerless against mountainous waves of despair.

This state of darkness did not disappear suddenly. The process was like a slow thaw after a hard winter. After some months of darkness, I was walking on the moors one afternoon while giving a retreat in Yorkshire. I discovered that I was enjoying the feel of the wind and the sight of the grass bending before it. I was conscious of bird song and the movement of the clouds. Then there would be another storm from my unconscious and darkness would envelop me again.

Of its nature, this kind of inner turmoil is unintelligible at the time and feels totally destructive. It did not suddenly vanish: the recovery was gradual and it still continues, but now I can look back on that period of darkness and feel grateful for it, although I never want to experience it again, nor would I wish it on my worst enemy.

Although during the darkness I mouthed the prayers 'You are my rock, my refuge and my strength', the real rock for me was me, my judgement, my ability to perform, my strength, my virtue. That was why I wanted to ignore my own weakness, helplessness, fickleness and sinfulness. My sin was self-importance and my sickness was complacency. Words are inadequate. I know I did not reason myself out of the depression. I was shaken out of it to my false foundations. I can look back on it now, can be grateful for this greatest of gifts, but I still have to pray God to keep shaking whenever I start building again on my own foundations, because I know I can so easily do so.

This experience of inner darkness which, at the time, felt totally destructive, is now, in memory, a creative energy. It has not led me to condemn my past as totally false and misguided. With my very limited consciousness I was genuinely trying to serve God: I was not being deliberately hypocritical. I was not, however, aware of the subtle egoism contaminating my relationship with God, and it was only through the pain I felt at the core of my being that I could begin to see the truth. Now I see more clearly why St Ignatius tells us to pray for the grace of bearing insult, injury and abuse, because these are the sledge-hammers which reveal our hidden and false foundations. Now, too, I know why that phrase of St Catherine of Genoa so fascinated me, long before I understood its meaning: 'My God is me, nor do I recognise any other me, except my God himself'.

The layers of consciousness seem infinite and each day's experience reveals further layers which have not yet acknowledged God's presence in all things. The clue to discovering these layers is to be found in reflecting on the emotional pain we experience. Where is it coming from? From God, or from my hurt ego? The poverty Jesus described as bliss – Blessed the poor, theirs is the kingdom of God – means living with every layer of our consciousness in the truth that God really is my rock, refuge and strength, and that there is no other. I began to see that there was an ego element in my spiritual vertigo over the issues raised by working on peace and justice. Much of my pain and frustration was ego pain, which enervates, demoralises and depresses. Letting go of the ego does not banish the pain, but the pain no longer enervates, is no longer so self-absorbing, no longer so depressing, but is suffused with a sense of hope. I could now see more clearly that true happiness is to live constantly in this inner knowing that God really is my rock, refuge and strength, and that no insult or injury, rejection or calamity, can ever destroy this truth.

When I returned from Jerusalem in July 1987, I continued working with justice and peace groups, based now in Birmingham at the Jesuit noviceship. During the walk, I had often reflected on our split spirituality and how it expresses itself in many different ways, in the distinctions we make between head and heart, between intellectual reasoning and feeling, words and actions, profession of belief and behaviour. In Jerusalem, I had met Bruno Hussar, a Jew, brought up and educated with Arabs in Egypt. He was now a Dominican priest and founder of the Neve Shalom village community near Jerusalem, where Jews, Arabs and Christians live together in community, devoting their lives to the promotion of peace and reconciliation. In our conversation he had constantly used the phrase, 'Do and you will understand' as distinct from 'study the question theoretically and you will understand'. Because of the disjunction between our hearts and our heads, it is possible for us to study a question endlessly without its affecting our behaviour in the slightest. There has never been more study on the causes of world poverty and world hunger than in the last forty years, but the problems have increased rather than lessened, because mere intellectual understanding, although important, does not of itself lead to effective action. I knew this failure in my own life. I was constantly thinking and talking about poverty, injustice and conflict, while living in the comfortable security of leafy Harborne, a middle-class suburb of Birmingham.

Before my walk to Jerusalem, Margaret Walsh came to see me. She belonged to the Congregation of The Sisters of the Infant Jesus and was then in her second year of living with two other sisters in Heath Town, a very depressed housing estate in Wolverhampton, with a bad reputation for violence and drugs. The unemployment rate was over 80 per cent, most of the households consisting of single-parent families, mainly Caribbean, with a minority of Asians. Very few on the estate were church-goers, but Margaret said that over the past two years she had learned more about Christianity from the tenants of Heath Town than in her previous forty years of Catholic upbringing, convent education, teacher training and innumerable courses on theology and spirituality. On my return from Jerusalem I visited Heath Town.

The sisters called themselves the Hope Community, kept open house, visited the estate, made friends and listened to the tenants. The Hope Community grew, partly thanks to volunteer workers, who would come and live in Heath Town for a year or more, but also because many of the tenants began to describe themselves as members of the Hope Community. One evening Margaret had a phone call from the police. They had arrested a Heath Town man, who claimed to belong to the Hope Community and was insisting that he must get in touch with the superior of his community, Margaret! In the course of their work, the sisters made contact with the local housing authorities, the social services, the local hospital, and often accompanied the tenants in their court appearances and visited them in prison. They lived in a world unknown to most people in Britain, a world of real hunger and deprivation, of fear and intimidation. They saw the reality of poverty in Britain which is denied by government officials and saw, too, the traplike effect of our social and economic structures in which so many are caught, while those outside the trap claim that the trapped are there because they are too lazy and work-shy to escape. The sisters were faced daily with the moral dilemma of whether or not to give food to the hungry who came to their doors. Handing out food could weaken the recipients by creating dependency, while refusal left them hungry.

The people among whom they lived and with whom they forged friendships are labelled 'the underclass' by some in the media. There were criminals among them, men and women who had been in prison and were now engaged in activity which would return them to prison if they were caught. It was from 'the underclass' that Margaret learned the meaning of Christianity. In spite of their poverty and the hopelessness of their situation, the tenants had a great gift of living in and enjoying the present moment. There was no pretence among them, they knew one another and each one's past, but they were tolerant and accepting. When they did have money or food they shared it, and birthdays were always celebrated with a party. After one riot in the estate, when a grocer's shop was looted, one of the principal looters threw money and goods to the crowd, keeping nothing for himself. Theft, prostitution and drug-pushing corrupt a society, but when one meets the guilty and hears of the desperation which led them into this activity, anger grows against the spiritually and materially comfortable who relish condemnation of the guilty while remaining obstinately unaware of the possibility that they might share the greater guilt. Frequently the guilty had entered into crime in order to feed and clothe their children or because of intimidation.

The Hope Community neither proselytised nor preached in words, but instead responded to the needs around them. They aroused the tenants' interest and some began to join the sisters at prayer. Now, nearly ten years later, the percentage of church-goers is still tiny, but every six weeks there is a religious service held in the community centre, prepared and celebrated by the tenants themselves, to which they invite local ministers. Each celebration is different, but includes much singing and music, with prayers, both spontaneous and prepared, and a Gospel scene is always acted out, based in a Heath Town setting. There is individual testimony in which people tell some part of their own story, and the service always ends with tea. Numbers vary from sixty to over a hundred. A number of tenants have been asking to be baptised. They do not understand Church divisions and have no desire to be baptised into a church in the city: they want to be baptised into the Hope Community, a request with which the Churches are at a loss to know how to deal. The early Christian Church would have had no such problem.

In January 1989 I went to live in the Hope Community. I had thought and prayed over the move and felt right with the decision. I tried to keep up outside work, seeing individuals and groups, and to continue working on *Walk to Jerusalem*, while living in a flat in Heath Town. After six weeks of living in the noise and discomfort, my health, normally robust, showed danger signals and I had to return to Birmingham, a blow which touched off again the depression from which I thought I had recovered. It was only later that I realised the source of my disappointment. At the time I felt a failure because I was, in fact, unable to live poor among the poor, even although that was what I thought I wanted to do. Later, I realised that the source of much of my disappointment lay in my failure to live up to an ideal I had proposed for myself. It was the ego again! The ideal was good in itself, but not for me in my particular circumstances and with my limitations. When I could accept the truth of this, the failure ceased to be depressing, and future possibilities became exciting. Life can become very dull when everything goes according to plan, so it is fortunate that it rarely does so. Religious people speak of 'God's plan for our salvation'. Whatever that plan may be, it is a safe bet that it will cut across any plans of our own.

I returned to Birmingham from Heath Town in February 1989, and continued to work with peace and justice groups and with writing my book. By this time, I knew there was no such thing as 'peace and justice spirituality', but I was still working mostly with people who were in some way active in justice and peace.

Two events occurred which led me to be less selective in the groups with which I worked. The first was an invitation from Lincoln Theological College to spend six weeks there giving courses on Ignatian spirituality to Anglican ordinands. I wrote to the principal suggesting that instead of giving lectures, I should offer a retreat in daily life to any of the students or staff who might be interested. The principal invited me to visit the college to explain the nature of this retreat. I did so, and told them that those making the retreat would have to undertake to pray on their own for about an hour on each day of the retreat and that once a week they would have a private conversation with a retreat guide. Fifty-four students and staff expressed interest. I knew I could not give a retreat to this number on my own, so I asked Ursula Burton, then working at St Beuno's as a member of the staff during the three-month course, if she would be willing to come to Lincoln, and she agreed.

Ursula had been one of the first laywomen to apply for the

St Beuno's three-month course in 1983. Having been accepted, she wrote a few weeks before the course began, asking if she might attend only the first six weeks, including the thirty-day retreat, and then return to do the final six weeks in a later course. She had cancer. The consultant advised immediate surgery, but having already had cancer surgery, she wanted to face the illness in a different way. I expected that her illness would become the focal point of her retreat, but while fully aware of her cancer, it was other events which engaged her in prayer, among them the fact that she was still recovering from the pain of divorce six years before. When she reported back to the consultant six weeks later and after the retreat, the cancer tumour had diminished and eventually disappeared. She completed the course the following year and from 1984 onwards she became a member of the three-month course staff at St Beuno's.

Meeting with twenty-seven different people for one hour each every week for six weeks is very exacting and exhausting, but Ursula and I were both encouraged by the effect the retreat was having. Through their prayer, and especially through imaginative prayer, retreatants began to get in touch with past memories which were still affecting their outlook and behaviour. They became more interested in the action of God in their own lives than in the lives of the Old Testament patriarchs, or in the structures and doctrines of the early Church. Most of them had never before had spiritual direction or any instruction in private prayer which related it to everyday life. This was not a defect peculiar to Lincoln Theological College: it was also true of most denominational theological colleges and of Roman Catholic seminaries. Prayer was emphasised in both, but its practice was limited to prayer in common. Private prayer might be advocated, but no detailed help was normally given.

After the Lincoln retreat, Ursula Burton gave similar courses with others at St Andrew's University and at Oscott College, the Catholic seminary for the Birmingham archdiocese. With a friend, Joyce Ferne, also a laywoman, she went annually to the theological colleges at Salisbury and Wells and to Queen's College, Birmingham. When those who had made such retreats were ordained, they introduced these prayer methods into their own parishes. Many went on to make eight-day residential retreats and to further training in retreat-giving and spiritual direction, and so prayer networks began to build up in different parts of the country.

Ursula Burton was a very intuitive and gifted listener, who could enable her retreatants to get in touch with themselves. At St Beuno's her retreatants had included some elderly Jesuits, who appreciated her skill. Knowing her effectiveness as a retreat-giver and spiritual director, I began to see that nurturing and developing the ministry of lay person to lay person was an urgent task for the Church of the future. There is enormous untapped spiritual wealth in the Church, but most people who are not in the ordained ministry, or living a consecrated religious life, are unaware of their own spiritual wealth. Also, the present structures of the Church are heavily clerical, and most church-goers complain that they are not given help in developing their own prayer life. If people who are not professionally religious come to know more about prayer, they seldom know how to share their knowledge with others, and if they do learn to share it, it can be difficult for them to find the opportunities to exercise their skills, because the opportunities are controlled by clergy or by professional religious people.

The second event which led me to work more widely with any groups interested in spirituality rather than exclusively those who were actively engaged in justice/peace work was a random encounter with Bishop Graham Chadwick a year after he had completed the St Beuno's three-month course. We were both engaged in giving a renewal course to L'Arche assistants at Ampleforth, the Benedictine monastery and school in Yorkshire. During the course we had a free day and walked in the Yorkshire Dales. Over a pub lunch Graham told me of the work he had been doing in giving retreats in daily life. Many were now asking if there was any kind of training available to enable them to accompany others in this kind of retreat. As far as I was aware, the only such courses available were the three-month residential course at St Beuno's and a two-year, one-day-per-week course in London. Both were too long as well as too remote and expensive for the people with whom Graham was working. One of the units in the St Beuno's three-month

course was a two-week session on retreat-giving and spiritual direction. Before leaving the pub we had decided to put on such a two-
week course in the following summer, designing it for people who
had already experienced an individually given retreat and were
interested in learning more of the basic skills of retreat-giving and
spiritual direction. Graham undertook to find a place in which we
could run such a course residentially.

The first course was held in July 1985 at Llysfasi, an agricultural
college in North Wales, and was given by Graham Chadwick, Sr Mary
Rose Fitzsimmons, who had worked occasionally at St Beuno's, and
myself. Twenty-five people attended from a mixture of denominations
and states of life, including religious and clergy. The course has now
been running annually for ten years and about five hundred people
have experienced it. Some of the former participants now help to
run the courses. Most who apply have already been engaged in some
form of caring work, religious or secular. The course does not set
out to produce qualified spiritual directors and retreat-givers, but
simply to offer practice in some very basic principles which are oper-
ative in every human relationship.

I have come to a much clearer understanding of the nature of the
Spiritual Exercises through giving spiritual direction and retreats to
individuals, as well as through Llysfasi and other training courses.
The Spiritual Exercises are not just for a favoured few, who then
possess something which others lack, but they offer a method of
seeing more clearly the treasure which is already given to every
single human being. I have given the Spiritual Exercises to many
people who do not consider themselves to be spiritual or religiously
inclined, but when they make the Spiritual Exercises, they discover
that its main themes are already familiar to them through their own
experience of life's struggles. Others, who may have had years of
practice in prayer and have made the Spiritual Exercises many times,
may have no such familiarity with its themes, because their lives
have been too sheltered. That is why Ignatius says that the Exercises
must be adapted to the needs, energy and willingness of the
retreatant, advice which had consistently been ignored through the
centuries. It is still being ignored in many places today, where

the Exercises are given as though they were washing-machine instructions – the full cycle to be given to all who make them, irrespective of their life experience.

Through the Lincoln College and Llysfasi experiences I began to see ways of working with others in Birmingham. One participant on a Llysfasi course was the Reverend Francis Palmer from Lichfield. He knew the need for some sort of spirituality centre in the West Midlands and summoned a meeting of those likely to be interested. Seventy people came. They were unanimous on the need for a spirituality centre and provided a long list of functions which such a centre should provide. Ideas and suggestions are always plentiful: the difficulty is in realising any of them. We had no money and no official authority, so we decided that the only possible course of action was to encourage those present to form their own networks, which would meet occasionally to exchange information and produce occasional newsletters.

Within this network, a small group, all Catholic priests and religious, gave a retreat in daily life to fifty people in St Mary's parish, Harborne. Those making the retreat were instructed and practised in ways of praying imaginatively, which allowed their everyday experience to become the substance of their prayer. The retreat began on a Sunday evening and ended the following Saturday. Those making it undertook to pray on their own each day and to have a daily conversation each evening with a prayer guide. Later I heard that a group of these retreatants were still meeting occasionally and wanted to communicate these ways of praying, so we offered them an elementary course in prayer guidance, which consisted of a two-hour session once a week for six weeks. Those on the course who were willing, and seemed to have the ability to listen to themselves, were then invited to become prayer guides on future retreats in daily life. This experience made them aware of their need for further training, so we put on an intermediate course, again for six weeks, exploring further the questions which practice had raised for them. Eventually, we put on a course of forty sessions, spread out over two years, each session held on a weekday evening and lasting two-and-a-half hours. The courses grew out of the demands of people who had experienced a retreat in daily life. There are now over 150 people in the Birmingham area who have had some training as prayer guides, practising their skills, not only in giving retreats in daily life, but in whatever situation they find themselves. Both the training courses and the retreats are always open to people of any Christian denomination.

God, where are you? In an earlier chapter I mentioned two criteria which St Ignatius of Loyola gives in the Jesuit Constitutions for choice of ministries. He writes of any ministry, '*Quo universalius, eo divinius*', 'The more universal a work is, the more it is divine'. He also says that if a work is of God, then the fruit of the work will be out of proportion to the resources invested in it. 'The more universal, the more it is divine' obviously points to the ecumenical nature of any Christian ministry, but the ministry must be ecumenical not only in the sense that it is open to all Christian denominations, but also in the fact that it involves every aspect of human life, the social and political, as well as the formally religious. One of the signs of the fruitfulness of any ministry is that the work has a momentum of its own and does not become dependent on any particular individual or group. The growth in Britain of these little spirituality networks has been remarkable, and they have grown from grassroots, not from national campaigns. The more ecumenical the training courses and retreats in daily life, the more likely they are to grow, develop and multiply.

Is it safe to encourage people to act as prayer guides to one another after such a short training and is it not likely to do more harm than good? There are serious risks in this kind of work. Prayer can put us in touch with depths of ourselves, and sharing that experience with another can make us very vulnerable and open to manipulation. That is why I have come to dislike the terms 'retreat director', 'spiritual director', even the term 'prayer guide'. Jesus said, 'Call no one teacher, you have only one teacher.' The teacher is the Spirit of God within us, and human teachers, religious or secular, are only useful in so far as they enable us to get in touch with our inner teacher. Through working on spirituality training courses, I now see them primarily as damage limitation exercises. All the people who come on these courses are already in some kind of caring role, whether as clergy, laity in caring professions or, most important of all, as parents. The more we care and feel responsible for others, the more damage we are able to inflict on them. That is why the main lesson in all these training courses is insistence on the role of accompanist as an enabler who helps the pilgrims discover for themselves. The accompanist's role is not to judge, assess, approve, disapprove, or give advice, however wise it may appear, or to try to solve the pilgrim's problems. The theory is simple: in trying to put it into practice, we become increasingly aware of the complexity in all human relationships, and of our tendency to file away whatever another may say to us in our own mental filing system, presuming that having done so, we then understand the other, whose mental filing system cannot be the same as our own, as it is built up and arranged out of every experience of their unique lives. I saw this truth vividly expressed in a drawing which an Australian psycho-therapist once showed to me, presented to him by one of his aboriginal clients.

The drawing was a simple outline of two facing chairs, connected at their foot by a slender wavy line. Leading into the line on either side was a large cone, filled with dots and squiggles, producing very intricate and different designs on either side. Working in spiritual direction over many years, I had become increasingly aware of the complexity there is in any conversation; of the many layers of meaning in each mind and of the innumerable possibilities for misunderstanding in any verbal communication. This drawing expressed the complexity vividly. I come to every encounter with my cone filled with dots and squiggles, representing every experience in my life, both the external happenings and my own reaction to them. Every event is indelibly registered in my neural system, is unique to me, and affects all my subsequent perceptions. I meet with another whose cone of experience is also unique, and we talk. The miracle is that we can understand one another at all, even when we speak the same language. The tragedy is that because we can fit the words of the other into the cone of our experience, we think that we have understood the other and react in accordance with our own cone pattern. Here lies the source of most human conflict and the roots of human violence. Aboriginal people, as I was to learn later, do not talk much with those who are close to them, for they know intuitively what is going on within the other, an intuitive knowledge which extends to the animals and plants of their own area.

Work in spirituality also throws light on the nature of the Church and on the meaning of Church unity. Michaelangelo claimed that in his sculptures he did not form the lump of stone into a masterpiece: he discovered the form within the stone. His genius was to let the pre-existing form emerge. This is a good image for the experience of working in spirituality with people of different Christian denominations and of none. Listening to their prayer experience, one becomes aware of the unity in which they are held in God. The denominational differences do not reach to the depths, but are largely culturally imposed barriers, which are real and also damaging. It is extraordinary that our Christian Churches, which all claim to be scripture-based and Christ-centred, give so little attention to nurturing the inner prayer life of individuals. It would make an interesting survey to ask of Church members, how much instruction in private prayer they had received, and how much help they had been offered in nurturing a form of prayer which was linked with their everyday experience. To conjecture a one per cent positive response from Church members would probably be over-generous.

It is because we are divided into our separate denominations and live in clerically dominated churches, and the clergy are so busy trying to keep their own churches going and in coping with the burdens of administrative work, that ecumenical activity is low on their list of priorities, if it has any place at all. Consequently the divisions remain and Church membership dwindles.

Those clergy who join with other denominations in encouraging individually given parish retreats, especially if they make the retreat along with their parishioners, discover that such joint activity is neither a threat nor an increased burden but, in fact, energises them and their parish.

CHAPTER 13

ᴄᴏᴏᴑᴄᴏ

God of Coincidence

Every moment is the message of God's will; every external event, everything outside us, and even every involuntary thought and feeling, within us is God's own touch. We are living in God, in God's action, as a fish in the water. (Dom John Chapman)

Eᴀʀʟʏ ᴍᴇᴍᴏʀɪᴇs become etched in the mind: later memories do not leave such distinctive traces. In the last four years I have travelled to Australia, New Zealand, Singapore and South Africa twice. My sister Edith, my two brothers, Ian and Joe, my close friend, Ursula Burton, and Julia McKinnon, who looked after me when I was a child and whom I mentioned in the first chapter, have all died. When I ask, 'God, where are you in all these events?', God's reply is characteristically vague, a vagueness with which I am now very familiar. God is always beyond us, beckoning us forward, a pillar of cloud ahead. I love that prayer, 'I said to the man who stood at the gate of the year, "Give me a light that I may tread safely into the unknown." And he replied, "Go out into the darkness and put your hand into the hand of God. That shall be better to you than light and safer than a known way."

As I look back on the last few years, I am amazed at the apparent coincidences, and how travel and bereavement were to interweave in ways I could never have imagined. I did not plan the worldwide travel: it happened through a series of apparently random events.

On holiday in the summer of 1991, I was walking along the shore in a remote part of the West Highlands of Scotland when I spotted a tiny isolated cottage by the edge of the sea. The picture of this cottage stayed with me. One of the few things I remember from school chemistry lessons is watching the liquid in a beaker being transformed into crystals when a drop of something was poured in. The picture of the little cottage acted like that drop on my psyche. The crystallisation began over a period of two years. At first, the memory of the cottage collected around it feelings of frustration, weariness, tedium, a longing for solitude, for time and space to reflect on the work in which I was engaged. In giving retreats, lecturing, running training courses, and writing, I often felt as though I was a gardener constantly digging and planting, but the soil was only a few inches deep: beneath this surface the soil felt rock-like.

Thirty years ago, sabbaticals were almost unheard of in religious and clergy circles. Today they are often encouraged. Theoretically, the sabbatical is a time for rest and renewal, for study and reflection, for taking bearings on life's journey. I longed for a sabbatical which would allow me to go deeper and release the energy in this compacted earth, so I asked for, and was granted, a year off from September 1993. At this stage, in 1991, I had no clear idea where I would go, nor how I would set about the digging, but I thought the cottage by the sea would be an ideal place, made inquiries, and found that it was not available.

Some time after seeing the cottage by the sea, I read an article in *The Tablet* on Australian spirituality, in which the author claimed that spiritual health could be recovered only if white Australians started to listen to and learn from the Aboriginal people. At this stage I did not even know that the Aborigines had a spirituality. Then I received a letter from an Australian woman, Bernadette Kennedy, who was working with Aboriginal peoples in Australia, asking if I could give her an eight-day retreat during her forthcoming visit to Britain. Bernadette had been a religious sister teaching in Australia for about twenty years. She felt attracted to working with Aborigines, was given a sabbatical which she spent with the Aboriginal people of Western Australia, and knew by the end of it that this was the work to which she was called. At that time her religious congregation was not prepared to engage in this work, so she left religious life and for the last twelve years had been working with Aboriginal people, mostly in adult education. Bernadette was not a romantic: she knew the dark side of Aboriginal life, but their spirituality had affected her profoundly, presenting her with a whole new way of looking at life, and putting her back in touch with her own Celtic roots.

After meeting Bernadette, I happened to be staying for a few days in Dublin at the Jesuit theological college in Milltown Park, where I heard that a sister from Australia, Clare Ahern, was doing post-graduate work, having worked with Aboriginal people for many years. She had written a thesis on Aboriginal spirituality, which she kindly lent to me. Later, I read Bruce Chatwin's *Songlines*, and a less-well-known but even more startling account of Aboriginal life in *Upside Down World*, written by an American doctor, who describes a three-month walkabout in the Australian desert.

In 1992, I received an invitation to spend two weeks in Melbourne in June 1993 to lecture and give workshops at a Catholic education conference. A few months later in 1992, I had a letter from an inter-church adult education committee based in Wellington, New Zealand. Every two years they invited someone to spend a month in New Zealand doing ecumenical work and asked if I would be free to come some time in 1993.

In 1992, one of the people to whom I was giving spiritual direction was a Sister Elizabeth Tham, from Singapore, who was doing post-graduate work in education at Birmingham University. She belonged to the Canossians, a religious congregation of Italian origin with a strong presence in South East Asia. Shortly after her return to Singapore, her provincial wrote asking if I would be willing to spend a month in Singapore towards the end of 1993, working with Canossian Sisters.

Nothing happens by chance! I had never in my life received an invitation from Australia, New Zealand or Singapore, nor had I met anyone who knew Aboriginal people, yet in the course of a year all these events happened. From these random events I began to see a possible plan for the sabbatical in 1993. What I had read and heard about Aboriginal spirituality fascinated me, and I knew that some Jesuits were living in an Aboriginal community in north-west Australia. Consequently, I accepted the New Zealand invitation to work there on ecumenism for a month, beginning in late September 1993. I also accepted the Canossian invitation to work in Singapore and Malaysia from mid-November till Christmas, planning then to spend about six months in Australia, learning what I could of Aboriginal spirituality.

At the Llysfasi two-week course in North Wales in 1991, one of the participants was the Reverend Robin Pryor, a Uniting Church of Australia Minister, who wanted to have a similar course in Australia, so I met with him on my short visit to Australia in June 1993. He and his colleagues organised a two-week course near Melbourne for January 1994, inviting Isabel Gregory from the Llysfasi team to join me. An earlier participant on the Llysfasi course, Dr Liz Carmichael, went to South Africa after the course. There she studied theology, was ordained priest, and began to work on peace and reconciliation in Alexandra township outside Johannesburg, where there were murderous clashes between Inkatha and the African National Congress, the ANC. In 1993, she invited Bishop Graham Chadwick to bring the Llysfasi team to South Africa to give courses in Johannesburg and Cape Town in May 1994. I agreed to join them although it would cut down the time I could spend in Australia.

The Catholic education conference in Australia included a workshop given by an Aboriginal woman, Vicki Walker, born of an Aboriginal mother and white father. She was currently engaged in a theology degree in which her particular interest was creation spirituality. Her workshop, with its glimpses of the way Aboriginal people see their world, fascinated me, because it helped me to locate more clearly the meaning of the garden plot and the compacted earth image. St Ignatius' spirituality has been described as 'Finding God in All Things'. I had been teaching and preaching this doctrine for years, along with its concomitant phrase, 'Finding God in Our Own Experience'. While I was convinced of the truth of both these phrases, I also knew my need further to explore them and their practical implications in my own life, the life of the Church, and in all human life. The Jesuits in Melbourne, with whom I stayed during the conference, put me in touch with Brian McCoy and Robin Koning, Jesuits living in an Aboriginal community in Balgo, in the north-west Australian desert.

As my sabbatical programme took shape, I realised that it looked more like a 'workathon' than a sabbatical, leaving very little time for study, reflection and writing. I asked for and was given an extension, so that from mid June 1994 until December I could have time for writing.

A week before I flew to New Zealand on September 24th 1993, I had an early-morning phone call. The caller was John Bickerton whom I mentioned in an earlier chapter. When a pupil at Stonyhurst in 1962, he had asked me at the end of one of my religion classes whether I realised that I was wasting my time because half the class, himself included, were atheists. I had kept in touch sporadically with John, our last meeting having been seven years earlier when he had visited me in Birmingham, telling me that he was giving up his computer business, had bought a haversack, and was about to embark on a world tour. I had the occasional letter from him from South America and a final letter from New Zealand. Like so many atheists, he was still preoccupied with religious questions. In his final letter he sounded ecstatically happy, describing New Zealand as 'God's own country'. I replied to the forwarding address he had given, but the letter was returned, addressee unknown. I was afraid he might have died, so it was a shock and a delight to hear that he would meet with me the following week in Wellington.

It is a strange experience to travel to the other side of the world in twenty-four hours, especially for a Scot travelling to New Zealand. The wind and rain of Wellington, the mountainous scenery and the people I met, so many of Scottish or Irish descent, made me feel I was still at home. John Bickerton presented me with a small library of books on the history of God's own country about which I knew so little. I never knew, for example, that women's emancipation was established in New Zealand in the nineteenth century, or that at the turn of the century New Zealand had a welfare state, initiated not by a Labour but by a Liberal government. After six weeks there I had decided that if there is reincarnation, and if we have any choice in the matter, then I would choose to be reborn in New Zealand. Wherever I

God of Coincidence

went, I felt at home. While working for a week in Christchurch, on the South Island, I lived in a house which was flanked on one side by Hagley Park Terrace – Hagley Road being one of Birmingham's main roads – and by Dublin Street on the other. Further along the road was Stonyhurst Street, then St Asaph Street, with Rabbie Burns Liquor store nearby. There was also an area called Burnside, the name of the Glasgow suburb where my brother Joe had lived for over thirty years. Later, when I visited Dunedin, an abbreviated form of Dundee and Edinburgh, the street names were even more familiar, and Rabbie Burns' statue dominated the city centre.

John Bickerton's library included a biography of Frederick Aloysius Weld, who first introduced sheep to New Zealand, so successfully that the sheep population is now over thirty million, ten times the number of human inhabitants. Frederick Weld became one of the early prime ministers of New Zealand and was a grandson of Thomas Weld, who had given Stonyhurst to the Jesuits in 1793. Frederick was educated at Stonyhurst, then spent two years travelling and studying in Europe, after which he decided to join his cousins, Charles Clifford and William Vavasour, and another Catholic contemporary, Henry Petre, in New Zealand, without having much idea of what he would do there. As a politician, Frederick shared many of the prejudices of the nineteenth-century English gentleman, including an innate sense of superiority over every other nation, including the native Maoris, but within his limitations he was scrupulously fair and did his utmost to ensure religious freedom in this new country.

The adult education committee had organised a series of workshops, retreats and lectures in Wellington, Palmerston North, Auckland and Christchurch, which made the first month of the sabbatical one of the busiest in my life, but I did not find it exhausting, because the people with whom I worked were so friendly and hospitable. There is a mysterious flow of energy in any encounter. After individual retreat-giving, or lectures, or workshops, I sometimes feel exhausted and empty, while at other times I feel energised and refreshed. Occasionally, I can account for the feeling, knowing that it is a projection of my own inner state. But there are other occasions when I cannot attribute the feelings to projection. Although in New

Zealand the programme was strenuous, and I sometimes felt tired before beginning a day's work, the encounters with individuals and groups were always energising.

After a month's work, I had twelve days free before going on to Singapore. At one of the workshops I had met Joy Cowley, novelist and author of many children's books. She and her husband, Terry, invited me to stay at their home in Fish Bay, on the Kenepuru Sound, and offered me a car with which to explore more of the South Island. I covered only a fraction of it, its scenery like a conflation of the Highlands of Scotland, the Alps, and the west coast of Ireland. What lingers in memory is the house at Fish Bay, the generous hospitality of Joy and Terry, who never imposed but let me be, and the call of the bell bird from the forest behind the house; the clusters of wild lilies in the garden, the friendly goat, the Labrador dog and the many cats. At low tide the shore was littered with large mussels and oysters. Walking the dirt road which skirted the shore brought back memories from twenty years earlier of walking the Road to the Isles in the Highlands of Scotland, from Inverailort to Mallaig, so similar was the scenery.

At Fish Bay and while touring the South Island I had time to reflect on the previous month. While I had enjoyed the work and the people I met, I doubted its long-term value, and so had not responded enthusiastically when the interchurch committee suggested another visit. During the month I had met many people of different Christian denominations, all of them interested in spirituality, and some very experienced and well trained, but there did not appear to be much close contact between them, or between the different denominations. When I returned to Wellington before leaving for Singapore, I suggested that if I were to return, I should do so with two others from Britain, in order to give a two-week workshop of the Llysfasi type to people of different denominations, who were engaged in some form of spirituality work. This would be followed by a one-week retreat in daily life in Wellington parishes, for which participants on the course would be the prayer guides, while the three of us would teach them how to conduct general supervision in groups, as well as providing individual supervision. The idea behind the suggestion was that once we had demonstrated a method, local people could then build up their own spirituality networks, learn how to conduct their own training sessions, organise ecumenical parish retreats, and provide general and individual supervision for the prayer accompanists. This suggestion was accepted, and two years later, in October 1995, I returned with Lister Tonge, an Anglican priest, and a Roman Catholic sister, Madeleine Prendergast, of La Sainte Union Congregation. We gave the course to an ecumenical group numbering twenty-five, followed by an individually given parish retreat in Wellington for over fifty people.

After my first visit to New Zealand, I flew to Singapore in mid November 1993. Emerging from the plane in the late evening was like entering the tropical greenhouses in Kew Gardens, hot and humid. When I went to bed on that first evening I soon discovered that a mosquito had prior occupancy underneath the covering net, so I slept fitfully, until wakened by a blast of music outside my room. The Canossian Sisters, who were my hosts, ran a school for the hearing impaired and the day began early with school gymnastics to loud musical accompaniment.

The school banned sign language and taught the children to lip-read, a system which my deaf nephew, Gerry, was forever denouncing. As a child, he had attended a school where signing was forbidden. His natural way of communicating was by signs, which can convey shades and depths of meaning which the spoken word cannot express. He claimed that as a child he was familiar with the meaning of words through his use of signs, long before he had learned to lip-read, or see the words in writing. Signing, he claims, is a language in its own right, and to forbid deaf children to sign is an oppression of the deaf by the hearing community, every bit as oppressive as the English attempts to ban Gaelic in Ireland and Scotland, or Welsh in Wales. In Singapore, government schools for the deaf allowed signing, but their pupils were then limited to menial jobs in later life. The Canossian sisters were trying to remedy this by training their pupils in lip-reading from an early age, so that as soon as possible these children would be able to attend ordinary schools, and so have a variety of possible careers open to them. In Singapore, however, there was a problem: examination results are held in such high esteem that one way of undermining a political opponent, for example, is to publicise his poor showing in school or university examinations. Schools are assessed on their examination results and league tables are published. Consequently, deaf children are not always welcome in hearing schools, as they may threaten the school's place in the league!

After one day in Singapore I travelled by bus to Melaka in Malaysia, to give an eight-day retreat to the Canossian sisters there. The house was at the foot of a hill on which stood an ancient church, where Francis Xavier had once preached in the sixteenth century on his way from India to Japan and China. He never reached China, but died within sight of it. His body was first buried in the Melaka church, but later taken to Goa, where his tomb is still a place of pilgrimage.

The Canossian sisters were mostly Chinese. After a first session with them I had no idea whether anything I said had been heard, or understood, because the room was accoustically bad and made worse by very noisy fans. Their facial expressions seemed impassive, and their appearance was uniform, for they were still dressed in habits and veils, which most Catholic women religious in Britain had abandoned many years ago. As I came to know them, both in Melaka and in Singapore, I recognised more clearly the rigidity of my own thought patterns. What is suitable for one country at a particular time may not be suitable for another. Religious have to work as best they can within the limitations and restraints which civil and ecclesiastical authorities impose. In Malaysia, they had to contend with the constraints imposed on them by an Islamic government, which made it very difficult to run their Catholic schools. In Singapore, religion was encouraged, provided it did not engage in political questions, which can be a more subtle and dangerous constraint than that existing in Malaysia. In Singapore, for example, the film *Romero*, the story of the life and assassination of Archbishop Oscar Romero of San Salvador, was not allowed to be shown in cinemas. Romero had been a conservative archbishop whose eyes were opened when he saw what was happening to the poor of El Salvador. He spoke out against the regime and was then gunned down in the chapel of a San Salvador hospital.

It is very difficult for religious men and women of any country to live with integrity within the constraints imposed on them without colluding with, or being subtly corrupted by, civil or ecclesiastical injustice. The task is impossible unless religious are sustained and enlightened by a robust inner life, nourished by personal prayer and the availability of good spiritual guidance. The Canossian sisters were very talented and doing excellent work in education and nursing, but they felt the need for spiritual guidance and for opportunities for training in it. As in New Zealand, so also in Singapore and Malaysia, there were many individuals trained in spiritual direction, but they tended to work in isolation, and in Singapore there seemed to be little ecumenical co-operation in spirituality or in any other aspect of Church life, nor much awareness of the need of it. Each Christian Church, or sect, was fully engaged in its own denominational pursuits.

Besides the eight-day retreat in Melaka, I gave another in Singapore, followed by a five-day workshop on spirituality and retreat-giving, all given to Canossian sisters. When invited to return, I suggested the same programme as for New Zealand. The suggestion was put into the hands of a committee, accepted, and in November 1995, the same team, Madeleine, Lister and myself, flew from New Zealand to Singapore to give a two-week workshop to thirty-six people, followed by a six-day individually given retreat to ninety in a Singapore parish.

The Singaporean nation, not yet forty years old, is a mixture of races – Chinese, Malaysian, Indian, European – and numbering about three million. The island is about the size of the Isle of Wight, with hardly any natural resources. Even for its water supply it is dependent on other nations. The ethnic mixture is potentially explosive. In the 1950s, while still under British control, there was massive unemployment and poverty. Today, it is one of the world's most prosperous trading centres with virtually no unemployment, and almost all the population owning their own homes. The streets, besides being free of litter and graffiti, are safe at night; the crime rate among

Singaporeans is very low, pornography and drugs are not easily available. Drug-dealing carries a death sentence. On both my visits, the centre of the city was ablaze with Christmas illuminations, which made Birmingham's look tawdry in comparison. At other times of the year the city celebrates Chinese, Muslim and Hindu festivals, stores and hotels competing with one another for the prizes awarded for the best decorations. In this way, the religious and ethnic divisions, potentially divisive, become an asset to the city.

Religion flourishes in Singapore, especially among youth, with a phenomenal recent growth in the Christian Pentecostal Churches. In one book I read, the author stated that while the Pentecostal and Charismatic Churches are increasing rapidly, the Roman Catholic Church remains static, but this was not the impression I received when I was taken to a Redemptorist church known as 'The Novena Church'. At 2.15 on a Saturday afternoon it was packed to its capacity of five hundred and there were as many again standing outside, almost as many men as women, and with more young than old. Every Saturday on the hour, starting at 8 am and continuing until 8 pm, thare is a half-hour novena service in honour of 'Our Lady of Perpetual Succour', at which prayers of petition and thanksgiving are said, a short sermon is given and traditional hymns to Our Lady are sung. It ends with Benediction, when the priest holds up the monstrance containing the Blessed Sacrament and blesses the congregation. It is reckoned that ten thousand to twelve thousand people come to the Novena church every Saturday, including a large percentage of non-Christians. Some of the Canossian sisters told me that their first introduction to Catholicism had been at the Novena church. I stood there in amazement, wondering how many would be likely to attend such services if they were put on in Birmingham: I reckoned that twenty would be a generous estimate.

Singaporeans have to work very hard to retain their prosperity. Their energies are so absorbed in business and money-making that they seem to have little energy for much else. In a recent poll, the favourite occupations of Singaporeans were watching television and eating out. As long as they are free to get on with their business, the majority seem disinterested in politics and are not greatly concerned about the strict press and media censorship, or the infringement of human rights. Those who are interested in these questions soon discover that independence of thought is risky.

Singapore is, in many ways, a model state, in which the vast majority of its citizens own their own houses, enjoy full employment, can feel safe at home and on their streets, have an efficient system of health insurance and an excellent public transport system. Their youth are protected from drug pushers and other corrupting influences. Foreign visitors and traders are made welcome and protected by fair trading laws from unscrupulous dealers. The various religions are encouraged to celebrate their festivals in ways which seem beneficial to all. During my two visits of one month each, I met with great kindness and most generous hospitality from people who worked extraordinarily hard, yet always seemed to have time for the stranger. The groups with whom I worked on both visits were very responsive and co-operative. In spite of all this, I felt uneasy, for Singapore's prosperity suggested a nightmare vision for the future of nations dedicated to a market-forces economy. What follows is not an indictment of Singapore: it is a spiritual reflection, arising from my Singapore experience, on a market-forces economy, and it is as applicable to Britain as to Singapore, or to any other nation which makes a prosperous economy its highest good.

In order to prosper, the more able and industrious citizens would be rewarded financially and protected from unwelcome intrusion within well-protected, well-equipped ghettos, with as much choice of television programmes as the government deemed suitable, and with a wide variety of restaurants and fashion stores. The less able would be few, being compulsorily aborted before birth, or put to death, if deemed a burden on the economy because of infirmity or age, the policy being presented as compassionate relief of suffering. Any menial tasks remaining in such a sophisticated country would be performed by visitors from poorer nations, paid a pittance for their labours, employed for a limited number of years, then forcibly returned to their own country. Training in citizenship would begin in nursery school when the children would be graded according to their technological promise and educated accordingly, learning to measure their own and everyone else's worth by their examination successes. Dissidents, who would be few, would be imprisoned, banished or, like the terminally ill, aged and infirm, put to death by the Ministry of Compassion. Religion would continue to flourish, provided it did not interfere with government policy. There is a novel, '2084', waiting to be written of a world in which market forces reign supreme, which could make George Orwell's Nineteen Eighty-four seem crude in comparison.

Our value system underlies every decision we make individually or corporately. When a nation's policies are dominated by economic considerations, then whether those responsible for the decisions are consciously aware of it or not, they are caught up in idolatry. The highest good has become the economy, and the economy has no regard for the sacred, the numinous, the infinite worth of every human being. Worshipping the economy, we become what we worship, as unfeeling and as callous, and so we can make decisions destructive of human life because they promote our economic prosperity, so that we increase, for example, our arms exports while cutting down on overseas aid.

As human beings we have to worship: the choice, as Jesus put it, is between God or mammon. Spirituality is concerned with choice, for in every decision, whether we are aware of it or not, we are choosing life or death, God or mammon. That is why I felt the spirituality work I was engaged in was worth doing. But mammon is all-pervasive and can infect the religiously committed just as much as the unbeliever.

Religiously, Singapore left me both impressed and puzzled: impressed by the obvious religious fervour, but puzzled by its insulation from other aspects of life. In the Catholic Church there had been a diocesan justice and peace commission, which no longer exists as some members had been imprisoned for their activity, one man receiving a three-year sentence. The Christian Churches appear to be insulated not only from political and social questions, but also from one another. In trying to arrange the second visit in November 1995, one of the organising committee suggested that the course and subsequent retreat would be much easier to organise if offered

exclusively to Catholics, and so 'would avoid the problems of ecumenism and of intercommunion', adding that the bishop had very
strict views on this subject! I replied that I would not come unless
both the course and the retreat were open to all denominations. The
committee promised to do its best, but out of the thirty-six participants on the course, thirty-five were Catholic and one was Anglican.

This problem of religious insulation is not peculiar to Singapore. I
have encountered it in every place and country I have visited. The
clergy of each Christian denomination tend to be so fully occupied
with their own parishes that they have little energy left for any
thought or activity beyond the upkeep of their plant and the provision
of church services. Co-operation with other Christian churches
appears to be a distraction from the main task. There was a car-
toonist, Calman, who used to specialise in God cartoons; in them
God appeared as a tubby figure seated on a cloud, reviewing his
creation. I imagine a cartoon in which God, looking down from
his cloud at the divided Churches, is saying, 'I do wish you would all
become atheists!' It is so easy to exclude the God of unity, the God
of all creation, from our Churches and church services.

While I found some of these reflections depressing, I also felt confirmed in plodding on with work on spirituality among people of all
denominations or none, for there can be no effective or lasting unity
among Christians unless it is rooted in prayer. The Spirit of God is
the source of our unity. It is only in-so-far as Christians are perceptive
of and responsive to that Spirit that unity can be recovered. What
form that unity will take, no one can predict. Being of God, it will
not be conformity, for the Spirit of God is a Spirit of infinite variety.

I was summoned back to Britain for a Jesuit meeting over
Christmas 1993, and then went to Australia in early January to give
the two-week workshop in Croydon, near Melbourne, organised by
Robin Pryor. This was followed by an ecumenical weekend in Melbourne, organised by lay people impatient at what they perceived as
hierarchical and clerical reluctance to move towards closer unity. At
the end of January, I was free to learn something of aboriginal spirituality until early May, when I was due to go to South Africa.

CHAPTER 14

↜⟨᠋᠍᠍᠍᠍᠍⟩↝

God of
'The Irreligious'

'See sky and sun, see tree and flowers, birds and insects, you, me?
We all one.' (Conversation with Hector, an Aboriginal from Turkey Creek)

I HAD HOPED to be living in the Aboriginal community at Balgo, in
the north-western Australian desert at the beginning of February
1994, but Brian McCoy, one of the two Jesuits living there, advised
against arrival before March, as the heat would be intolerable. Unfortunately, the rainy season began in March, making access to Balgo
by road impossible.

I spent February in the Jesuit house of theology in Melbourne which
was, in fact, a series of terraced houses, six people in each one, an
arrangement which fostered a closer community life and avoided the
dangers inherent in large institutions. The Jesuits were part of a
larger ecumenical faculty, with shared lectures and courses. The
Jesuit community itself included priests and brothers engaged in
other apostolates, working with refugees, street children, the homeless, and some members of the theology faculty lived in nearby
parishes, so that there was a wealth of experience in the house. On
Sunday afternoons, the large garden behind the houses was usually
filled with different groups of refugees from Vietnam, Cambodia, or
Thailand. They would have Mass together in their own language,
followed by a meal. It was a most welcoming and interesting house
in which to live.

I visited the Catholic bookshop in Melbourne in search of books
on Aboriginal spirituality, but they had none. There was a large selec-
tion of European and American publications, including those of

Darton, Longman and Todd, who had published three of mine, though none was included on the well-stocked shelves. I asked the manager whether he stocked a book called *God of Surprises*. He paused, then said, 'Oh yes, I know the book. It's by Sheila Cassidy, isn't it?'

There is a Catholic Aboriginal Centre in Melbourne with a good library, where I met up again with a number of people, including Vicki Walker, who had presented the workshop at the Catholic Education Conference in Melbourne eight months before.

Besides reading what I could of Aboriginal spirituality, I found the month in Melbourne also gave me time to reflect on the spirituality work in which I was engaged; reflection which was stimulated by the comment of one elderly and forthright Jesuit who, after years of work in retreat houses, announced, 'Personally, I would not put a spirituality person in charge of a piss pot!'

There are many dangers inherent in spirituality work. Like religion in general, it can easily become insulated from ordinary life. In spirituality the insulation is like a mystical foam in which its practitioners can be safely cocooned, mystifying non-practitioners and robbing them of any self-confidence in spiritual matters. They therefore assume the guru knows best and obey unquestioningly. This can give the gurus illusions of grandeur, inflating their egos with compressed flattery. I have rarely encountered full-blown examples, but it is a risk for all who work in spirituality. We need frequent exposure to the messy side of life, some part-time activity which exposes us to the equivalent of piss-pot management, and strong doses of the grace for which Ignatius prayed, of 'bearing, insults, injury and abuse'.

More subtle and pervasive than flattery is the modern tendency to confuse holiness with what is called 'wholeness', so that spiritual growth becomes a preoccupation with one's own development and calls itself 'holistic spirituality'. This is a potential trap for both practitioner and client. We all want to be whole, but the search for wholeness can become totally self-centred, a kind of narcissism, leading to spiritual blindness, because the soul cannot see beyond its own narrow notion of wholeness. The temptation is subtle, because without a love of self there can be no love of others. The healing of memories and of life's hurts are both necessary for spiritual health, as is a sense of our own worth. The narcissistic danger is that we never progress beyond these needs. Holiness demands the eventual dismantling of our ideas on wholeness. The people I have met, who seemed holy, were neither models of wholeness themselves, nor preoccupied with their own development.

Aboriginal spirituality is not a subject which preoccupies most white Australians. I was presented with a best-selling book, *Reinventing Australia* by Hugh Mackay. The back cover included the sentence, 'Because we are living through an Age of Redefinition, many of us are suffering from the anxiety, stress and insecurity which are the inevitable consequences of having to adjust to such radical social, cultural and economic upheaval. The question is: how will we cope?' In over 300 pages, the Aboriginal peoples are granted only one short paragraph, which ends, 'Aborigines throughout the 1970s and 1980s clearly positioned themselves at the bottom of the heap, and reinforced the general view that, if there were a lower class in Australia at that time, then it was populated by the homeless, the unemployed and the dispossessed. Aboriginal peoples were seen as the quintessential symbol of that state.' The author evidently did not share the view expressed in *The Tablet* article, which had first aroused my interest in 1992, namely that salvation would come to the Australian nation through the Aborigines.

No one knows how many Aborigines inhabited Australia when Captain Arthur Philip founded the first convict settlement at Sydney in 1788, but it is reckoned there were about a million, with over 200 different languages among them. By the end of the eighteenth century they were heading for extinction, although they had existed in Australia for at least 40,000 – some claim 100,000 – years, living as hunters and gatherers, and in such harmony with their environment that they had no permanent buildings, nor did they wear clothes. They had no written language, although some of their art has survived on rocks and in caves. However, all their painting was part of religious ceremonial, so in most cases their canvas was the desert sand, and not designed to last longer than their dreamtime celebration.

Until the white settlers arrived, the Aborigines had no notion of private property, which could only be an encumbrance to those who are constantly on the move. Nor did they have our understanding of person. We think of ourselves as individuals, absorbed in our need for self-development and self-advantage. Aboriginal people do not think in this limited way. As one of their poets, Bill Neidje, has put it:

> Listen carefully, careful
> and this spirit e come into your feeling
> and you will feel it . . . anyone that.
> I feel it . . . my body same as you.
> I telling you this because the land for us,
> never change round, never change.
> Places for us, earth for us,
> star, moon, tree, animal
> no matter what sort of an animal, bird or snake . . .
> all that animal same like us. Our friend that.

The Aboriginal people not only do not share our idea of person and of private property; they do not share our idea of time. Their geographical surroundings tell them the story of creation, which is not a past event, but a present happening. Their landscape tells the story of the creating spirits, still at work in their surroundings and in all who dwell in them. Therefore, it is important to live in harmony with these creating spirits, and the purpose of Aboriginal Law is to instruct the people in this harmony. When the white settlers arrived, confiscating their land, desecrating their sacred sites, disrupting their existence as hunters and gatherers, that harmony was broken and the Aboriginal people, too, were broken. In the last century they were in danger of becoming extinct and many Christian missionaries thought that all they could do for them was 'to smooth their pillows' before death. It was not until the 1970s that they were accorded civil rights, and it was only in the 1990s that their right to their traditional lands was legally recognised. Frank Brennan, a Jesuit and a lawyer, was the main advocate of this recognition. Previously, all land in Australia not already occupied by the settlers was called '*Terra Nullius*', 'nobody's land'.

At the beginning of March 1994, I set out from Melbourne for Balgo, hoping to complete the journey in twenty-four hours, flying first to Alice Springs and proceeding from there by bus and plane. In fact, because of flooding, the journey north to Balgo took a fortnight, for I had to wait for several days at Alice Springs, and another few days at Katherine, 650 miles further north, for the floods to subside. Instead, they rose steadily. Eventually I went to Darwin by bus, then on to Balgo by plane, car and another small plane, arriving on March 14th. During the fortnight en route, I saw plenty of evidence of the brokenness of the Aboriginal people who were sitting in small groups with their cans of beer and boxes of wine, or else begging in the streets of Alice Springs, built to cater for the wealthy tourist. Off the tourist route I visited some Aboriginal settlements, enclosed areas under Aboriginal control, where alcohol was banned. The tourist does not realise that many of the Aborigines to be seen drinking in the streets have been expelled from their own communities, yet they are taken as representative of the whole people. An Aboriginal visiting London's Embankment area might make the same judgement of all British people.

Aboriginal art shops were one of Alice Springs' few compensations. In one, I met a charming Irishman who spent part of every year travelling into the desert in search of Aboriginal artists. He claimed to have learned more about spirituality from this work than from his Catholic upbringing. The Catholic churches I visited on the way to Balgo showed little sign of Aboriginal influence. Much more evident were the messages from visionaries of Medjugorje, Fatima and Garabandal, and the sayings of Pope John Paul II. The liturgies I attended seemed untouched by Aboriginal thought and culture.

Balgo lies at the heart of the most arid region of Australia, about 200 miles from the nearest metalled road, its dirt roads making it inaccessible during the rainy season. Like many of the present Aboriginal settlements, it had been a Christian mission station, in this case, Catholic. At first the mission had been situated about 40 miles from the present site and was founded by two remarkable German Pallotine missionaries, Brother Frank Nissl and Fr Alphonse. They chose such a remote spot because they were under threat of internment as enemy aliens at the beginning of the Second World War. I visited the ruins of this former mission, the shells of its school, hospital, church tower and bakery still standing. The mission had to move to its present site in the early Sixties because of a land claim. It was not 'Terra Nullius', but belonged to a white farmer. For many years the new mission at the present Balgo was simply a school for Aboriginal children. In accordance with Government policy, children were taken from their families, sometimes forcibly, and educated to become proper Australians, uncorrupted by family influences! In Balgo, the parents came and camped close to the mission to be near their children, whom they were only allowed to visit on Sundays!

Balgo now has a population of about 400, with three smaller satellite settlements within a 40 mile radius, all under Aboriginal control. The landscape is majestic, with its escarpments and red desert, which blooms in the rainy season: the settlement itself is sordid, littered with rubbish, wrecked cars and other debris. Most of the Aborigines are unemployed, receiving what they call 'sit-about money'. There are lots of children, but few men between the ages of eighteen and thirty. Most within this age group either have moved to the cities, or are in prison, or have committed suicide, or have died in detention. Alcohol is banned, but it is still smuggled in from the nearest town, about 250 miles away, causing havoc, especially in family violence, the women being the most vulnerable. There is a school, medical clinic, art centre, adult education centre, as well as basket-ball and football pitches, which were floodlit until the lighting was vandalised. Although the settlement is under Aboriginal control, the teachers, nurses, social workers and engineers are almost all white, with a few Aboriginal assistants. The whites live in buildings protected by wire fences and set apart from the Aboriginal homes.

I was impressed by the dedication of the nurses and teachers whom I met, battling against the apparent hopelessness of the situation. The Aboriginal people have been disgracefully treated in the past, but every step taken to try to remedy the situation creates further problems. When they were recognised as citizens, and therefore entitled to a wage if employed, or to social security if they were not, most of them became unemployed. Their white farmer employers had provided them with food and land on which to camp, but they were not paid full wages. When the farmers were forced to pay full wages, they dismissed them from their land. As there is little *'Terra Nullius'* left, the Aboriginals congregated in settlements where they received 'sit-about money', which keeps them alive but leaves them demoralised, especially the men.

In 1798, David Collins wrote in *An Account of the English Colony in New South Wales*, 'It has been observed by an eminent divine that no country has yet been discovered where some trace of religion was not to be found. From every observation and inquiry that I could make among the people, from the first to the last of my acquaintance with them, I can safely pronounce them (the Aborigines) an exception to this opinion.' And the opinion that the Aborigines were religionless persisted for years. A modern anthropologist has stated that they are probably the most religious people who have ever lived. The problem is not Aboriginal atheism, but our difficulty in understanding the complexity of their thought. Also, they are reluctant to reveal their thinking to strangers. One missioner, who had worked with them for over thirty years, told me, 'When you have been with them for twenty-five years, you are likely to get an answer to your questions.'

Because the Aboriginal way of living and of seeing reality is so different from our own, it is not surprising that some Christian missionaries have doubted whether Aborigines can ever become true Christians. Being a nation of hunters and gatherers, they could accept Christianity as many of the poor in Britain would, for example, accept the ministrations of The Salvation Army, ready to sing hymns fervently in exchange for a meal and a bed. When one mission station was running out of funds, the Aborigines stopped coming to church. On being reproached for his absence, one man gave the succinct answer, 'No tobacco, no alleluia!' Near Balgo there was one evangelical minister whose method was disastrously simple. He worked on Aboriginal fears of the spirit world, assuring them that they would all be damned unless they renounced their own beliefs and customs and accepted 'The Lord Jesus'. He had a large following!

While at Balgo, I visited Turkey Creek, about 300 miles north, where Sr Clare Ahern, whose thesis I had read in Dublin, had worked for many years and founded an Aboriginal Spirituality Centre. There I met Hector, an elderly Aboriginal artist, learned in Aboriginal Law. He told me about his youth, spent working on farms, where they were kicked, beaten, and given very little to eat by their white employers. He also told me the story of 'Mistake Creek', a place only a few miles from where we were sitting. In the 1940s, a farmer lost a cow. Suspecting it had been stolen by the Aborigines, the farmer, with two of his Aboriginal stockmen, rounded up thirty men, women and children, killed them and burned their bodies. Next day the cow reappeared. The police were called. They shot the two stockmen and warned the white farmer to clear out of the area. I asked Hector how he coped with this trauma and whether he did not feel great bitterness. He claimed to feel no bitterness, no hatred, and said that what had sustained him was his Aboriginal way of seeing the world. We were sitting in a garden at the time. He turned to me and said, 'See sky and sun, see tree and flowers, birds and insects, you, me? We all one.' Yes, I believe God is in all things, but listening to Hector's story I saw the shallowness of my own belief.

The church at Balgo was a beautifully constructed building with shell-fish fossils embedded in some of its stones, reminders that this inland desert had once formed an ocean-bed. The walls were hung with Aboriginal paintings on Christian themes, presented by the artists. Sunday services were rarely well attended, despite the attractiveness of the church and the attempts by Brian and Robin to speak the native language in the prayers, readings and songs, and to preach not from a text, but from one of the many paintings. On weekday evenings there was a Mass attended mostly by the white Catholics working in the school or the clinic, but a few Aboriginal children always joined us. If they were too young to receive Holy Communion, they always came up for a blessing.

Holy Week at Balgo was the most liturgically chaotic and spiritually moving I have ever experienced. For weeks beforehand, Brian and Robin had been preparing the church leaders, of whom there were many in Balgo and the outlying settlements, consulting them about the form the ceremonies should take and encouraging them to produce paintings. All the services were held in the open, outside the south wall of the church. Aboriginal people are more at home in the open air than inside buildings.

On Palm Sunday, I was taken to one of the satellite stations for the evening Mass. As darkness fell, we proceeded with our palms to a hilltop where Mass was celebrated. I was walking with a group of Aboriginal children to whom I had been introduced. At one point, I stumbled on a stone. A seven-year-old child, called Deone, took me by the hand and led me to the hilltop, herself barefoot. Her gesture became for me a symbol of my time at Balgo. These people, labelled primitive, the underclass, broken and despised, were leading me to a place from which I could have a better view of God. As we were leaving after the ceremony, we saw a large group sitting motionless under the starlit sky, all watching an American soap opera. Electricity had been installed only a few months earlier and now it was drawing this desert people, who had lived for thousands of years at one with earth and sky, into the shadowlands of American soap, perhaps doing more lasting and devastating damage than the early white settlers had ever inflicted.

Almost everyone in Balgo attended the Holy Week services, which were held in the open air, and large numbers came in trucks from the surrounding areas. The trucks formed a half circle around the chapel's south wall. The congregation sat on the ground, including a large number of children and an even greater number of mangy dogs. Every household seemed to possess several dogs, which served a double purpose: they provide warmth – a cold night is called a two-dingo night – and they also detect and ward off evil spirits. During the ceremonies, dogs and children roamed free. Aboriginal people tend not to discipline their children until they are twelve years old, when boys undergo a most severe initiation ceremony. Once initiated, they belong no longer to their family, but to their group. Before the initiation ceremony, mothers mourn the loss of their sons for two days. The girls can be given away in marriage from the age of thirteen, usually to much older men. During the long ceremonies the dogs and children fought and played, which did not seem to disturb the adults. During the Easter Vigil service, I saw two children sitting together, both in nappies, one of them passing the time by hitting the other on the head with an empty plastic cola bottle.

On Good Friday morning the ceremony of the Stations of the Cross was scheduled for nine o'clock and began just before ten, which was prompt by Balgo standards. Instead of the usual fourteen stations there were only four, each taking place outside one of the houses. The front of each house had been carefully swept and displayed a painting, commissioned for the occasion, illustrating one of the scenes of Jesus' journey to Calvary. Each picture was decorated with flowers and candles. At each station, one of the Aborigines would explain the picture and then lead the prayers. Large numbers attended this service, accompanied by their dogs, but this time there was an addition. One of the women had a kestrel on her shoulder, which kept its perch whether she was sitting, standing or walking. The ceremony lasted one-and-a-half hours, with many dogfights taking place between stations, but no one seemed unduly disturbed. Walking between the stations with these Aboriginal people was a most moving experience, for it symbolised the reality of their own passion in the last two hundred years as victims of the authority of Church and State. Caiaphas had said, 'It is expedient that one man should die for the people.' His words echoed in Australian history. 'It is expedient that the Aborigines should be driven off their land so that it can be mined and its wealth extracted, so that it can be profitably farmed. It is expedient that Aboriginal children should be taken from their families and educated free from corrupting influences.' Apart from the occasional yelping of dogs, there was a deep silence as they walked their own and Jesus' way to Calvary.

On Good Friday evening there was a three-hour service, attended by almost everyone in Balgo and by many from outlying areas. Although Fr Brian McCoy was the celebrant, he played a very minor role. In Balgo and the outlying districts, church leaders were appointed from among the Aboriginal people, and for the Holy Week services they stood around the altar with enormous and colourful stoles draped over their shoulders. The passion account was given through Aboriginal paintings. After the passion story in Catholic churches, there is a Veneration of the Cross, when the congregation come up and kiss the foot of the crucifix. In Balgo, the church leaders congregated on one side of a large cross, and laid their hands and prayed over anyone who came to venerate it. I had never before experienced the wonder of God's forgiveness as I then felt it as I stood with these Aboriginal hands on my head and shoulders while they prayed over me. These people who had suffered, and continued to suffer so severely from exploitation by the whites, were reaching out in a gesture of forgiveness. The Veneration of the Cross was followed by a smoking ceremony when all who wanted to be purified, which included almost the whole congregation, passed through a gauntlet of smouldering branches. At the end of the service the Cross was carried into the church and the floor outside the church was carefully swept, just as they sweep a house after someone has died.

As Robin and Brian had spent many hours preparing the church leaders for each ceremony, they felt there was no need for another meeting before the Easter Vigil service on Holy Saturday evening, but the church leaders nevertheless appeared early on Saturday morning, demanding another meeting.

The Easter Vigil service begins with the blessing of fire, symbol of Christ's resurrection. The Paschal candle, symbol of Christ, light of the world, is lit from this fire and carried in procession into the church. In Balgo, the ceremony began with a fire dance performed by two elderly men and four small children, their legs and arms garlanded with laurel wreaths. As they danced, stamping the ground with their feet, the flames leaped higher from the burning branches. The Paschal candle was in the form of a message stick, the Aboriginal method of communication between different tribes. The history of salvation from creation until the present was told through another set of pictures hanging from the church wall. This was followed by a lengthy blessing of all the church leaders, followed by an even lengthier blessing by these leaders of those who were to become leaders. Then the twenty-six adults and children who were to be baptised, and the four adults who were already baptised but were asking to be received into the Catholic Church, were prayed over. When the baptisms were finished, all the adults were invited to speak, which many did at length. The whole congregation was then invited to contribute to the prayers of intercession and proved tireless in their demands of God!

During this lengthy ceremony I often looked up at the clear night sky and felt the mysterious joy of Easter seep into me, bringing with it the knowledge that God is in every human being, in every movement of our devious minds and hearts and in every human tragedy, drawing us out of death into life. Sitting in the congregation was one particular Aboriginal couple. That morning the wife had appeared at the clinic, so badly beaten by her husband that they thought she might have to be flown to hospital. That evening husband and wife were sitting together, reconciled.

A few days after Easter, I was in the art centre, a large hut, where canvasses were hung and stored ready for inspection by art dealers who would occasionally fly in from Melbourne or Sydney. The art centre also served as a social centre where the people met and children played. On this occasion there was a fierce row going on between one of the Aboriginal women, Bridget, and the deputy director of the centre. Bridget was demanding a further advance on a picture which she had not yet completed. The deputy director was refusing. Eventually, Bridget, with ill grace, sat down on the floor, unrolled her canvas and began to paint. Two days later, two small planes flew out of Balgo bearing Bridget's sons and grandsons to a football match 300 miles away. Bridget had completed her picture and the money earned paid the plane fares! In spite of white influence, Aborigines are still unaccustomed to the notion of private property: what they earn belongs to the family or the group. In the Balgo region there are over 200 registered artists, none of whom have ever graced an art school. Some of them can earn fairly large sums of money quite suddenly, enough to enable them buy a second-hand car. This quickly becomes common property, which accounts for the large number of wrecked cars around.

It is only in recent years that acrylics have become available to Aboriginal artists, who formerly worked with only four basic colours. Their wonderful sense of colour, expressed in their acrylic paintings, now attracts worldwide attention. To the Aboriginal artist, the colouring is of very minor importance. Their paintings are expressions of their inner mind, of their way of seeing reality, and they are always centred on the dreamtime, the celebration of creation, which is timeless. Their paintings, like icons, contain many layers of meaning. It will include their landscape and stories of the creating spirits who formed it. But there are other layers of meaning, some only to be understood by those initiated in dreamtime rites. Many of the older Aborigines are not happy about the sale of Aboriginal paintings, fearing that their exposure to non-Aboriginal people could do harm. It is as though their paintings are extensions of themselves, so that they render themselves personally vulnerable to any who look on the paintings.

On April 24th, I left Balgo after Mass, strengthened by a final blessing from the church leaders. I spent a few days in Darwin, and a weekend in Perth, before flying to Johannesburg, just as the results of the first democratic South African elections were being announced. The elections had been peaceful, in spite of the crises and killings beforehand, caused by clashes between the ANC and Chief Buthelezi's Inkatha party supported by white security forces. I heard and read many stories of the delight among the people, black and white, as they queued to vote together for the first time in their lives. Waiting in queues for many hours was not a problem for the blacks who had been waiting for this moment for centuries. Even the police, I was told, looked happy and relieved to be doing their job of protecting the people, instead of attacking the black majority. Johannesburg was a city transformed. Formerly a white preserve, with the blacks confined to menial tasks by day and forced back into the townships at night, the streets were now thronging with blacks, many setting up their stalls on the streets and selling fruit outside expensive supermarkets.

There were some gloomy predictions of economic disaster under ANC rule, of the withdrawal of big business, of the likely outbreak of uncontrollable violence. The South African economy was already precarious. The problems of education, unemployment, homelessness and health care were formidable and, to judge from statistics, insuperable, but these gloomy predictions omitted to mention the extraordinary spiritual resilience of black South Africans. Centuries of oppression and poverty have engendered a spirit of endurance. Freedom is much more precious to them than economic security.

In Johannesburg, I again met up with Bishop Graham Chadwick and his wife, Suzanne, with Sr Mary Rose Fitzimmons, Sr Madeleine Prendergast and Isabel Gregory. We were to give a two-week, Llysfasi-type workshop at the Good Shepherd Convent in Hartebeespoort, a most beautiful place not far from Pretoria. There were forty participants, of whom half were black. For most of them, it was the first time they had ever met together on a basis of equality, and for many it was their first meeting with Christians of other denominations. The course is so constructed that participants spend much time simply listening to one another, avoiding discussion or argument. The team's initial nervousness was soon dispelled by the extraordinary community sense that quickly developed. This was especially apparent in the daily celebration of the Eucharist. The blacks did not need hymn sheets or musical scores. They sang spontaneously, harmonising naturally: and occasionally they would begin to dance. Our only problem lay in ensuring that the kitchen staff were not kept waiting too long to serve the meal which followed.

During the workshop, Nelson Mandela was installed as President of the new South Africa. We cancelled our morning programme so that all could watch the ceremony on TV and the excitement could not have been greater had we all been at the ceremony itself. The black viewers clapped, trilled, danced and sang. As the South African Air Force performed a fly-past, they pointed with excitement, crying, 'They're ours'.

The hurts of centuries cannot be healed in a two-week workshop, but at least the healing can start, and the blacks have an extraordinary gift of forgiveness, personified in Nelson Mandela, whose gentleness and courtesy have won over some of the most intransigent white supremacists.

It was a wonderful coincidence that we were engaged in giving a workshop based on Ignatius' Spiritual Exercises at such a historic moment in the history of South Africa. The collapse of apartheid was a triumph of the Spirit. The causes for this sudden change from white minority rule to full democracy are complex, but underlying all the causes is the power of the Spirit, who sustained the blacks in their struggle and afflicted the consciences of the white world. It is significant that all the South African freedom and protest songs are scripture-based. The workshop at Hartebeespoort provided a glimpse of what is possible when black and white Christians of different denominations meet together in the Spirit. In theological language, the workshop was an eschatological sign, that is, a sign of our future state when 'all things will be reconciled through Christ and for Christ, everything in heaven and everything on earth' (St Paul, Colossians c. 1).

When the workshop finished, we had a week off before beginning a different type of course in Cape Town. The Hartebeespoort course was for those who had already experienced an individually given retreat. The Cape Town course was open to anyone interested in spirituality; it was non-residential, and held on five evenings, beginning on a Sunday, but with one full day, which was a bank holiday. Between workshops, Graham had organised a trip by minibus from Johannesburg to Cape Town, via his former diocese of Kimberley, including an overnight stay at a game reserve.

On May 24th, after overwhelming hospitality in Kimberley, where the people showed their gratitude to Graham and Suzanne for all they had done for them in the apartheid days, we left for the game reserve, a long drive, much of it on a dirt road. I was driving, with Graham next to me, and we were the only passengers wearing safety belts. Mary Rose, Madeleine and Isabel were in the seat behind, and Suzanne was in the back seat with all our heavy luggage behind her. As we came round a slight bend I felt the car go out of control, as though sliding on an icy road. For a few hundred yards we slithered from side to side, then slewed to the left into a shallow sand ditch where the van went over on its side, then righted itself, facing the opposite direction.

Suzanne was the most seriously injured, being thrown out of the rear window along with the luggage and suffering, as we discovered later, a badly fractured pelvis. Mary Rose, Madeleine and Isabel were badly thrown about, and suffered whiplash, bruising and minor scratches. Graham and I were physically unhurt. A passing motorist took me to the nearest town, about six miles away, and the police and a nurse arrived within an hour. The police examined the car's tracks and discovered the skid mark 400 yards further back where a tyre, possibly both tyres, had blown. It was another two hours before the ambulance arrived to take Suzanne to hospital in Kimberley, where she was to remain for three months before she was fit to return to the UK. Graham accompanied Suzanne, and the rest of us were taken to Kuruman, where Madeleine, Mary Rose and Isabel were X-rayed, and Madeleine detained overnight, as her whiplash was more severe. Fortunately, there was a motel just opposite the hospital where we were able to find rooms.

The mind's ability to insulate events one from another is both a curse and a blessing. It is a curse in that it enables us to live content-edly with a split spirituality, worshipping religiously but acting inhumanly. It is a blessing in that it enables us to act in an emergency without disintegrating. In the three-hour wait for the ambulance and during the subsequent months, I was grateful for the mind's defences for, as T. S. Eliot wrote, 'humankind cannot bear very much reality'. At first, the shock of the accident penetrated only the surface of my consciousness, producing a flow of adrenalin which enabled me to make the practical arrangements. The flow continued until evening when I could neither eat nor sleep, as the horror of what had hap-pened began to seep into my consciousness. The phrase 'You were responsible' hammered insistently on my mind. Eventually I was driven to do something which was of lasting help. I faced into 'You were driving', into fears about Suzanne's survival and into the damage that had been done to the others. With Christ present as I did so, I begged to see the truth of the matter and not run away from my own sense of guilt. I cannot explain clearly what then happened. I had no sudden enlightenment, but I did feel an assurance that all would be well, and managed to sleep.

The aftermath of the accident taught me more about levels of consciousness, for the night of the accident did not put an end to the trauma. The memory kept recurring, and each time it had to be faced again, as though for the first time, but with diminishing inten-sity. This has helped me to understand more clearly that Gospel passage in which Peter asked Jesus, 'How many times do I have to forgive my brother? As many as seven times?' And Jesus answers, 'Not seven times, but seventy times seven times.' I had always found this passage difficult, because if the brother is forgiven for one offence, and follows it up with another 489, then forgiveness does not seem a very effective way of coping with him. I now understand the text differently. The brother may offend me only once, but I may have to forgive 490 times, as the magnitude of his offence, whether real or imagined, sinks down into deeper layers of my consciousness. Similarly, guilt for our own sins and offences has to be confronted at each level of descent into our consciousness, even if there are 490 different levels, otherwise it will infect the whole psyche.

On Sunday, May 30th, we were due to begin the one-week course in Cape Town. I was in favour of cancelling it, but Mary Rose and Isabel, both moving with difficulty because of bruising and whiplash, were in favour of continuing. Madeleine was so badly affected that she could not stand for long. On Friday, May 28th, we travelled by car to Kimberley where I was able to visit Suzanne in hospital, relieved to find her in good form in spite of the pain and enforced immobility. Next day we flew to Cape Town where we were magnificently lodged in the chaplain's house of Archbishop Desmond Tutu's residence.

The course began on Sunday evening with 130 participants, of whom only one was black. A physiotherapist, who attended Mary Rose and Isabel, forbade them to continue after Tuesday, so I finished the course on my own. Each evening after the session I used to walk for an hour in the wooded grounds of the archbishop's residence, which lies at the foot of Table Mountain, looking at the night sky. I would remember the Aboriginal Hector's words that we are all one, which helped me to see the trauma of the accident and the stress of finishing the course on my own in a wider perspective. The truth of 'in God we live and move and have our being' was reaching down to deeper levels of consciousness.

During the course itself, participants began to admit to themselves the fears which lay below the surface of their relief that apartheid had ended, and they were encouraged to bring these fears into prayer and to share them with one another. The effect of this openness was to increase their joy at the ending of apartheid.

A year later, in September 1995, I was back in South Africa with a recovered Madeleine and with Lister Tonge, giving another two-week course at Hartebeespoort to the thirty-eight people who had been unable to come in May 1994. Again we had a very good mixture of races and of Christian denominations, and this time we had three of the participants from the previous course now acting as team members. Their effectiveness was very encouraging, for we knew that South Africans could now continue this method of training using their own resources. After the workshop, we then moved to Soweto with about half the participants, so that they could give a retreat in daily life to the parishioners of St Martin de Porres in Orlando West. About forty made this retreat, including a few Methodists and Anglicans, and there are plans to repeat and spread this work in Soweto.

In mid June 1994, I returned to Britain, with the pleasant prospect of a few months of relative quiet living in Edith's flat in Wemyss Bay, where I would be free to start writing.

CHAPTER 15

୧ଚ୨ଚ୬

God Whose Answer Echoes Down the Arches of the Years

And what the dead had no speech for, when living,
They can tell you, being dead: the communication
Of the dead is tongued with fire beyond the language of the living.

(T. S. Eliot, 'Little Gidding', Four Quartets)

OUR CONSCIOUSNESS, with all its thoughts, feelings, emotions and memories, can be compared to a large symphony orchestra, new instruments and themes being introduced with every event we experience. Some events become a dominant theme, which may enhance the harmony, or cause dissonance. In this final chapter I shall recall some recent events which have for me resolved some of the earlier dissonances. The underlying theme of this symphony is one of my earliest memories, of sitting on the edge of the bed at the age of three and saying 'God', because I wanted to see what would happen.

The symphony will continue until death, with further dissonance and further resolution. What I now write is reflection on my own experience in light of my own Christian, Catholic and Jesuit upbringing. I know that many Christians, Catholics, and even some Jesuits will not agree with my present conclusions: it would make very dull reading if they did. If there is any value in what I write, it is not in the answers I offer, but in the questions experience has raised, for the questions are common to us all.

The death of my own father when I was seven, of Marie, of my mother, and then of Margot, had become dominant themes in my life, affecting everything.

On Good Friday 1992, my sister Edith had a severe stroke and died two months later. In January 1993, my younger brother, Joe, died of a heart attack. In October 1993, Ursula Burton died of cancer. In February 1994, my elder brother, Ian, the last surviving member of my family, died in his sleep.

'Death, where is thy sting?' St Paul asks. I had never experienced death as a sting: it was much more devastating; as though a plug had been removed from the base of my psyche draining away all physical and spiritual energy, leaving only an inner void, 'a strange and innermost collapse of all that makes me man'. Yet recently, when I experienced so much loss within two years, although I felt an initial sadness, the inner void soon filled with a sense of peace and of the life-giving presence of the dead. It was not only my attitude to death which had changed, but to life, too. The change was not sudden: it had been going on for years. It was my friendship with Ursula Burton and the travel abroad, especially in Balgo, which clarified the process.

While I was living on the Isle of Skye in 1984, Ursula Burton had invited me to give a retreat at Moniack Castle, near Inverness, home of her friend from childhood, Philippa Fraser. Among those attending the retreat were Ursula's daughter, Vicky, and her husband, Angus. On the last evening of the retreat I was walking with Vicky and Angus when we met a straying herd of cattle. We chased them back into the field from which they had come, Vicky showing a good turn of speed in the chase. A few days later she had to go into hospital for a minor operation. I had returned to Skye when I heard that Vicky had not recovered consciousness. She remained unconscious and totally paralysed for almost two years in Edinburgh Royal Infirmary. Ursula visited her daily, bringing flowers and tapes of her favourite music, convinced that Vicky was aware in spite of her immobile, unconscious state. I visited her on several occasions. At the end of a visit Ursula would comment on Vicky's state, 'She is struggling today' or 'She is much more peaceful today'. I could observe no change.

Vicky's paralysed condition was more distressing than death for those close to her, for her colour was healthy, her eyes open but without movement, and the family knew that there could be no recovery. Yet there was always a feeling of peace in her room, which the nurses also experienced. Ursula grieved over her, but beneath the grief she had an inner assurance that Vicky, although unconscious and immobile, was still active, an activity which was not confined within the limitations of her physical body. I was glad, for her sake, that she had this inner assurance, but I did not share it.

Ursula was very intuitive and had healing gifts, about which she was both reticent and wary. I used to drive her to the limits of her great patience by constantly asking her to express her ideas more clearly and coherently, requests which would end in her declaring that I would never understand as I was far too rational. I still believe that our rationality is a God-given gift which we ignore at our peril, but our conversations made me more aware of the limitations of reason.

St Anselm said, 'Faith seeks understanding'. Intuition, too, must seek understanding. Although I often disagreed with Ursula's reasoning, or lack of it, I respected her intuitive gifts. She confirmed for me something I had read years before in a theological periodical. The author claimed that the function of theology is not to answer questions, but to keep questions open for further exploration. Heresy, he described as closing questions, giving definitive answers requiring no further exploration. Heresy leads us down cul-de-sacs: orthodoxy keeps pointing us to the road ahead. It is ironic that it is the fundamentalists in any religion who claim to be the truly orthodox, but who are also the most enamoured of cul-de-sacs!

Ursula's notion of the human soul was that it was not only coterminous with all creation, but also beyond it, because anchored in God. She therefore did not see Vicky as locked within her paralysed body. For Ursula, this was an intuitive knowing. I have heard other people, who have had near-death experiences, say that they could remember looking down on themselves lying on the bed and hearing the conversation of the onlookers. After Vicky died, Ursula had many experiences of her presence and later wrote *A Bridge between Two Worlds*, an account of Vicky's illness and death.

Ursula's intuitions battered on my rational mind. I was fascinated when I read some books on modern nuclear physics, and in particular by the comment of one physicist addressing the question of the ultimate particles of matter, who stated that 'there are no ultimate particles. Within every particle exists every other particle'. Some nuclear physicists lapse into the language of the mystics.

'In God we live, and move and have our being.' In Christian understanding, there are three persons in one God, so united that each one shares totally with the other two. The Divine Persons are essentially relations, as distinct from being Persons who relate. We are made in the image of God. Essentially, we too are, insofar as we are in relationship with the rest of creation. Our personality is not something we possess and with which we then relate to other people and things: personality is something we discover through our relationships and is itself a relationship. Ursula's notion of the soul being coterminous with all creation, and reaching beyond, was not as outlandish as I had at first thought.

When studying theology, I found the Doctrine of the Trinity the most difficult, boring, and irrelevant to everyday life. Now it seems to me most exciting and relevant. All doctrines are imperfect expressions of something intuited, they are examples of faith seeking understanding. When the understanding tries to operate without the intuition, its formulations become sterile. In light of the Doctrine of the Trinity, I began to see more clearly the damage done by our Western over-emphasis on the individual, with its pursuit of individual development at the expense of the communal. In spirituality this over-emphasis on the individual leads to spiritual narcissism, the cultivation of deep egocentricity, which can lead to most inhuman behaviour. In social life it leads, among other things, to the exaltation of market forces, the new god of competitiveness, before which all life must be immolated. Ursula's intuitions, which at first I had found incomprehensible, were beginning to make sense.

A few years after Vicky's death, Ursula rang me one evening to say that she had just been told she had to have urgent surgery on another cancerous growth. Eight years previously, when she had first applied for the St Beuno's three-month course, a diagnosed growth had disappeared. Having delivered this bombshell, she went on to describe the extraordinary beauty of Edinburgh's Botanic Gardens, where she had walked after receiving the news. Had I received the same news, I should probably have walked through the beautiful gardens seeing nothing but stretchers, operating theatres and tombstones. Three years later in Australia, as I sat with Hector in Turkey Creek listening to his understanding of the world around him, I was reminded of Ursula's description of the Botanic Gardens. Because Hector saw himself as at one with everything and everyone else in creation, he had therefore been able to survive the cruelty of his white employers without bitterness or resentment. Because Ursula lived with a permanent awareness of the limitations of her own consciousness, and with an intuitive knowing that she was caught up in something much greater, she had therefore the inner freedom to look up and delight in the beauty of the Botanic Gardens in spring, while still knowing that death was probably close.

A year after her cancer operation she was returning to her cottage at Kilmuir, near Inverness, when she felt a sudden stab of pain. At the moment of pain she was looking at a broken-down barn, known as the Coach House, a solid building inhabited by pigeons and used for storing hay. That evening she had decided to put all the money she could gather into the purchase of the Coach House, to convert it into a retreat house, open to anyone who might like to come. Two years later, in 1992, the Coach House was opened, a beautiful conversion providing five bedrooms, all looking out across the Moray Firth, two meeting rooms, and a large attic prayer room.

Ursula's health deteriorated, and in summer 1993 she phoned to tell me that she had been given three months to live. She was momentarily shaken by the news, but was soon busy organising a family reunion for her birthday, to be celebrated in the Coach House. She joined in the dancing, which was medical folly, but she had no regrets, even when severe pain followed.

Before I left for New Zealand in September 1993, I went to stay with her in Kilmuir. I had to drive her down to Edinburgh one day to see her consultant, meaning to return with her that evening, but she was too weak, and never returned. When she had the energy, she loved to talk. On one occasion I asked her, 'Tell me honestly, do you really feel peaceful?' There was slight indignation in her reply. 'I not only feel peaceful, I feel positively joyful.' She went on to say that she did not want 'May she rest in peace' to be inscribed on her tombstone. 'I have no intention of resting in peace. I look forward to the next stage when I shall be much more free to do what I really want to do: to change attitudes towards death, so that instead of making us fearful, the thought of death should help us to relish life more.'

One afternoon when she had returned to Edinburgh, she insisted on going to a nearby park, even though managing the stairs from her flat caused her agony. Her joy at the prospect of death was not a dislike of life. She had suffered traumas in life, but she now looked back in gratitude for everything, even the traumas, for she saw them as necessary stages on the journey. Her only regret was that she would be unable to finish a book on which she was engaged on 'Death and Dying'!

When we said goodbye, knowing that we would never meet again on earth, it felt no different from the many goodbyes we had said at parting in the past, for I knew she would still be around, her intuitions battering against my rational mind. I phoned her one Sunday from New Zealand. Her voice was weak, but she was in good spirits, having seen all her family. I was going to call the following Sunday, but on the Wednesday I had a phone message from Ursula's friend, Joyce Ferne, to say that Ursula had died peacefully just after midday on October 8th and that she was smiling as she died.

In autumn 1994, when I was living in Edith's old flat by the Firth of Clyde, I celebrated Mass on the feast of All Saints in the local church, where I had been baptised, and where all my family had worshipped, including grandparents and many relatives. The sense of their presence was almost overwhelming on that occasion, and remained long after the celebration. The sense of presence included many other friends and acquaintances who have died. It was as though we were all meeting again with every tear wiped away, they assuring me that they were with me, I assuring them that I wanted to live for them. The experience felt genuine at the time, and it still feels genuine, and brings hope and peace whenever I recall it.

The Christian creed states, 'I believe in the resurrection of the body and life everlasting', but of the nature of this life after death in a glorified body, we know nothing. In what follows, I am not attempting a theology of death and the afterlife, but simply recounting my own experience. Reflecting on it, I cannot see that it contradicts traditional teaching, but it does raise questions about the way in which we interpret the teaching.

God is eternal, which means that for God past, present and future are all 'in the now'. We are time conditioned: God is not. The Aboriginal notion of time, so different from our own, fascinated me. For the Aborigines creation was not a past event, but a present happening, a truth they celebrated ceremonially in the 'dreamtime'. In the All Saints' Day experience, the dead were present to me in the now. It was as though I was still living their life, so that their destiny and mine were inextricably linked. Their strengths and goodness were mine, but their weaknesses and failures were also mine. Their inner conflict between good and evil was continuing in me. My failure could still affect them, just as their past failures could still affect me. When I write these thoughts, I know they could be wrongly interpreted. Managing our own lives is quite difficult enough without having responsibility for all our dead relatives and friends as well, but to me this did not seem depressing, but encouraging, because the experience was set in the context of the Eucharist. God, who manifested Godself in Jesus, is present in all creation, has entered our sinfulness, suffering and death and, in Julian of Norwich's words, 'All will be well, all will be well, all manner of things will be well'. As I reflected on this thought, I began to see that the relationship was not only with my own family, but with all people who have ever lived. In ways I cannot hope to understand, we are all interconnected and interdependent. We are all in this world for better or worse, for richer or poorer. What we do to the other, we do to ourselves. Individual, group, national, or multi-national greed, which ignores the need of the other, must eventually lead to our own impoverishment. 'As you do to one of these least, you are doing to me.' Hector's 'See sun, sky, birds, flowers, rocks, you, me? We all one', and Ursula's belief that the soul is coterminous with all creation and beyond, were beginning to flow into my understanding of life, of Eucharist and of

Church, new notes in the orchestra of consciousness, resolving many of the dissonances.

After the experience of celebrating Mass on All Saints' Day and the peace and joy which it brought me, my rational, common-sense mind began to object. 'Your peace and joy springs from vague and woolly thinking. You are spinning a cocoon of wistful fantasy around you, as substantial as gossamer, and it will be blown away by the first breath of reality. This fantasy that you are one with all your family, relatives, ancestors and friends may represent how you would like things to be, but you know perfectly well that in a crisis you do not think that way and have no sense of their presence.'

My intuitive self answers, 'I acknowledge your criticisms. I know that this intuitive knowing is easily blown away in a crisis, but that does not mean it is not true. What is true is that I am more in the habit of listening to you, my rational, common-sense self, consequently I stifle my intuitive self. But thank you for your criticism, for it helps me to see more clearly that which I had only vaguely grasped before.'

It was only many years after Marie's and Margot's deaths that I could bring myself to speak to them in imagination. When I did manage to do so, the conversations were always life-giving and strengthening. Although I still experience a slight reluctance to start on these conversations, they are always reassuring. I now think of the dead as being like shy visitors at a party. They remain on the fringe, do not intrude, but once engaged in conversation, they often turn out to be the most interesting people in the room. And now I see that God, too, is like this, a hidden God, who does not intrude, can easily be ignored and has little small talk, but if I just stay, as it were, by God's side, slowly God's presence becomes 'tongued with fire beyond the language of the living'.

Someone once said, 'When I pray, coincidences keep happening: when I stop praying, they cease.' God is in the harmony of things. It is therefore to be expected that the more we can let God be God in us and through us, the more likely we are to see connections which previously escaped us. 'Wisdom is to know the harmony of things: joy is to dance to its rhythm.' 'In Your light, I see light', as the psalmist wrote.

The brief time I spent among the Aborigines also clarified a question which had first agitated me twenty-five years earlier when I met the Gorbals group of the Iona Community in Glasgow and attended their Eucharist, but did not receive Holy Communion because the Catholic Church does not allow intercommunion. I have been faced with this same problem on many subsequent occasions and am constantly meeting others who are troubled by it.

The Aborigines see reality as sacramental, that is, as signifying a reality not perceptible to the senses. Their art represents this vision. Their paintings, at one level, represent their desert surroundings, but contain many other layers of meaning, and portray the actions of the creative spirits. In their 'dreamtime', their ceremonies focus the attention of the participants on the reality of these creating spirits, and on the consequent responsibility on those present to live in harmony with them.

One effect on me of the Aboriginal experience was to raise questions about my own understanding of the sacraments and sacramentality, questions I had been asking myself for years. The first time the question became real, as distinct from academic, was when the Polish woman from the Soviet Studies Department of Glasgow University asked to have her child baptised in the Catholic chaplaincy. Preparing the ceremony for a congregation which, I knew, would be predominantly non-Christian, I realised clearly that I did not believe that this baby, whom I was about to baptise, would be given a share in God's life, from which non-Christian babies were excluded. I understood the ceremony as a celebration of our Christian awareness of God's action on every child, whether Christian or non-Christian. It took a long time before I began to apply the implications of this way of understanding the sacraments to the Eucharist, and to the meaning of Christian mission.

In the Eucharist we are celebrating our awareness of the nature of God in whom all creation exists. God is the God of self-giving. Jesus is the sacrament of God, Emmanuel, God-with-us, a sign to us of the God in whom we live and move, and in whose image we are made. On the night before he suffered, Jesus took bread, which he blessed, broke, and gave to his disciples, saying, 'This is me, given for you.

Do this in my memory.' The heart of the universe, the source of all things, of all life, is this mysterious and utterly gratuitous love of God for all creation. As Christians, it is right and necessary that we should celebrate this reality in special ceremonies, not in order to make God be present to us, for God is already 'closer to us than we are to ourselves', but to celebrate our awareness of the reality of God's omnipresence. 'Do this in my memory' is an invitation not simply to perform a celebration, but to live the celebration we perform, allowing the self-giving God to live in us and through us, a God whose providence includes the just and the unjust alike.

As I began to understand the Eucharist in this way, so my unease with the Catholic ruling banning intercommunion increased. I no longer felt able to celebrate the Eucharist on any occasion when it was made clear to non-Catholic participants that they could not receive, nor did I normally feel able to abstain from receiving Holy Communion at a Eucharist celebrated by a minister of another Christian denomination. In stating this I am stating a personal conviction, not the official teaching of the Catholic Church. Nor am I advocating the abolition of all regulations governing the celebration of the Eucharist. Whatever regulations are imposed, they must be consistent with the truth that we are celebrating; the truth that God, who is love, who manifested Godself in Jesus, is the heart of the universe. Our present Catholic regulations can leave the impression that it is not primarily God's love that we are celebrating, but our own virtue, orthodoxy or denominational correctness.

As a Catholic priest, I do not believe it right for me to flout the regulations of the Church to which I belong while acting in its name, and this has been the source of difficulty in the intercommunion question. When faced with the question, 'Do you believe that when acting in an official capacity within the Catholic Church you are free to ignore the Church's regulations and follow your own convictions?' I have no hesitation in answering, 'I must follow the Church's regulations', but in the matter of intercommunion the question is not as simple as that. There is a deeper and more basic principle which must govern all our actions, whether as a priest or a lay person, namely the fundamental right of people to follow the promptings of their own conscience. Consequently, whenever I celebrate a Eucharist to which other Christians have been invited, I explain to them both the Catholic ruling forbidding Holy Communion to those who are not Catholic, but I also give the Church's teaching on the obligation of each one to follow the promptings of their own conscience, assuring them that none who present themselves will be refused. To refuse to give Holy Communion to someone who approaches in good faith would be not only a violation of the person refused, but also a contradiction of the meaning of Eucharist itself, a denial of God's self-giving nature.

Would it not be enough to say at the beginning of any Eucharist, 'Whoever wishes to celebrate God's love, uniquely manifest in Jesus Christ, image of the Unseen God, and present in all things and in all peoples now, is welcome to join fully in this celebration'?

Having worked in ecumenism for many years, I am grateful for the experience of many different Christian traditions, yet the division of the Churches is a scandal and destructive of the Church's mission. It is not the differences in themselves which cause the disunity of the Church, but the way in which we approach those differences. In every Christian denomination there must be individual customs, traditions and ways of worship, otherwise there would be no point in their separate existence. In St Ignatius' meditation on the Two Standards, it is not riches, honour and status which are destructive, but the way we relate to them. When we make attainment of any of these things our life's ambition, then we make idols of them and destroy ourselves. So, too, in religion we can become so attached to particular forms of worship, particular observances and rituals, that we regard them as absolutes, threatening to leave the Church at the very suggestion of change. Much of the energy of clergy and parishioners can be expended on trivial changes, draining everyone of the energy required to love and to serve. That is why those who pride themselves on being the most loyal, committed and orthodox may also be the most Christless in their attitude to those who disagree with them.

As a Roman Catholic, I must respect my own tradition, listen to and obey its injunctions, insofar as these are compatible with Christian teaching, but I also believe there are countless people of other denominations, of other religions, and of no religion, who are nearer to God than I, because they are more generous in obeying the law of love in their hearts. This thinking does not lead me to discount the Catholic Church: it helps me to remember that the point of all its ritual, teaching and observances is to help us to love God above all things and our neighbour as ourselves. Any ritual, teaching or observance which fails in this should be changed. That is why the Church needs continual penance, a need acknowledged in this century in the Second Vatican Council.

In my youth I thought that working for God's Kingdom meant trying to persuade everyone to become a good Catholic. Now I understand the mission of the Church differently. It is to learn to recognise the action of God in everyone. This is a much more demanding task than simply announcing the truth, as we see it, to others, promising them eternal life if they agree, eternal damnation if they do not. This different way of seeing mission demands that we listen carefully to what others have to say, face the doubts with which we are confronted through that listening, and allow other people's outlook to modify or change our own. If we refuse to do this, then we are open to the charge of being committed to an ideology, rather than to the God of mystery, of truth and of love, who dwells in all creation.

This mission of Christ, to which every Christian is bound, means that we have to work hard to find a language, signs and symbols which speak to the people of our day. If God is at work in everyone, then there must be some way of recognising this action of God in our lives. In a recent investigation in Britain by the Alister Hardy Institute in Oxford, about 70 per cent of those questioned claimed to have had some experience of God in their lives, while only about 10 per cent claimed to be regular church-goers. The constant complaint of most churchgoers I meet is that the ceremonies and sermons are dull, the language obscure, the signs and symbols unintelligible, and that religion, as they experience it, seems to have very little to do with ordinary life. Non-church-goers make the same complaint.

Religion has everything to do with ordinary life. Professionally religious people – clergy and members of religious orders and congregations – are subject to the temptations which afflict every human being, the desire to dominate. Professionals in every discipline of life tend to become a closed circle, jealous of their position and expertise. They develop a language of their own, intelligible only to the initiated. The more successful they become, the more powerless they render those whom they profess to serve. The Church's mission must never be to control, but to empower people, and not only to empower its own members.

> The spirit of the Lord Yahweh has been given to me . . .
> He has sent me to bring good news to the poor,
> to bind up hearts that are broken,
> to proclaim liberty to captives,
> freedom to those in prison.
>
> (Isaiah c. 61)

Working with people committed to justice and peace issues caused many inner dissonances at first, but the cumulative effect has been a deeper understanding and appreciation of Jesus' Sermon on the Mount and a clearer perception of the roots of violence.

In Marx's vision of the ideal Communist state, there would be no need of coercion by the rulers. The vision is attractive. To progress towards such an ideal state, Marx believed that coercion would be necessary as a temporary means towards that end. The means used in Russia and other Communist countries brought about the downfall of Communism, because the coercive measures used destroyed the ideal itself.

Jesus, in his life and teaching, exhorts, invites and persuades, but he never coerces. He rejects Satan's temptations, which are all to do with the exercise of power over others, by referring every temptation back to God. 'Man does not live on bread alone.' 'Thou shalt not tempt the Lord, thy God.' 'You must worship the Lord your God and serve him alone.' He tells his disciples, who are arguing as to who will have first place in the coming Kingdom, 'The rulers of the pagans lord it over their subjects, and their great men make their influence felt. With you it must not be so. The greatest among you must become the least of all and the first among you must be the servant of all, for the Son of Man came, not to be served, but to serve, and to give his life as a ransom for many.' In the Sermon on the Mount he exhorts the people, 'Be perfect, as your heavenly Father is perfect', but the perfection is God's compassion for all people. 'Love your enemies, do good to those who hate you, pray for those who persecute you', because 'God, the Most High, is himself kind to the ungrateful and the wicked'.

It is extraordinary that as Christians we can live quietly and co-operatively in societies which are acquisitive, both individually and nationally, which foster competitiveness rather than co-operation, which struggle for power and advantage over others, and which have an awed reverence for rank and status.

When I look back at many of the dissonances in my own life, I see that much of the hurt came either from failure or from fear of failure, from being or feeling powerless or overlooked. Those dissonances begin to resolve when I realise that there is no lasting security in success, power or in being noticed.

St Luke's version of the Sermon on the Mount includes, 'Why do you notice the splinter in your brother's eye when you cannot see the plank in your own? . . . Take the plank out of your own eye first, and then you will see clearly enough to take out the splinter that is in your brother's eye.' (Luke c. 6). This touches the roots of violence in everyone and it is from these roots that all human violence grows. What we cannot see within us, we project on to others, without any awareness that we are doing so. This enables us to act unjustly in a spirit of self-righteousness. We do this individually, as groups, as Church and as a nation. Hurling abuse or weapons at another enhances our feel-good factor, at least temporarily, but it also fuels violence. I have found enormous help in recent years in the writings of Réné Girard, the French anthropologist who has made a special study of violence and its links with the sacred. Violence is, of its nature, imitative, and it spirals. All primitive societies have their tabus, which act like fire-breaks against the flames of violence. When the tabus fail to prevent or stem the violence, then they have the scapegoat mechanism, whereby enemies are reconciled by combining to put the blame for the violence upon the scapegoat, which may be an animal, a human being, or a group. This scapegoat mechanism is universal, according to Girard, is endemic to all societies and is a source of further violence.

It was through his study of violence that Girard became a Christian, for he saw Christ's life, passion and death, his non-violent resistance to evil, his opposition to scape-goating – 'Take the plank out of your own eye first' – as the only antidote to spiralling violence.

From my experience in working with peace groups and in giving individual retreats, I began to see more clearly that the most important thing any of us can do in the cause of peace is to practise non-violence in our own lives and within our own minds and hearts. The only thing we can change is ourselves, and the only thing we can change in ourselves is the way we think and the way we perceive reality. Peace, like violence, begins in the human heart. Like violence, peace is imitative and it can spiral outwards, affecting people and events beyond our consciousness. Buddhists have been teaching this for centuries.

This truth, that peace and violence begin within our individual hearts and minds and that the effects spiral outwards, can bring harmony to the dissonance which a sense of powerlessness engenders. In justice and peace work, the problems are so formidable, complex and intractable, that if we reflect at all, our efforts seem utterly futile. Our minuscule individual efforts are ineffective if measured quantitatively, in terms of the power we can exercise to effect change. If we dare bring this pessimism into prayer, we can begin to glimpse our own atheism. My depressing sense of powerlessness is based on the assumption that the promotion of peace and justice in the world depends on my ability as an individual to exercise enough power to change things as I think they should be changed. In my reasoning, I have omitted God, God's loving providence, and my interconnection with everything else in creation. My sense of powerlessness and hopelessness is God standing at the door and knocking. When God is invited in, I begin to see more clearly where the real struggle lies. It is not in my trying to impose my ideas for peace and justice on the world, but in my allowing God to take over my ego so that I can become an instrument of God's peace, not a manufacturer of my own. There is no greater contribution any individual can make to the world's peace. We do not have to be powerful, learned, able, healthy, wealthy or good looking: all we have to do is to acknowledge our powerlessness and entrust it to God who, as St Paul said, is at his most powerful in our weakness, whose folly is wiser than human wisdom, and whose weakness is stronger than human strength.

Nothing happens by chance. Before leaving for South Africa, New Zealand and Singapore in September 1995, I returned to Wemyss Bay for a week's holiday. I visited Julia, who had looked after me as a child. She was now house-bound with terminal cancer. Before I left, we celebrated Mass in her house with two of her friends. I could sense all my family around me joining in thanking God for the gift of Julia. A few days later she died, and I flew up from Birmingham to conduct the funeral, two days before leaving for South Africa. Her own children, grandchildren and great grandchildren numbered over fifty and most of the village of Skelmorlie attended, together with other friends and acquaintances. Few of them were church-goers, but they recognised Julia's wonderful generosity and wanted to be there. As I celebrated the Eucharist before the funeral, I felt great gratitude for Julia's life and for having been able to be with her a few days before her death. Many of those attending her funeral may not have been familiar with God language in church, but they recognised God's self-giving in Julia.

'God' I said at the age of three to see what would happen; 'God' I am still saying seventy years later, and still waiting to see what will happen.

'Now I know that You are always greater than anything I can think or imagine, and for this I am most grateful. I am glad that I cannot locate You, define You, describe You. I used to worry about self-identity, about who I was. Now I am glad not to know, and I can thank You for the mystery of my being. The Greeks said, "Call no one happy until they are dead." I do not know how much longer I shall live, nor what shall become of me. I do not know if the way I am trying to live now really is your will. You have shown me something of the depths of self-deception that are in me, and I may still be deceiving myself. But what I do know is that You are the God of every situation, God in our darkness drawing us to light, God in our sinfulness offering us healing, God in our self-deception leading us into truth, God who is for us, even when we are against ourselves. So I know that even if I am unwittingly deceiving myself, if I follow what truth there is in me, then You will draw me further into Your truth, and that there is no situation, no state, no place I can reach where You will not still be closer to me than I am to myself.'